Brazil's Developing Northeast

Paper $2.00   Library edition in cloth $3.50

STEFAN H. ROBOCK

Brazil's Developing Northeast

A Study of Regional Planning and Foreign Aid

The Brookings Institution *Washington, D.C.*

Foreword

For a little more than a decade, the United States has been actively engaged in technical assistance and capital aid programs for under-developed countries. Only since 1960 has Latin America been a high priority area for these efforts. It is not surprising, therefore, as Stefan Robock emphasizes in this book, that we do not adequately understand the Latin American environment within which the Alliance for Progress is attempting to achieve higher levels of social and economic welfare, and we know too little of how to influence the development process. In particular, the Brazilian Northeast is poorly understood both outside and inside Brazil. It presents an unusually complex development problem because it involves the issue of an underdeveloped region within an underdeveloped country—an important matter that has been neglected in the growing literature on development and foreign aid.

Northeast Brazil has only recently received significant attention from the United States foreign aid program. Yet the region has a long history of indigenous efforts to stimulate development and substantial experience with external technical assistance. This study of the area's development history, problems, and prospects yields valuable insights into the complexities of the development process. It also helps to clarify the potentials and limitations of foreign aid. And it provides a more profound and balanced understanding of a specific area that has become highly important in the Alliance for Progress effort.

Professor Robock has been both a student of and active participant in economic development activities. As a result, his study considers both theoretical and practical aspects of the development problem and political as well as economic factors. He first became familiar with the Brazilian Northeast during World War II, while stationed in the area as a Naval air intelligence officer. In 1954, while serving as Chief Economist for the Tennessee Valley Authority, he was invited by the Brazilian government to undertake a long-term assignment as

United Nations Economic Development Adviser for Northeast Brazil. He served in this role and later as chief of the United Nations technical assistance mission to Northeast Brazil for two and a half years until late 1956. Since that time, he has maintained close continuing contact with the development efforts of Brazil and its Nordeste through several short technical assistance assignments.

This book is a case study of an area that is important in its own right. But in a broader sense, it is a general commentary on the development process, development planning, and foreign aid. The author begins with a statement of his general concept of development. He then lays a factual foundation through a brief overview of the total Brazilian setting, recent regional patterns of Brazilian development, and the structure and trends of the Northeast economy. The history of indigenous development efforts, beginning almost a century ago, are then traced through the "fighting the drought" approach to the affirmative economic development programs now becoming established as national policy for the region. After reviewing past and present foreign aid activities to assist the Northeast, the study presents a series of general views on future development issues and prospects for foreign aid which emerge from the Northeast experience.

Professor Robock is Director of International Business Studies in the Graduate School of Business, Indiana University. His practical experience in economic development includes five years with the Tennessee Valley Authority and overseas assignments in India, the Philippines, Liberia, Nyasaland, Colombia, Chile, Venezuela, and Bolivia. While doing the work for this study, he was associated with the Foreign Policy Studies Division of the Brookings Institution.

Professor Robock and the Institution gratefully acknowledge financial support from the Ford Foundation which made this study possible. They wish to acknowledge and thank a great many Brazilian and American officials, scholars, and other individuals and organizations for their interest and help. These include the study's Advisory Committee: John Adler and Gerald Alter of the World Bank; Joseph Grunwald, Yale University; Cleantho de Paiva Leite, Inter-American Development Bank; Reuben Sternfeld, Agency for International Development; Philip B. Taylor, Jr., Johns Hopkins University School of Advanced International Studies; William V. Turnage, U. S. Department of State; Alfred C. Wolf, Inter-American Development Bank; and

Robert E. Asher, Brookings. The study was under the guidance of H. Field Haviland, Jr., Director of Foreign Policy Studies at Brookings.

The views expressed in the publication are the author's and do not necessarily represent the views of those consulted during its preparation. Neither should they be construed as reflecting the views of the trustees, the officers, or other staff members of the Brookings Institution.

Robert D. Calkins
President

June 1963
The Brookings Institution
1775 Massachusetts Avenue, N.W.
Washington 36, D.C.

Author's Preface

When I returned to Northeast Brazil in mid-1960, after an absence of four years, I was tremendously impressed with the progress the Northeast was making. And I concluded that a scholarly study of this important "country within a country" would be a worthy project. Such a study, I felt, would enlarge the understanding of an important area and provide valuable material for the use of policy makers and development technicians in other underdeveloped areas.

A pessimistic and alarmist picture of this vast region has become widely accepted and contrasts sharply with the optimism of this study. My principal explanation for this phenomenon is that I am evaluating Northeast Brazil against its own situation in the past, rather than in relation to other more fortunate areas. Also, I give more weight to the momentum of development than I do to static comparisons of the current situation.

The individuals in Brazil who gave me assistance are so numerous that I cannot mention all of them. Dr. Raul Barbosa gave generously of his own time and placed the staff of the Bank of the Northeast at my disposal for collecting information and for reviewing the factual details of my study. Dr. Celso Furtado interrupted his busy schedule on numerous occasions to give me the benefit of his views and experience. And I must give special thanks to Francisco Oliveira, Jader Andrade and Juarez Farias of SUDENE, Carlos Costa and Fernando Mota of the Bank of the Northeast of Brazil, and Isaac Kerstenetsky of the Getúlio Vargas Foundation.

Several distinguished Brazilians with long experience in the Northeast had migrated to Washington to work with Inter-American agencies. Among these individuals who were accessible for invaluable assistance and advice throughout the project, I am specially indebted to Rubens Costa and Joaquim Batista Fernandes of the Inter-American Development Bank and João Gonçalves de Souza of the Pan American Union.

My sincere thanks are also due to a number of persons who critically reviewed the draft manuscript. These include Diogo Gaspar, Romulo Almeida, Ambassador Lincoln Gordon, Albert O. Hirschman, Edwin M. Martin, Paul Fisher, and my colleague John P. Lewis. I benefited greatly from the detailed comments of these reviewers, but I should make clear I do not hold them responsible for the final results of this effort.

I am also grateful to the Brookings Institution and to H. Field Haviland, Jr., Director of Foreign Policy Studies, for making it possible for me to undertake this study. And I value the encouragement, professional assistance and technical guidance that was unselfishly given throughout the project. Robert E. Asher, with his keen insights and broad background in foreign aid and development, reviewed and gave advice on my work as it progressed. Herbert C. Morton and Evelyn Breck handled the publication and editing of the manuscript with helpful and sympathetic guidance, and Helen Eisenhart prepared the Index.

Finally, this book would not have been possible without the assistance of my wife Shirley Robock. Throughout the many months of data gathering, analysis, drafting, and checking, she has been my principal helper. Her knowledge of Brazil and of Portuguese, and her ability to critically review the facts, the analysis, and my writing have contributed in a crucial way to the completion of this study.

Stefan H. Robock

June 1963

Contents

CHARTS AND MAPS

1

The Development Process
and Northeast Brazil

ECONOMIC DEVELOPMENT is a complex, dynamic process, and the currently popular techniques for accelerating this process are development planning and foreign aid. Within the setting of world competition of economic systems and a revolution of rising expectations, it has become imperative that both the developed and the underdeveloped nations learn more about the development process and the means of influencing it. Toward this end, the present study examines the issues of development planning and foreign aid. The issues are studied not by generalized or abstract analysis, but through the history, experience, current situation, and future prospects of the major underdeveloped region in the Western Hemisphere—Northeast Brazil. The study does not separate the issues into conventional academic fields, such as economics, politics, administration, and ethics, but instead attempts to merge the various professional disciplines as they are relevant to the experience of Northeast Brazil.

Northeast Brazil, like other geographic areas, has unique characteristics. Yet the long development experience and current problems of the vast Brazilian Northeast embrace the full range of issues confronted by most underdeveloped areas in their efforts to achieve economic, political, and social progress. The examination of this "nation within a nation" also highlights an important aspect of economic development that has been neglected in the formulation of development and assistance programs—the issue of underdeveloped regions in underdeveloped countries. In practice, the issue of the internal geography

1

of development occupies a major share of the time and energy of government officials and politicians in the developing countries.

In the foreign aid field, Northeast Brazil provides an excellent setting for evaluating the potentials of outside assistance in solving essentially internal problems. It is hoped the results of the evaluation will provide guidance for both donors and recipients of foreign aid.

History of the Northeast

If the Brazilian Northeast were a separate nation, it would rank second in population and third in area within South America. With its present population of about 25 million, Brazil's "bulge" has as many people as Thailand, more than Argentina, and almost three times the number of people in the New England region of the United States. In area, the Northeast is larger than Italy, Spain, and Portugal combined.

The Northeast was the earliest settled region of Brazil and among the first areas in the "New World" to be colonized. In 1532, sugar cane production started there, and in less than a century Northeast Brazil became one of the most important sugar producing areas of the world.[1] But with the development of the sugar industry in the Caribbean, world prices of sugar fell sharply in the last half of the seventeenth century and continued at low levels during the next century,[2] and the era of Northeast prosperity based on a sugar and slave plantation economy came to an end. At a later stage, cotton agriculture became important, but the Northeast never regained its position of economic leadership in Brazil. During subsequent periods gold, rubber, and coffee became the nation's principal products, and the economic frontier and the center of economic gravity of the country migrated with the changes in the leading commodities.

With the decline in sugar prosperity, the expanding Northeast population shifted in ever greater numbers to the semiarid interior where subsistence agriculture and cattle raising became the principal eco-

[1] J. F. Normano, *Brazil: A Study of Economic Types* (University of North Carolina Press, 1935), pp. 19-20.
[2] Celso Furtado, *Formaçaõ Econômica do Brasil,* Editôra Fundo de Cultura, Rio de Janeiro (1959), p. 29.

nomic activities. The accelerated transfer of population and economic activity from the humid coastal areas to the semiarid interior made the periodic droughts that hit the interior increasingly calamitous for the region.

Motivated by an unusually disastrous drought in 1877, the federal government finally recognized the Northeast *sêca* as a national problem, and initiated a special large-scale program of building dams and reservoirs as "works against the drought." The intensity of the "fight against the drought" fluctuated greatly over the decades. As is true of public works programs in many countries, the effectiveness of the activities was greatly reduced by politics and, in some cases, administrative irregularities. Many controversies occurred about specific technical details of the general strategy. But the general strategy itself, and the diagnosis of the Northeast problem on which it was based, were rarely questioned.

Beginning in the late 1940's the growing world interest in economic development and economic planning concepts and ideas began to permeate professional and governmental circles in Brazil. Soon the economic development point of view became strong enough to prevail over the traditional engineering approach to Northeast Brazil. When another serious drought occurred in 1951, President Getúlio Vargas was persuaded to make what he called a "revision, if not a complete change, in traditional methods" and to "give a definite economic and social orientation to the study and solution of the [Northeast] problem."[3]

The economic, or New Era, approach was first implemented by creating the Bank of the Northeast (BNB), a regional development bank with broad responsibility to stimulate economic expansion in the area. But political realities and vested interests permitted the traditional engineering approach to continue along with the New Era activities. The BNB initiated its operations in 1954 headquartered in the area. The BNB requested and received technical assistance for economic development from the United Nations. The United States was frequently asked for specific types of expert assistance, but for reasons explained in Chapter 7, the Northeast program evolved without any significant participation by the United States aid program.

The new approach has had its share of failures and has encountered

[3] *Message to the Congress No. 363 of 1951*, Oct. 23, 1951.

great resistance from politicians, technicians, and others. But it has continued to advance. In 1956, on the recommendation of the BNB and its United Nations advisor, President Juscelino Kubitschek took a first step toward coordinating all federal development activities in the Northeast. When another major drought occurred in 1958, the economic and regional coordination approach became firmly established with the creation of the powerful federal agency, the Superintendency for Development of the Northeast (SUDENE). In early 1960, within a few months after it was established, SUDENE prepared and presented a five-year plan to the Congress.

At this time, the United States became concerned about the Castro-Communism threat in Northeast Brazil and intensified its interest in the region. The SUDENE plan was approved by the Brazilian Congress in December 1961 after an extended and often bitter political struggle. By April 1962 the United States made its first major commitment to help the region.

From Obscurity to International Fame

The Brazilian Northeast first became known to many North Americans during World War II. Numerous airfields on the Brazilian "bulge" were bases for antisubmarine operations, and the air terminal at Natal on the southern ferry route became at one time the busiest airfield in the world. The Northeast also received major attention and assistance from the United States as a source of critical war materials. But with the conclusion of the war, the area dropped from the international limelight. By 1960, the United States foreign aid program had only a few technicians and was spending no more than $250,000 a year on technical assistance in this region. And many Brazilians were frank in complaining that they did not have enough Communists to warrant United States attention.

Then the "winds of change" blew on the Northeast. In mid-1960 the United States Embassy became aware of and greatly concerned with Francisco Julião, an obscure state legislator in Pernambuco, and the Peasant League, an incipient land reform movement, struggling along with some minor success. An enterprising American reporter then visited the Northeast, and on October 31, 1960, the front page of the *New York Times* urgently warned, "The makings of a revolutionary situation are increasingly apparent across the vastness of the poverty-stricken and drought-plagued Brazilian Northeast." Shortly thereafter a film of the National Broadcasting Company, "The Troubled Land," which had been prepared in the Northeast, provided visual proof to millions of American television viewers of the Northeast crisis and serious Castro-Communism threat.

The increasing concern in the United States for Latin America and an almost hysterical fear of creeping Castroism made Francisco Julião an exciting new event. As a leader of the Socialist party in one of the nine northeastern states, Julião was a "Marxist." Furthermore, Julião had visited Cuba earlier in the year and at the time of the news story was on a tour of Communist China. Also, Julião and members of the Peasant League had recently occupied a large plantation in Pernambuco and distributed the land to the workers. The state government, unwilling or unable to remove the squatters, subsequently paid for the land and legalized its de facto occupation by the peasants.

But the United States overlooked a number of other relevant facts. Brazilian politics has its own exuberant style. The Northeast, as one of the most turbulent examples of this style, has a long history of revolutions or protest movements. In the Pernambuco revolution of 1817, local priests were the revolutionary leaders and champions of social reform.[4] In 1874 a virtual civil war, the *Guerra dos Quebra-Quilos*, swept the interior of the region in protest against the adoption of the metric system of weights and measures. The famous bandit rebellion of Antonio Conselheiro in 1896-97, chronicled by Euclides da Cunha in the literary classic, *Rebellion in the Backlands*, was suppressed only after the federal government had dispatched four army expeditions to the Northeast. In 1935, a serious communist revolution started in Rio Grande do Norte and Pernambuco and threatened to spread to the rest of the country.

As is true in much of the world, "socialism" does not have the bad connotation in Brazil that it has in the United States. One Brazilian in the Northeast is a leader of the Socialist party and at the same time a large landowner in the region. In the late 1950's numerous politicians, including former President Jânio Quadros, made trips to Cuba, and

[4] Gilberto Frayre, "Misconceptions of Brazil," *Foreign Affairs* (April 1962), p. 455.

many Brazilians accepted the all-expense invitations of the Chinese Communists to visit their country. The membership of the Peasant League was minute in comparison with the almost 5,000,000 farm workers in the region and about 900,000 in the state of Pernambuco alone.

From the auspicious publicity beginning, the attention of the news media and the United States government to Northeast Brazil accelerated to near crisis pitch. As one keen Brazilian observer explained, "Julião received from the international and conservative Brazilian press publicity beyond his wildest dreams. As they customarily do to all their enemies, the conservative press made him an important force."

Shortly after President Kennedy took office in 1961, his administration gave prompt and high-level attention to Northeast Brazil. Numerous Washington officials and United States legislators visited the area. A technical mission headed by former Ambassador Merwyn Bohan was dispatched to review development plans. And in April 1962, the United States announced its major foreign aid commitment for the region. The April 1962 agreement implied a tremendous increase in United States assistance—from a level of about $250,000 to $65,000,000 a year. During the first year of the program, however, only a small part of the increased aid has been disbursed.

Misconceptions About the Northeast

Unfortunately, the circumstances of the "discovery," the inevitable bias of the news media toward reporting unusual and sensational events, and the absence of comprehensive and scholarly studies in English on Northeast Brazil,[5] have combined to create many misconceptions in the United States about this important area. But misconceptions about the development problems of the Northeast are also widely prevalent within Brazil. Brazil is a large country—larger by another Texas than the United States minus Alaska—and most Brazilians from the South have no personal acquaintance with their Northeast region.

[5] A major section in Albert O. Hirschman's *Journeys Toward Progress: Studies of Economic Policy-Making in Latin America* (Twentieth Century Fund, 1963) presents for an English-speaking audience one of the first scholarly studies on the development problems of Northeast Brazil. It focuses primarily on the history of federal policy toward the drought phenomenon.

Moreover, among Nordestinos and many other Brazilians, the Northeast is a highly emotional subject. The following description, written recently by a civil engineer who is a government official in the Northeast, is representative of a widely prevalent emotional approach to this area. He says:

> The word "Northeast," in reference to Brazil, suggests to all the Nation much more than a simple geographic position. It signifies a world of problems—many insoluble—a way of life, a psychology, a strange people in a land sometimes strange. The word recalls only DROUGHT, HUNGER, MISERY.[6]

The so-called "Drought Polygon" of the interior, constituting about half of the nine-state area, is semiarid but not a desert. And the Northeast is not continually drought-plagued. The rainfall pattern in the polygon is uncertain, and much of the total annual rainfall is concentrated within a short period. The most recent serious drought year, 1958, followed by six years the drought of 1951-52, which in turn was the first major drought in the region for nineteen years. The widely reported drought and food crisis of 1962 (*Time*, May 18, 1962) was brief and limited to only a few small areas.

Nor is all of the Northeast poverty-stricken and stagnant. Bahia has the expanding petroleum production fields of Brazil and a reasonably prosperous cocoa bean area. Pernambuco has a growing phosphate rock and fertilizer industry. Ceará has valuable long-staple cotton production and tropical waxes and oils. Paraíba has a booming sisal growing and sisal products industry. The small but expanding manufacturing sector of the region includes "growth" industries such as cement, chemicals, certain consumer goods, and even machinery.

Per capita income levels in the Northeast are only one-half of the national average and about one-third of the average for the "heartland" of Brazil. But contrary to well publicized "gospel," economic disparities (on a relative basis) between the Northeast and the South are not widening. Over the last decade, real output in the Northeast expanded at a faster rate than the annual 2.5 percent per capita goal established by the Alliance for Progress. From 1955 to 1960, the Brazilian Northeast had the fastest rate of growth for any region in Brazil, and average per capita income rose from 42 percent to 50 percent of the

[6] Jorge de Oliveira Netto, *Sergipe e o Problema da Sêca,* Edição da COTEF, Aracaju (1955), p. 9.

national average. By 1960, Northeast per capita income had reached a level of about $140 and was above that in Paraguay and Bolivia and approaching income levels in Peru, Guatemala, Honduras, and Ecuador.

Nor is the region a cultural desert. In fact, cultural richness seems to have been stimulated by economic poverty, and literature, poetry, music, and politics have flourished in the Northeast. This is the area that produced, in 1934, sociologist Gilberto Freyre's *The Masters and the Slaves,* which together with other brilliant professional contributions earned this Nordestino an honorary degree from Columbia University; and in 1947, Josue de Castro's *Geography of Hunger,* which has been translated into nineteen languages and which inspired the election of this scholar-politician as President of the Council of the United Nations Food and Agriculture Organization.

Northeast Brazil has an increasing number of universities in which the quality of education, though still deficient, is rapidly improving. The area also has large numbers of healthy and educated people. It is urbanizing rapidly and had twenty-two cities with more than 100,000 population in 1960. And of key importance for the future, the Northeast has in recent years, without any significant United States aid, made substantial progress in training technicians and in becoming institutionally prepared for a new era of affirmative and accelerated economic development.

The *sêcas,* as the Brazilians term the drought phenomenon, still dominate much of the regional thinking and politics. But with the development of an extensive transportation network and reservoir system in the interior, the *sêcas* have become less a period of human suffering and more a political phenomenon. The traditional political style for securing federal aid for the Northeast distorts the national and international "image" of the region. For decades, Nordestino politicians have based their claims for increased national attention and resources on reports of drought and famine. And the human tragedy of past droughts has been chronicled in vivid detail in brilliant Nordestino literary contributions. But the region now has the roads and transportation facilities to prevent humans and animals from dying of thirst and starvation. From the standpoint of formulating development programs for the region, it is crucial to recognize that the most basic problem of the Northeast is not the periodic drought but continuing poverty.

The Development Process and Development Planning

The development problem confronting Northeast Brazil and other underdeveloped areas can be stated in simple terms. The system—or society—is not operating efficiently enough in the economic and political spheres to provide an adequate flow of economic and social benefits. In a subjective sense, the system is inefficient because it does not satisfy the expectations and aspirations of the people. From an objective point of view, the inefficiency may be measured in terms of the quantity of the flow, the qualitative mix of the output, and the distribution of the benefits among people. The challenge confronting Northeast Brazil, therefore, is to improve the operating efficiency of its entire society—of people as individuals, of private institutions, and of government organizations—on a continuing basis.

As the case of Northeast Brazil reveals, the development process encompasses much more than preparing economic blueprints or plans and injecting more capital into an area. The plans must be a product of a planning process that enlists the maximum participation of all groups in the society. Until many preconditions for investment are achieved, increased capital investment is unlikely to produce significant results. In fact, if efforts are successful to create the preconditions—such as improving the skills of people, the administrative capacity of private and public institutions and the technical and factual knowledge of an area's resources, development potentials, and bottlenecks—an increased flow of capital may automatically result.

These and other political, social, and economic dimensions of the complex development process are the focus of what is to follow in this study. To deal with these issues concretely in a realistic setting, some factual background on Brazil in general and the Northeast in particular is presented. But some of the substantive findings of the study might be of interest here.

The history of Northeast Brazil demonstrates that a government's willingness to promote development through the expenditure of large amounts of money is no guarantee of development success. Almost eighty years ago, Brazil began supporting special federal programs for "recuperating" the Northeast. And for many decades, as has been noted, the lack of success from these efforts was attributed to ineffective administration and political irregularities. Only recently has Brazil recognized that an invalid diagnosis of the Northeast problem was the basic difficulty and that the direction of the development program must be changed.

A radical revision of long entrenched policies is a difficult task for any society. Thus, in the Northeast the changing of directions in development policies, by injecting more of an economic substance into the area of political decisions, has been one of Brazil's most significant accomplishments during the decade of the 1950's. The recognized failure of the "fighting the drought" approach was not a sufficient condition for a fundamental policy change. Well formulated alternatives had to be available at crucial periods of political decision-making. Furthermore, as the Northeast experience reveals, a radical shift in development policy is likely to find an area unprepared in terms of technically qualified and experienced personnel, adequate technical and economic data, and effective supporting institutions to implement the new policies.

The new policies required a major commitment by government for leading and guiding Northeast development. And the institutional framework for comprehensive development planning has gradually evolved along with political and popular acceptance of a revised governmental role. The short experience of the Northeast with development planning, however, has disclosed many gaps and weaknesses in accepted planning concepts and techniques, which result from a failure to conceive of development as a dynamic process. The conventional wisdom frequently does not recognize, for example, that development planning is primarily a political activity and must be knit into the mainstream of a government's decision-making process. The time limits for preparing development plans, therefore, are most likely to be dictated by political considerations rather than by the time requirements for producing plans that are technically sound and operational. A plan was needed in Northeast Brazil at a specific time as a symbol for popular support and to secure certain key political decisions. A plan was quickly prepared that served the political purposes even though it was critically deficient by technical criteria and as a basis for guiding operations.

The responsibility of development planning for allocating scarce resources and establishing priorities is also more complex than generally conceived. It is common to assume that capital is the scarcest resource and to establish priorities among specific projects by comparing their respective contribution to increased output per unit of capital required. Scarcity, however, is a relative question. Capital is scarce in Northeast Brazil, but, at the present stage of development, administrative and institutional capacity to use funds effectively is even scarcer.

Development planning must be concerned with the identification of the scarcities in a particular area and at a particular time. But it must go even further and initiate actions to eliminate the scarcities and bottlenecks as they are identified. The latter problem is similar to that of strengthening a chain. When the present weakest link is discovered and replaced by a strong link, another link becomes the weakest one. The performance of the chain can be continuously increased by a process of strengthening the weakest link of the moment.

Another point is that specific plan targets should never be considered an end in themselves. They can be achieved by using up available resources or by relying on external aid, which cannot be expected to continue. In such cases, the targets may be achieved, but the system has become exhausted. Specific target accomplishments do not mean development success unless they are clear products of a significant and lasting improvement in the operations of an area's institutions.

In these and many other respects, when development is recognized as a problem in momentum, the content and strategy of development planning activities may have to change radically.

The development experience of Northeast Brazil illustrates the sizable influence, both positive and negative, that external factors can have on development aspirations. An example of external factors largely outside of the Northeast's control is the favorable international market conditions for major regional products that have stimulated recent economic gains. There are other external forces with great potential for aiding the region that can be influenced by the Northeast through the national government. An example of these is agricultural resettlement projects in the interior of Brazil which can draw off surplus farm population from the Northeast. Development planning, therefore, must identify and keep under surveillance the external factors most significant to the area. Where these are independent of the region's action, internal adjustments to changing conditions should be programed. Where the external factors can be influenced, development planning should program activities and policies that can be recommended to other areas.

The matter of expectations and satisfactions of people deserves brief mention because they can be either an affirmative or a disruptive force for development. Dissatisfaction and rising expectations can be a powerful stimulant and pressure in support of development activities. But unrealistic and impossible expectations can be disruptive and a serious barrier to progress. It is important, therefore, as part of development activities to create realistic though ambitious expectations through sound technical studies and making their findings available, as is finally happening in Northeast Brazil.

The Regional Disparities Issue

The greatest accomplishment during the 1950's in federal policy toward Northeast Brazil was to reexamine the long accepted diagnosis of the Northeast problem and to develop a better diagnosis and understanding of the factors underlying the low economic and social levels in the region. But one important issue still has not been carefully reexamined; namely, the question of regional disparities in economic levels and rates of expansion. Many Brazilians consider the wide economic disparities between the various regions—in particular between the Northeast and the South—as a unique and special development problem that Brazil alone faces. A corollary of this conviction is that regional disparities are abnormal and should not be allowed to persist. Furthermore, the position is accepted by many economists that natural forces at work tend to create ever greater regional inequalities.

But as Furtado has recently noted, the regional disparities phenomenon is universally observed.[7] Even the United States and the Soviet Union have significant disparities in levels of living and rates of growth between rural and urban areas and between regions within each country. In fact, regional disparities in the United States some three decades ago were roughly comparable to the current disparities in Brazil. In the prosperity year of 1929, average per capita income in the United States ranged from 52 percent of the national average in the Southeast to 138 percent in the Middle Atlantic and Northeast

---

[7] Furtado, op. cit., p. 264.

states. This compares to a range of 51 to 146 percent for Brazil's major regions in 1960.[8]

The universal occurrence of regional disparities also suggests that they may be inevitable. The natural and human resources of a country or a subarea are not homogeneous or evenly spread over physical space. Economic production units involve what the economist calls "economies of scale" and are not completely divisible so that they can be spread evenly over the surface of an area. Steel, for example, must be produced in units of efficient size concentrated in a small number of locations. Many types of economic activity are interrelated and must be grouped in one area for efficient operation. Historical factors such as favorable locations with respect to international trade, navigable rivers, and proximity to coal fields also explain regional variations in the amount and productivity of economic activity within a country. And within most subareas of a country similar disparities exist.

As Hirschman has observed:

> We must take it for granted that economic progress does not appear everywhere at the same time and that once it has appeared, powerful forces make for a spatial concentration of economic growth around the initial starting point. . . . An economy, to lift itself to higher income levels, must and will first develop within itself one or several regional centers of economic strength. This need for the emergence of "growing points" or "growth poles" in the course of the development process means that international and interregional inequality of growth is an inevitable concomitant and condition of growth itself. Thus, in the geographical sense, growth is necessarily unbalanced.[9]

The issue whether regional disparities become cumulative and the rich areas become richer while the poor areas become poorer has been discussed from a theoretical point of view but has not been the subject of much empirical research. The distinguished sociologist-economist, Gunnar Myrdal, discusses this question in his book, *Rich Lands and Poor*,[10] and reaches the pessimistic conclusion that the normal situation —without serious governmental intervention—is a tendency toward greater regional inequalities. Hirschman, on the other hand, argues that economic pressures eventually are generated that will remedy

[8] See Chap. 2, Table 5.
[9] Albert O. Hirschman, *The Strategy of Economic Development* (Yale University Press, 1958), pp. 183-84.
[10] Harper & Brothers, 1958.

such a situation. There is general agreement, however, that government action can influence the regional pattern and that a policy of
greater equalization can be valid. At the same time, it is abundantly
clear that complete equality is unrealistic and a goal that can retard
total economic progress.[11]

Reliable regional statistics covering a significant period of time are
hard to find in most countries. The Economic Commission for Europe
attempted about a decade ago a pioneering study of regional disparities within European nations which did not reach any definitive
conclusions whether the gap between poor and rich regions within
countries has been widening.[12] The best available data are the personal
income estimates by states and regions in the United States. These
data extending over a period of three decades clearly reveal a narrowing of regional differentials in the United States.

The regional deviation in 1960 of average per capita income in the
United States ranged from 72 percent to 117 percent of the national
average as compared to a range of from 52 to 138 percent in 1929.[13]
The regional data for Brazil which extends back only to 1947 also
shows a narrowing of regional disparities, particularly since 1955.

If it becomes better recognized that regional disparities occur in all
developing countries, that they are "an inevitable concomitant and condition of growth itself," and that they are likely to narrow over time—
particularly with a rapid national rate of growth, the preoccupation
of the Northeast and backward regions in other countries with egali-
tarian arguments for regional justice might become less intense. And
more promising development directions might be followed. One such
direction is to focus on the welfare and the contribution of the people
rather than inanimate political units or physical geographic areas.
This suggests that migration can improve the welfare of individuals
and reduce regional disparities. It also suggests that investment in
human resources creates mobile capital that contributes to economic
and social progress at any location in a country.

[11] See, for example, Walter Isard and John H. Cumberland (eds.), *Regional
Economic Planning*, Organisation for European Economic Co-operation, Paris
(1961), p. 23.

[12] United Nations Economic Commission for Europe, *Economic Survey of Europe in 1954*, Geneva (1955), pp. 136-72.

[13] Charles F. Schwartz and Robert Graham, Jr., *Personal Income by States Since
1929*, U. S. Office of Business Economics, *Survey of Current Business*, *Supplement* (1956), and *Survey of Current Business* (August 1961).

A related change in thinking that ought to be encouraged is for the Northeast to focus on its absolute gains and its potentials for further growth rather than being exclusively concerned with how well it is doing in relation to São Paulo. Furthermore, the maldistribution of income within the Northeast may be a much more serious problem to the region than the income disparities between regions. Social and political pressures generated by a real or imagined inequality in sharing the rewards of economic progress can frustrate as well as stimulate development efforts.

The Challenge for Foreign Aid

Northeast Brazil is destined to remain for some time in the foreign aid limelight as a major Alliance for Progress project. Despite its recent progress, it is still a poor region with major economic problems and a high potential for political and social disorder. But it is clearly apparent that the Brazilian Northeast, like most other developing areas, presents too complex a situation for either Brazil or the donors of foreign aid to be guided by much of the traditional thinking and simple clichés that now dominate the scene.

First, it must be recognized that a nation can achieve rapid economic progress, as Brazil did over the 1950's, without relying on foreign aid. Foreign aid of the proper kind, right amounts, and given to the appropriate groups can help to accelerate economic growth. But foreign aid has an equally great, if not greater, potential for distorting and frustrating a country's development efforts, particularly if it creates unrealistic expectations.

A second principle is that foreign aid programs are successful only if, over a reasonable period, they work themselves out of a job. That is, foreign aid must do more than temporarily improve economic and social welfare in the aid recipient country. Its more fundamental role is to improve the operating efficiency of the system so that the aid recipient has a permanently increased and self-sustaining capacity to satisfy needs and expectations. If the country is not permanently better off when aid is withdrawn, external aid has performed only a special relief or welfare function.

Foreign aid discussions characteristically devote a great deal of attention to the obligations of the aid recipient. His responsibilities include such matters as comprehensive long-range development planning, fiscal and monetary policies, social reforms, and honest and efficient development administration. But foreign aid is a joint venture, the success of which is also dependent on the extent to which the donor recognizes and fulfills the obligations he implicitly assumes by encouraging the arrangement.

If the foreign aid donor is motivated by what he considers to be political dangers, he must have an adequate background and evaluation system for gauging accurately political events and political factors in the aid recipient's country. The case of Northeast Brazil presents the interesting situation of the United States acting on the basis of its own political evaluation that a critical Castro-Communist threat exists in the region, whereas the key Brazilian officials in the region, who know the history and style of their region and evaluate the situation differently, are not responding favorably to the types of foreign aid activities being offered.

The donor has an obligation also to develop an accurate and detailed understanding of the economic structure and trends of the aid-recipient's country. Short missions like the Bohan Mission can be useful, but it is unlikely that they can provide the depth of understanding needed for operating an effective aid program.

The donor's chances for success will depend heavily on the extent to which he assumes a responsibility for equipping himself with the types of assistance likely to be required either for fulfilling the aid conditions established by the donor or for achieving rapid and significant development results in the area. For example, the United States insists that aid recipient countries undertake comprehensive economic planning. Shouldn't it undertake, therefore, to train a supply of United States personnel in economic planning in order to respond to the requests for technical help in this field and to prepare the AID staff itself to evaluate the planning work it is likely to be asked to support? To fulfill this kind of a responsibility, the donor must do long-range planning to anticipate and have available with the proper timing the kinds of assistance that are likely to be needed and that are crucial for achieving the donor's foreign aid goals.

In general, this study reaches a reasonably optimistic conclusion about future development potentials for Northeast Brazil and about possible foreign aid successes that can be significant for the Alliance for Progress. But both Brazil and the United States must understand that development success and foreign aid results cannot be achieved quickly, that only a share of the foreign aid projects can be expected to succeed, and that foreign aid is a two-sided affair in which the goals of the donor and the recipient may conflict, and the giver as well as the receiver may be handicapped by inadequate knowledge and understanding.

2

Brazil's Economy and
Its Regional Patterns

WHAT IS THE TOTAL Brazilian setting for the Northeast problem? What has been the pattern of recent Brazilian economic expansion? And in what way has the Northeast region participated in over-all economic growth?

Brazil has progressed in developing economic statistics and studies. But for such a large and complex country much of the information is inadequate for a complete understanding of the current situation and past trends. As is true in most countries, developed as well as under-developed, regional economic patterns are less well studied than over-all national trends. But despite the many limitations of statistics and basic economic studies, a reasonably reliable overview can be presented of Brazilian economic expansion, regional patterns of development, and the role played by the Northeast in the total picture.

Geography and Resources

Brazil covers an area larger than the continental United States and as great as the rest of South America together. Brazil's population, which exceeded 75 million in 1962, increased at a rate of 3.1 percent per annum in the 1950's. Despite long standing efforts to develop the interior, including the recent establishment of Brasília, the major

18

concentrations of population and economic activity are along the coast.[1]

Unlike the United States and Canada, Brazil has no Pacific Coast as a western objective in expansion. The "Go West" inspiration that sparked the settlement and development of the United States and Canada, and that was stimulated by the various attractions of the west coasts, has not been a similar force in the development of Brazil.[2] In Brazil, westward movements inspired by the search for gold and diamonds did not result in permanent farm settlements when grasses proved too poor for cattle and the land did not serve for crops. But contrary to widely held impressions outside of Brazil, the central and south interior that Brazil has been so anxious to settle is not jungle. The tropical jungles are in the Amazon River basin of the far North.

Certain physical characteristics have impeded the development of Brazil's interior. The high coastal escarpment that runs southward for 2,000 miles from Salvador in the state of Bahia has made the construction of roads and railroads into the interior difficult and costly. Only a few rivers cut through these mountains to the sea. The principal rivers of the Southeast flow away from the coast and, after traversing falls and rapids, empty into the tributaries of the Rio de la Plata and thence into the Atlantic between Argentina and Uruguay. River transportation, therefore, has not played a major role in the development of Brazil.

The location of a large part of the Brazilian territory in the tropical region of the Amazon is another retarding physical factor. Almost half of Brazil's total area is in the Amazon basin of the North. Such physical barriers as the climate, poor soils, and tropical vegetation have limited the settlement there to only 2.6 million people.

The size of the country, the limited development of overland transportation, the geographical variations in resources and historical factors have separated Brazil into regions with widely different characteristics. The principal concentrations of people and economic activity are in the eight states of the Southeast and South. These two regions with only 18 percent of Brazil's total area have 60 percent of the popula-

[1] See Preston E. James, *Latin America*, 3d ed. (Odyssey Press, 1959), for general background on the geography and resources of Brazil.

[2] See Vianna Moog, *Bandeirantes e Pioneiros*, Editôro Globo, Rio de Janeiro (1955), for an interesting study of the contrasting patterns of settlement in Brazil and the United States.

TABLE 2.1. *Characteristics of Brazil's Regions*
(Percentage Distribution)

Region	Land Area	Population 1960	Total Income 1960	Electric Power Capacity Dec. 31, 1961	Per Capita Income as Per Cent of National Average—1960
North	42	4	2.2	1.0	61
Northeast	18	32	15.9	8.8	51
Southeast	8	25	28.8	38.6	116
South	10	35	50.6	51.2	146
Central-West	22	4	2.5	0.4	62
Brazil Total[a]	100	100	100.0	100.0	—

Source: For area, and population, Instituto Brasileiro de Geografia e Estatística, *Anuário Estatístico do Brasil,* *1961,* Conselho Nacional de Estatística, pp. 13, 46; for income data, Getúlio Vargas Foundation, Brazilian Institute of Economics; for electric power data, Banco do Brasil, S.A., *Relatório 1961,* Brasília (1962), p. 194.
[a] Brazil's total area is 8,511,965 square kilometers; total population, 1960, 70,799,000; total income, Cr.$1,901,177 million; electric power capacity, Dec. 31, 1961, 4,352,512 kilowatts; per capita income, 1960, Cr.$27,000.

tion and generate almost 80 percent of the national income. (See Table 2.1.)

Brazil is well endowed with natural resources. Hydroelectric potential is large, and abundant deposits of iron ore, manganese, and other minerals are known. Vast equatorial forests exist in the Amazon basin and one of the largest reserves of pine forests is in southern Brazil, in the cool highlands of Paraná, Santa Catarina, and Rio Grande do Sul. Most extensive of the vegetation types in Brazil, however, are the savannas, covering most of central and west Brazil, and the scrub forests (caatinga) of the Northeast. On the negative side, Brazil has small deposits of coal, generally of low quality, and limited but growing production of petroleum. Also, there has been inadequate systematic investigation of Brazil's mineral riches, particularly in the interior.

Recent Economic Growth

Brazil has achieved over the decade of the fifties one of the fastest rates of economic growth in the western world, despite its turbulent political situation and a spectacular inflation in the later years of the decade. Overall growth in real output is conservatively estimated at more than 6 percent a year (about 3.5 percent on a per capita basis). This compares with a gross national product (GNP) growth rate from 1951 to 1960 of only 2.6 percent for the United States and 5.3 percent for the six Common Market countries of Europe. Germany was the only country in Western Europe that exceeded the GNP growth rate of Brazil. In Latin America, only Costa Rica and Venezuela, over the period from 1950 to 1957, experienced faster growth rates than Brazil. On a per capita basis, however, Brazil was the Latin American leader.[3]

But economic levels in Brazil still ranked behind Venezuela, Argentina, Chile, Uruguay, Costa Rica, and Colombia. Brazil's estimated $332 per capita GNP (1960) and its growth rate were both higher than in Mexico. But income per head was only about one-eighth of the United States level and about one-fourth of the economic levels in western Europe.

The dominant factor in Brazil's sustained and cumulative economic development has been a phenomenal industrialization supported by rapidly expanding activity in transportation, electric power, and mining. Agricultural output also experienced steady growth, but at a less spectacular rate than industry. In terms of real output, agricultural production increased by 52 percent from 1950 to 1960, but industrial output gained by 140 percent over the same period. Manufacturing as a source of income has become almost as important as agriculture in Brazil; but in terms of employment, agriculture is still dominant.

Brazil achieved its phenomenal economic growth with virtually no foreign assistance from the United States except for "hard" loans from the Export-Import Bank, without a steadily growing export sector, and despite, or perhaps because of, a serious domestic inflation situation. From 1945 through 1959, Brazil received only about $50 million in grants from the United States, and a large share of this amount was military assistance. Over the twenty-year period from 1940 to 1959, Brazil received about $1 billion in hard loans from the Export-Import Bank and repaid 44 percent of the principal plus $130

[3] For the latest comparative statistics on Latin America, see Inter-American Development Bank, *First Annual Report, 1961*, Social Progress Trust Fund (1962). For U.S. and European statistics see Chase Manhattan Bank, *The New European Market: A Guide for American Businessmen* (1962), p. 39.

Index of Real Output in Brazil, 1949-1960

(1949 = 100)

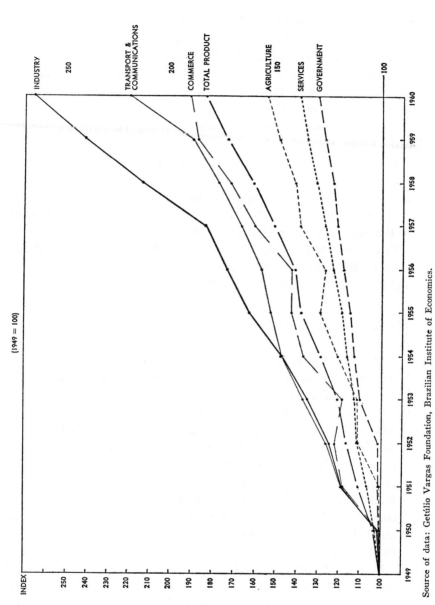

Source of data: Getúlio Vargas Foundation, Brazilian Institute of Economics.

23

million in interest and commissions.[4] However, the United States also made available about $150 million worth of agricultural surpluses, which saved Brazil some valuable foreign exchange.

At the end of World War II, Brazil had a substantial accumulation of foreign exchange. Foreign exchange controls were established in 1948, but much of the foreign purchasing power was used for luxury consumption goods before the controls became effective. During the early 1950's, foreign exchange earnings from coffee and cocoa beans were high. Yet throughout the entire postwar period, Brazil was normally in a situation of foreign exchange crisis. A large flow of private foreign investment, an increase in foreign debt through commercial credit loans from the United States, and loans from the World Bank in the early postwar period were Brazil's principal means of coping with the foreign exchange situation. As of 1962 the World Bank had loaned $267 million for the foreign exchange costs of electric power and transportation projects in Brazil.

The Pattern of Industrialization

Textile manufacturing and food processing industries have long been important manufacturing activities in Brazil,[5] and as of the latest industrial survey in 1958 one out of every three factory workers was still employed in these industries.

Next in importance is the chemical and pharmaceutical industry, which has been one of the leading growth sectors for Brazil. Petroleum refining is included in this industry group. The nine oil refineries in Brazil—only one of which was in operation before 1950—processed 80 million barrels of crude petroleum in 1961. Rapid expansion has also occurred in phosphatic and nitrogen fertilizers, synthetic fibers, industrial chemicals, and pharmaceutical products.

Steel production began in Brazil on a major scale at the end of World War II with the establishment of the government controlled Volta Redonda plant supported by a United States Export-Import Bank loan. Over the decade, steel production increased about two

[4] Brazilian Embassy, *Survey of the Brazilian Economy, 1960*, Washington, D.C. (September 1960), pp. 95-97.
[5] Stanley J. Stein, *The Brazilian Cotton Manufacture* (Harvard University Press, 1957).

TABLE 2.2. *Brazilian Industrial Growth, Selected Industries, 1950-1960*

Industry[a]	1950	1960
Cellulose	52 (1953)	210
Cement	1,386	4,474
Fertilizers	—	521
Flour (wheat)	1,032	2,570 (est.)
Paper	247	474
Steel ingots	789	1,843
Steel shapes (laminados)	623	1,358
Sugar mills	1,403	3,319
Tires (motor vehicle)	1,353	3,253
Tractors	—	1,653[b]
Trucks and Automobiles	—	133

Source: Instituto Brasileiro de Geografia e Estatística, Conselho Nacional de Estatística; *Anuário Estatístico do Brasil, 1952, 1954,* and *1961;* Banco do Brasil, S.A., *Relatório 1961.*
[a] In thousands of metric tons except tires, trucks and automobiles, which are thousands of units, and tractors, which are in units.
[b] 1961.

and one-half times to a level of approximately 2 million ingot tons—still a small steel production for a country of over 70 million population.

The most dramatic industrialization feat was the creation within a five-year period of the seventh largest automobile industry in the world. Before 1956, activities in the automotive field were limited almost exclusively to the manufacture of parts and minor assembly plant operations. But by 1960, in response to special government incentives, ten major concerns were producing over 130,000 automobiles and trucks in Brazil with about 90 percent of the parts domestically manufactured.[6]

Other major expansions occurred in paper and pulp, heavy mechanical and electrical equipment and, more recently, in tractor production. Almost half of Brazil's capital goods in the early 1960's was being produced internally. This includes machine tools, motors, transformers, turbines and generators, mining, transportation and refrigerating equipment. The shipbuilding industry, now being established, will have a capacity of 160,000 tons deadweight per year by 1963. The

[6] Lincoln Gordon and Engelbert L. Grommers, *United States Manufacturing Investment in Brazil: The Impact of Brazilian Government Policies, 1946-1960* (Harvard University, 1962), Chap. 4.

tractor industry started in 1960 and produced 1,600 units in 1961. The production goal for 1962 is 5,000.

What accounts for Brazil's surge of industrialization? A main factor has been the government's determination to "emancipate" the country from its traditional role as a producer of raw materials.[7] Another crucial factor was the growing vigor and influence of private business, particularly in São Paulo, which explains why government policy has relied mainly on private enterprise for industrial expansion. The only fields completely reserved to government enterprise are petroleum exploration and the railroads. Petroleum refining is both public and private, but the three government refineries (Presidente Bernardes, Landulfo Alves, Duque de Caixa) have 82 percent of the country's total refining capacity.[8] Since the passage of the PETROBRAS law in 1953, no new refineries can be built by private enterprise nor can the existing six privately owned refineries expand. The distribution of petroleum products is completely in the private sector. In the steel industry, the government pioneered by establishing the first large integrated steel plant, Volta Redonda. The government also owns dominant interests in other major steel plants. About 40 percent of the industry is private. In electric power, the government's role is growing; as of 1960, only one-fourth of total capacity belonged to mixed public-private corporations or state enterprises. Virtually all of the government capacity is newly constructed facilities. Until recently the expropriation of private utilities has been very small. The private power industry is largely foreign owned—Canadian and United States—and nationalistic forces have become strong for the government to take over these enterprises.

The process of industrialization started in the early 1930's when coffee production became unprofitable for a prolonged period. World War II acted as a strong stimulant to industrial growth because a severe shortage of shipping sharply curtailed imports of manufactured goods. During and after the war, government aid to industrial expansion became of decisive importance. Encouragement and protection were given to industry through manipulation of foreign exchange privileges, tariff and quota protection, and selective exemption from

[7] The most recent comprehensive study of Brazil's industrialization is the Brazilian Embassy, *Survey of the Brazilian Economy, 1960.*

[8] *Conjuntura Econômica,* International ed. (January 1962), pp. 42-43.

import duties. However, differential tax treatment and outright subsidies played only a minor role in governmental policies.

Both domestic private enterprise and foreign entrepreneurs have played major roles in Brazil's industrialization. In many cases, the new industries have been joint ventures of foreign and Brazilian interests.[9] The flow of foreign capital into manufacturing enterprises has been large, but the technological and managerial know-how imported along with the foreign capital has undoubtedly been of greater importance.

Complete statistics on the inflow of foreign investment are not available. But a partial picture of the many foreign countries investing in Brazil and the wide variety of manufacturing that has attracted foreign capital is shown by the recent registration in Brazil of some of the foreign private investment. Of the $511 million registered for the 1955 to 1961 period, about 40 percent came from the United States and 20 percent from Western Germany. Other countries in order of importance were Switzerland, France, Canada, England, Japan, and Italy.[10]

The automobile industry attracted 45 percent of the registered investment. But electrical and nonelectrical machinery, heavy chemicals and petroleum, pharmaceuticals, vegetable oil, and a variety of other types of manufacturing were also financed by foreign capital. Since 1960, however, with growing competition from the European Common Market for United States investment and a turbulent and uncertain political situation in Brazil, foreign investment has dropped off sharply.

Three features of Brazil's industrialization are of special interest. First, the expansion of manufacturing was almost completely directed to the domestic market. Second, despite the popular preference in Brazil as in most other countries for starting with the so-called "basic" industries, the industrialization pattern in most industries was for the assembly, finishing, or packaging stages to develop first and for the processing of intermediate and primary goods to follow successively. Third, the phenomenal growth in real manufactur-

[9] See, for example, Wolfgang G. Friedmann and George Kalmanoff, *Joint International Business Ventures* (Columbia University Press, 1961). Also Gordon and Grommers, *op. cit.*, pp. 138-44.

[10] Banco do Brasil, S. A., *Relatório: 1961*, Brasília (1962), p. 232.

ing output was achieved despite rapid inflation, which averaged about 25 percent a year over the last half of the decade and reached more than 40 percent annually in 1961.

Agricultural Trends

Over the last decade, agricultural production and farm income have expanded steadily, at a lesser rate than the dramatic gains in industry but still at a faster rate than population growth. Real output gained 52 percent and population increased 36 percent from 1950 to 1960. Consequently, agriculture has maintained its contribution to national income at between 26 and 31 percent of the total. The high of 31 percent was reached in 1960.

Coffee is the dominant single crop, but Brazil is much more than a coffee economy. In 1960, coffee accounted for only 17 percent of the crop area being cultivated and less than 15 percent of farm income. Other farm crops, each one almost as important as coffee, are corn, rice, cotton, and beans. Sugar, manioc—an edible root used for making flour and tapioca—bananas, wheat, and cocoa beans follow in importance. The farm sector also includes a rapidly expanding livestock industry and some stagnating extractive agricultural products such as tropical waxes and oils.

Agricultural raw materials and foodstuffs are the dominant foreign exchange earners for Brazil. Despite recently depressed world prices, coffee still accounts for half of the value of Brazil's total exports. Cocoa beans, although meeting growing competition from African producers, remain important. Cotton exports have expanded greatly in a favorable world market, and sugar has become the third most valuable export item as a result of Cuba's loss of the United States market. Other important agricultural exports include meat and by-products, tobacco, sisal fiber, castor bean oil, and carnauba wax. In coffee, Brazil is the world's leading producer. In cocoa beans, it is next after Ghana and Nigeria. In sugar, Brazil follows the Soviet Union and Cuba. And in cotton, it is the second producer in the Western Hemisphere after the United States.

Food crops for domestic consumption all have expanded significantly. Rice and corn production have almost doubled over the decade, and manioc and beans have increased by about 50 percent.

Brazil has one of the largest livestock populations in the world—over 160 million head in 1960—but despite recent progress this sector is still far from fully developed.

The gains in agriculture resulted mainly from increased land utilization and only slightly from productivity increases. The area cultivated for the principal crops expanded from 16 million hectares in 1948 to 26 million in 1960. Yields per hectare have increased significantly for coffee and cotton, only slightly for corn, beans, manioc, and sugar and not at all for rice, tobacco, bananas, oranges, cocoa beans, and potatoes.

Minerals Development

The most significant recent development in the minerals field has been the increase in production of iron ore and manganese ore. The excellent quality of Brazilian iron ore, compact hematite with an iron content as high as 68.9 percent, and the existence of vast reserves, have been recognized for many years. But the problem of transportation from the interior over the coastal escarpment and a reluctance to permit foreign investors to exploit Brazil's mineral wealth have long retarded iron ore development. With an expanding domestic iron and steel industry, an improvement in transportation facilities, and a change in policies toward foreign investment, iron ore production has grown from about two million to more than nine million metric tons over the 1950 to 1960 period. At the same time, iron ore exports increased from about one million to over five million tons. Furthermore, exports are projected to reach 25 million tons by 1975.

In manganese ore, Brazil ranks with India and the Soviet Union as the world's largest producers. During the late 1950's, a major manganese mining project was completed in the territory of Amapá in the North by a Brazilian company associated with Bethlehem Steel. The ore is now transported to a new port over a newly constructed railway 200 kilometers long. Largely as a result of the Amapá project, manganese ore production has increased fourfold to a level of one million tons, and exports to more than 800,000 tons.

Other important minerals are tungsten ores, mica, bauxite, uranium, and thorium. Brazil also has sizable deposits of phosphate rock, limestone, fluorite, dolomite, and other minerals indispensable for the chemical industry. But, in the main, Brazil's mineral resources are not yet well known, since most of the national territory has not been adequately surveyed. As only one example, Brazil's large phosphate rock deposits were discovered accidentally by a group looking for underground water only a few years ago at a short distance from Olinda in Pernambuco—a city over four hundred years old in the center of one of the most densely settled areas in Brazil.

In petroleum, Brazilian production of crude oil has grown rapidly since oil was discovered in 1939 in the state of Bahia. But the country still imports a major share of its requirements. In 1953, the government created a government corporation (PETROBRAS) which has a monopoly of the exploration and production of petroleum, owns and operates the bulk of refining capacity, and is expanding its activities in ocean and pipeline transportation and in petrochemicals. The production of crude petroleum, located completely in the state of Bahia in the Northeast, increased from about 340,000 barrels in 1950 to 29,600,000 barrels in 1960.

Coal production in Brazil has fluctuated between 2 and 2.3 million metric tons over the last decade. Production could be greatly increased, but the quality of the coal is low, and only a small share of output can be used to meet the growing demand for metallurgical coal.

Transportation and Electric Power

Shortages in transportation facilities and electric power have long been considered the key bottlenecks in Brazilian economic expansion. The problem in transportation is the size and topography of the country. The difficulties in electric power have been the large investment requirements of the industry, restrictive government controls in an inflationary situation which have made the electric power field unattractive for private investment, and changing public policies toward private investment, particularly foreign private investment, in public utilities. Despite these problems, the transportation and electric power sectors have grown rapidly over the last decade.

A look at the map of Brazil will demonstrate the inherent difficulties faced by Brazil in transportation development. The extensive coastline and three river basins—the Amazon in the North running from the west to the east, the San Francisco in the Northeast flowing from the south to the north, and the Rio de la Plata in the South with little penetration into Brazilian territory—are Brazil's natural lines of communication, but all are underused. Inland transportation, especially the railroad system, is oriented from the coastal cities to the interior with few and deficient connections between cities. Most railroads and roads were developed to channel raw materials to the ports for export and not to provide a national transportation system. And to make matters even worse, the railroads are of different gauges. Thus, the country became divided into economic islands with coastal shipping providing a weak link between these islands.

An overall indicator of progress in transportation is a doubling of the index of real production for transportation and communications in the last decade. A government corporation was established to run all the railroads, and traffic has increased along with improvements in the rights of way and large-scale acquisition of diesel locomotives. But the government corporation has been running substantial deficits, and the railroads still do not play the major role in transportation and probably never will.

Highway transportation has expanded the most rapidly. The government pays for the roads, but private capital finances the transportation equipment. The federal and state highway system has been almost doubled in the 1950 to 1960 period, but still totalled at the end of 1960 only about 120,000 kilometers of which about 13,000 kilometers are paved. But the number of trucks and automobiles has doubled, and the number of buses has tripled over the decade. Motorcycles and motor scooters have also become widely used.

Air transportation has developed rapidly and has become an important carrier of cargo as well as passengers. Port installations have been improved. Merchant marine and coastal shipping are being reequipped and expanded, and a shipbuilding industry is being initiated. But coastal shipping in particular still remains one of the major transportation bottlenecks.

Brazil's expansion of electric power capacity and output has been rapid, but the availability of power has generally lagged behind the demands of such a fast growing economy. Installed capacity has grown by 2 million kilowatts over the decade, to 4.8 million in 1960, according to official statistics, and production has expanded from 8 to 23 billion kilowatt hours. These data, however, do not include a substantial amount of capacity and production from installations of private business firms which have been stimulated by a long-existing power shortage. To meet the expanding power needs of the nation is still one of the major tasks of Brazil.[11]

Regional Patterns of Recent Expansion

What has been the regional pattern of Brazil's recent economic growth? Have all regions shared in the country's rapid progress or have certain regions been stagnating while others advanced at a very fast pace? And have regional disparities within Brazil been increasing?

Contrary to popular belief in Brazil, over the last decade all the major regions have been sharing in the nation's growth. Furthermore, although wide regional disparities in income levels still exist, these disparities have begun to narrow—particularly over the last half of the decade.

Regional statistics in Brazil have serious weaknesses and must be interpreted with caution. Moreover, the analysis of comparative growth rates within the country is a complex problem. It involves differential rates of population increases as well as of output and prices in different sectors. Nevertheless, despite statistical limitations and analytical complexities, the following general conclusions, derived from available statistical data and reasonably supported by independent external evidence, can be accepted with considerable assurance.

The geographical patterns of the 1950-60 decade in Brazil can be summarized as follows: (1) All regions have made rapid absolute gains in both total and per capita income. (2) Each region has certain subareas or sectors of economic activity which have experienced unusually rapid growth over the period. (3) From 1950 to 1955 the fastest growing regions were the South and Central West where the coffee sectors were booming. (4) From 1955 to 1960 the Northeast

[11] For a discussion of expansion problems in electric power see D. F. Cavers and James R. Nelson, *Electric Power Regulation in Latin America* (Johns Hopkins Press, 1959).

and the North progressed more rapidly than the South and Central West, where the setback in the coffee sectors offset much of the gains from industrialization. (5) The narrowing of regional differentials is clearest and most significant in terms of average per capita income. Because of internal migration, Northeast population increased by only 25 percent for the decade as compared to 45 and 73 percent for the South and Central West. (See Table 2.3.) The gains in per capita income for the Northeast were even greater, therefore, than in terms of total income.

Why is it so widely believed in Brazil that regional disparities are growing and that virtually all of the Nation's expansion is occurring in the South? Probably the principal reason is Brazil's underdevelopment in objective regional analysis. Although this professional field is making progress, there have not yet been any continuing comparative regional studies for the country as a whole. The amount of data is increasing, but it is not being analyzed. In the absence of technical studies, the usual tendency in Brazil and elsewhere is for politicians in some areas to accent only the lags in their region in the hope of securing more government support, thus creating a popular impression of greater and greater regional disparities.

Another reason for the erroneous impressions is that such studies as have been done on regional disparities have made an error in using point-to-point comparisons or index numbers. For example, the brief analysis of regional patterns included in the Brazilian Embassy report on Brazil's economy compares data for only three years: 1948, 1952, and 1958.[12] Because 1958 was a drought year in the Northeast, its share of national income was naturally down. The Celso Furtado report, based on data only up to 1956, compares only two years— 1956 and the immediate postwar year of 1948—in arguing that regional disparities are growing. The report also presents an index of production for the regions with 1948 as a base.[13] Although the index technique uses data for all the years, it is still only a comparison of each year to the base year. If the base year is a typical year and well chosen—and 1948 is a doubtful choice—the calculations may be useful for showing trends within the region. But comparing indexes of

[12] Survey of Brazilian Economy 1960, p. 4.

[13] Conselho de Desenvolvimento do Nordeste, A Policy for the Economic Development of the Northeast, Rio de Janeiro (1959), p. 12; Table 4, p. 13.

TABLE 2.3. *Population in Brazil by Regions and States, 1950 and 1960*

Regions and States	1950 Number (thousands)	1950 Percent of Total	1960 Number (thousands)	1960 Percent of Total	Increase 1950 to 1960 Number (thousands)	Increase 1950 to 1960 Percent Increase
NORTH	1,845	3.6	2,601	3.7	756	41.0
Amazonas	514	1.0	721	1.0	207	40.3
Pará	1,123	2.2	1,551	2.2	428	38.1
Rondônia	37	.1	71	.1	34	92.2
Acre	115	.2	160	.2	45	39.1
Rio Branco	18	—	29	—	11	61.2
Amapá	38	.1	69	.1	31	81.7
NORTHEAST	17,974	34.7	22,427	31.9	4,455	24.7
Maranhão	1,583	3.1	2,492	3.5	909	57.4
Piauí	1,046	2.0	1,263	1.8	217	20.8
Ceará	2,695	5.2	3,338	4.8	643	23.9
Rio Gde do Norte	968	1.9	1,157	1.6	189	19.6
Paraíba	1,713	3.3	2,018	2.9	305	17.8
Pernambuco	3,395	6.5	4,137	5.9	742	21.9
Alagoas	1,093	2.1	1,271	1.8	178	16.8
Sergipe	644	1.3	760	1.1	116	18.0
Bahia	4,835	9.3	5,991	8.5	1,156	23.9
SOUTHEAST	13,264	25.6	17,698	25.1	4,434	33.4
Minas Gerais	7,728	14.9	9,799	13.9	2,071	26.8
Espírito Santo	862	1.7	1,189	1.7	327	38.0
Rio de Janeiro	2,297	4.4	3,403	4.8	1,106	48.2
Guanabara	2,377	4.6	3,307	4.7	930	39.2
SOUTH	16,997	32.8	24,681	35.0	7,684	45.3
São Paulo	9,142	17.6	12,975	18.4	3,833	42.0
Paraná	2,129	4.1	4,110	5.8	1,981	93.0
Santa Catarina	1,561	3.0	2,147	3.1	586	37.8
Rio Gde do Sul	4,165	8.0	5,449	7.7	1,284	30.8
CENTRAL WEST	1,737	3.3	3,007	4.3	1,270	73.2
Mato Grosso	522	1.0	910	1.3	388	73.4
Goiás and Dist. Fed.	1,215	2.3	2,097	3.0	882	72.6
BRAZIL	51,976	100.0	70,799	100.0	18,823	36.3

Source: Instituto Brasileiro de Geografia e Estatística, Conselho Nacional de Estatística, *Anuário Estatístico do Brasil, 1954* and *1961.*

regions against each other can be highly misleading. For example, by shifting the base in the Furtado calculation to either 1951, 1952, or 1953 the gains for the Northeast exceed those for the Central South.

A final factor is that until results of the 1960 population census became available in early 1962, all of the per capita income estimates for 1950-60 were based on the assumption that population in each of the states was continuing to increase at the same rate as experienced during the 1940-50 decade. These per capita income data now have to be revised in light of the results of the latest census. There has also been a time lag in other new data finding their way into the irregular and limited pattern of regional studies. The regional income data for 1959 and 1960 were included in the analysis for this study. But the studies in Brazil had not as of the time this was written incorporated this material. Remembering that 1958 was a drought year for the Northeast, it is apparent that the latest available comparisons will show a distorted economic picture for the region.

TABLE 2.4. *Brazil's Income, Regional and State Shares, 1950-1960*
(Percentage Distribution)

Region	1950	1951	1952	1953	1954	1955	1956	1957	1958	1959	1960
NORTH	2.2	2.2	2.2	2.0	1.9	2.0	2.3	2.4	2.2	2.1	2.2
Amazonas[a]	1.0	0.9	0.9	0.8	0.8	0.8	1.0	1.0	0.9	0.9	0.9
Pará[b]	1.2	1.3	1.3	1.2	1.1	1.2	1.3	1.4	1.3	1.2	1.3
NORTHEAST	16.4	15.5	15.0	14.2	14.4	13.9	14.4	14.9	14.3	15.3	15.9
Maranhão	1.0	1.0	1.0	1.0	1.0	0.9	0.9	1.0	1.0	1.2	1.2
Piauí	0.6	0.5	0.6	0.5	0.5	0.5	0.5	0.5	0.5	0.5	0.5
Ceará	2.4	2.0	2.0	1.8	1.7	1.7	1.9	2.0	1.4	2.0	2.1
Rio Grande do Norte	1.0	1.0	0.9	0.7	0.7	0.8	0.8	0.8	0.7	0.9	0.9
Paraíba	1.6	1.4	1.3	1.2	1.3	1.3	1.3	1.3	1.1	1.3	1.5
Pernambuco	3.9	3.9	3.6	3.5	3.4	3.3	3.4	3.6	3.7	3.6	3.5
Alagoas	0.9	0.9	0.9	0.8	0.8	0.7	0.8	0.9	0.9	0.9	0.9
Sergipe	0.6	0.6	0.6	0.6	0.5	0.5	0.6	0.6	0.6	0.6	0.6
Bahia	4.5	4.2	4.1	4.1	4.5	4.2	4.1	4.2	4.3	4.4	4.7
SOUTHEAST	31.3	31.4	30.6	30.8	30.8	30.5	31.8	31.4	30.9	30.4	28.7
Minas Gerais	10.8	10.7	10.5	11.2	11.3	11.1	11.2	11.3	10.3	10.3	9.7
Espírito Santo	1.3	1.5	1.2	1.3	1.3	1.3	1.2	1.3	1.1	1.1	1.0
Rio de Janeiro	4.4	4.3	4.5	4.3	4.2	4.2	4.6	4.6	4.5	4.5	4.5
Guanabara	14.8	14.9	14.4	14.0	14.1	13.9	14.8	14.2	15.0	14.5	13.5
SOUTH	48.2	48.8	50.0	50.3	50.3	51.0	48.9	48.9	50.0	49.8	50.7
São Paulo	32.3	33.6	33.8	33.0	33.9	32.9	31.4	31.5	32.3	32.0	32.3
Paraná	4.7	4.6	5.3	5.3	4.5	5.6	4.6	5.1	5.7	6.2	6.6
Santa Catarina	2.5	2.2	2.4	2.7	2.4	2.7	2.7	2.7	2.7	2.6	2.7
Rio Grande do Sul	8.7	8.4	8.5	9.3	9.5	9.8	10.2	9.7	9.2	9.0	9.2
CENTRAL WEST	1.9	2.1	2.2	2.7	2.6	2.6	2.6	2.4	2.6	2.4	2.5
Mato Grosso	0.7	0.7	1.0	1.1	1.2	1.1	1.1	1.0	1.1	0.9	1.0
Goiás	1.2	1.4	1.2	1.5	1.4	1.5	1.5	1.4	1.5	1.5	1.5
BRAZIL	100.0	100.0	100.0	100.0	100.0	100.0	100.0	100.0	100.0	100.0	100.0
Total income in Cr.$ billion	214	254	293	360	456	579	732	872	1,040	1,418	1,901

Source: Getúlio Vargas Foundation, Brazilian Institute of Economics.
[a] Includes territories of Rondônia, Acre, and Rio Branco.
[b] Includes territory of Amapá.

The trends in total income and income per capita for Brazil's regions and states are shown on an annual basis in Tables 2.4 and 2.5, and the widely varying rates of population increase between 1950 and 1960 are shown in Table 2.3. An examination of these data clearly reveals the distortions that result in comparing regional trends by using a single base year for all regions in an index or by using only two or three years of the entire period. Also, it should be noted that the emphasis in such comparisons is on relative rather than absolute rates of growth. A region can be expanding steadily, but its share of total national income can increase only if its rate of expansion is greater than the average for the nation.

How the regions have shared in recent growth can be better understood by examining briefly the structure and trends in each region.

TABLE 2.5. *Brazil's Per Capita Income, Regional and State Shares, 1950-1960*

(Percentage National Average)

Region	1950	1951	1952	1953	1954	1955	1956	1957	1958	1959	1960
NORTH	65	64	63	59	56	57	65	68	62	59	61
Amazonas[a]	76	71	70	63	61	63	75	78	72	67	68
Pará[b]	58	58	57	54	51	53	59	61	55	54	56
NORTHEAST	48	46	45	43	44	43	45	47	45	48	51
Maranhão	34	33	32	32	31	29	29	30	31	34	34
Piauí	29	28	29	26	25	25	27	28	26	29	29
Ceará	47	39	42	37	35	30	40	42	30	42	45
Rio Grande do Norte	53	54	52	43	43	45	50	49	40	53	57
Paraíba	48	46	44	38	41	42	43	43	39	47	54
Pernambuco	61	61	57	57	56	54	57	61	62	61	60
Alagoas	44	44	43	42	40	39	44	49	51	50	51
Sergipe	49	53	53	52	48	46	52	54	56	57	55
Bahai	50	46	46	47	51	48	48	49	50	52	56
SOUTHEAST	126	126	124	125	125	123	128	127	124	122	116
Minas Gerais	74	74	74	79	80	79	79	81	74	74	71
Espírito Santo	79	94	77	80	79	77	72	77	67	66	64
Rio de Janeiro	102	98	102	98	94	93	101	98	97	96	95
Guanabara	334	331	322	312	312	308	325	311	324	315	291
SOUTH	151	151	155	155	154	154	147	146	147	145	146
São Paulo	189	194	195	190	194	187	178	177	180	177	178
Paraná	117	112	123	120	99	118	91	99	106	111	111
Santa Catarina	84	76	81	91	82	91	90	88	90	87	90
Rio Grande do Sul	112	107	110	121	123	127	132	127	119	118	120
CENTRAL WEST	60	64	64	77	75	73	69	64	67	62	62
Mato Grosso	72	71	94	105	110	97	93	84	94	71	78
Goiás	54	60	51	64	59	63	58	54	55	58	55
BRAZIL	100	100	100	100	100	100	100	100	100	100	100

Source: ETENE, Bank of the Northeast of Brazil. Based on data from National Income Unit, Getúlio Vargas Foundation.
[a] Includes territories of Rondônia, Acre, and Rio Branco.
[b] Includes territory of Amapá.

The Northeast will not be reviewed in this chapter, however, because it will be discussed in greater detail subsequently.

The North

This region with almost half of Brazil's total area had a 1960 population of only 2.6 million people even after a 41 percent increase over the decade. Its two states of Amazonas and Pará and four federal territories of Acre (Acre became a state in 1962), Amapá, Rondônia, and Rio Branco encompass virtually all of the Amazon River basin situated in Brazil. This is the region which monopolized world rubber production during the last part of the nineteenth century. But the rubber boom was short-lived. Seeds and plants from Brazil became the basis for the rubber industry of Ceylon and Malaya, which now dominate the field. Brazilian rubber exports reached a peak of 42,000 tons in 1912,[14] but rubber production declined thereafter until the pre-World War II period when the industry began to revive. Production in the Brazilian North recovered to about 30,000 tons a year during World War II and has since remained at about that level. But this amount of rubber, although close to Brazil's output in the rubber boom era, is now only a small share of greatly expanded world production.

The North's economy is heavily dependent on extractive agriculture and minerals, but also has a small and growing industrial sector. The agricultural sector is almost evenly divided between extractive products, crops, and livestock production. The principal extractive products are rubber, brazil nuts, pepper, and starch extracted from tropical fruits. The leading cultivated crops are jute and manioc. Animal production includes both cattle raising and poultry. Fishing is also important.

The industrial sector consists of a wide variety of small manufacturing establishments in textile, food, lumber, and leather products, and manganese in the minerals field. The region also has a petroleum refinery. A cement mill is being completed, and a large paper mill project promoted by Chinese capital appears to be going ahead.

The most spectacular major contributors to recent growth have

[14] Caio Prado Júnior, *História Econômica do Brasil*, 6 Edição, Editôra Brasiliense, Rio de Janeiro (1961), p. 245.

been the Amapá manganese ore project and the expansion of jute growing. Brazil nuts, pepper, fishing, poultry raising, cattle, and rice also experienced sizable increases in output. The vast forest resources of the North, although the focus of considerable technical assistance from the Food and Agriculture Organization of the United Nations, have not yet become a major source of income or employment.

The federal government has assisted development in the Amazon region through a special Credit Bank of Amazonia, originally created in 1942 to encourage rubber production. And in 1953, the federal government established a regional organization, the Superintendency for the Economic Valorization Plan of the Amazon (SPVEA) which is supposed to receive the 3 percent of total federal tax revenues allocated in the 1946 Constitution for Amazon development.[15] In practice, however SPVEA has been receiving only a share of this money, and the Amazon development project has had little momentum. Nevertheless, in relation to its small population, the region continues to make considerable progress, and of many ambitious projects being discussed, some will undoubtedly add to future growth.

The Southeast

The Southeast region with its 18 million population is a highly diversified and relatively high income area. Most of the region's area and more than half of its population are in the interior state of Minas Gerais. The states of Guanabara (the city of Rio de Janeiro and its metropolitan area), Rio de Janeiro, and Espírito Santo constitute the rest of the region. Per capita income for the region as a whole is about 20 percent above the national average, but within the region ranges from 64 percent of the national average in Espírito Santo to about 300 percent for Guanabara.

The region's agricultural sector produces a large share of Brazil's rice, corn, beans, oranges, bananas, and grapes. Some coffee and sugar are raised in the area but relatively little cotton. In livestock, the state of Minas is second only to São Paulo. In mining the Southeast

[15] Two additional sources of recent economic information on the North are the 2 volume SPVEA report, *Política de Desenvolvimento da Amazônia*, Presidência da República (1960) and the CAPES (Campanha Nacional de Aperfeiçoamento de Pessoal de Nível Superior) *Estudos de Desenvolvimento Regional* for Pará and Amazonas (1959).

is the dominant region with Minas Gerais accounting for 99 percent
of iron ore production, all of the nickel ore, and a significant amount
of manganese ore. As a source of regional income, mining and manufacturing together have long been more important than agriculture.
The manufacturing sector, heavily concentrated in the city of Rio
de Janeiro, includes food processing and consumer goods industries
as well as petroleum refineries and cement production. Most of Brazil's
basic iron and steel industry is in this region and located in the state
of Rio de Janeiro and at Belo Horizonte in Minas.

From 1950 to 1955, the Southeast's rate of growth was roughly
similar to the national average. The agricultural sector, in which coffee
is a minor item, except for Espírito Santo, prospered less than in the
regions to the South and West. Industrial growth was sizable and
rapid, and in 1956, with a burst of industrial expansion, the region
reached a peak in its contribution to the nation's income.

Since 1956, however, the Southeast has steadily lagged behind the
nation. The industrial sector, which includes the region's greatly
expanded output of iron ore and other minerals, maintained a rapid
growth rate. The agricultural sector, on the other hand, continued to
lag. Just as in the case of coffee, the region does not have enough of
a stake in cotton growing and sugar to have shared in the improved
situation for these commodities. But even more significant was the
slow down in commerce, government income, and the financial sector—
most likely due to the transfer of the nation's capital from the Southeast region to Brasília.

In 1960 Southeast per capita income was only 116 percent of the
national average as compared to 128 percent in 1956. For the state of
Minas Gerais, per capita income was only 71 percent of the national
average in 1960 as compared to 81 percent in 1957. Espírito Santo
was 64 percent in 1960 and 77 percent in 1957. Over the decade,
Guanabara changed from 324 to 291 percent of the national average.

The South

The South, Brazil's dynamic "heartland," consists of the four states
of São Paulo, Paraná, Santa Catarina, and Rio Grande do Sul. With
35 percent of Brazil's population, this region accounts for half of
Brazil's total income. After an increase of 45 percent from 1950 to

1960, the region's population of 25 million now exceeds that of the Northeast. And the South's average per capita income of 147 percent of the national average is almost threefold that of the Northeast.

For the region as a whole, agriculture is the dominant source of income and employment. Although its industrial sector has now surpassed agriculture, the state of São Paulo is Brazil's leading agricultural area.[16] And in agriculture Paraná and Rio Grande do Sul play a large regional and national role along with São Paulo. Coffee is still "king" and accounts for about one-fifth of total agricultural income in the region. Paraná is the fastest growing state in Brazil and the leader in coffee production. Paraná is also the second most important producer of beans, third in wheat and potatoes, fourth in castor beans and corn, and fifth in rice and cotton. The only major products in which Paraná is not a significant producer are sugar cane and fruits. In livestock production it is one of the fastest growing areas in Brazil.

São Paulo is second to Paraná in coffee and first in livestock, cotton, rice, sugar, peanuts, and tomatoes. Rio Grande do Sul is Brazil's foremost producer of wheat, potatoes, manioc, and onions in addition to being important in corn, tobacco, rice, and livestock. Santa Catarina is predominantly agricultural and produces mainly such food crops as corn, beans, rice, manioc, and wheat.

The South is Brazil's major industrial center with the state of São Paulo alone accounting for almost half of the nation's industrial income. The phenomenal expansion of the automobile industry in recent years, concentrated largely in São Paulo, has received much attention. But the region's industrial sector is highly diversified with food processing, textiles, and chemicals and pharmaceuticals still the principal manufacturing activities. The metals industry, machinery, apparel, printing, cement, paper, and wood products industries are also well developed. Although overshadowed by São Paulo, Rio Grande do Sul, Paraná, and Santa Catarina are all important industrially. Food and lumber products industries are extensive in all of the three states. In addition, Rio Grande do Sul produces on a large scale chemical, apparel, metal, and tobacco products, and the state's industrial income almost approximates the total industrial income for the Northeast region.

[16] For an analysis of São Paulo economy, see II *Plano de Ação Do Govêrno: 1963-66*, Estado de São Paulo, 1962.

In the minerals field, the South is not a major region. Santa Catarina is Brazil's principal coal producing area, but as mentioned before, coal production has been stagnant. Also the South has not shared in the country's expansion in production of petroleum, iron ore, and manganese ore. On the other hand, the region's financial and commercial activities are significant and have been a rapid growth sector for the South.

Nevertheless, a well developed region needs a tremendous amount of new expansion to stay ahead of other areas. And in this respect the gap has been narrowing since 1955 between the South and the Northeast. One factor has been heavy internal migration to São Paulo and Paraná in particular, with a resulting rate of population increase almost double that of the Northeast. A second major factor has been the deterioration of the international coffee market over the last half of the decade, which has been only partially offset by regional gains in sugar and cotton output. The South's share of Brazil's agricultural income contracted from a high of 56 percent in 1955 to 51 percent in 1960. Over the same period, average per capita income changed from 151 to 147 percent of the national average.

The Central West

Over recent decades, the vast central interior—the states of Mato Grosso and Goiás—has been Brazil's principal frontier area.[17] The population of the Central West region increased by 73 percent over the 1950 to 1960 decade, but still totals only 3 million. Brasília, which is located on the eastern edge of the region, had a 1960 population of 140,000 but the new capital accounted for only a small part of the 1,300,000 population gain for the decade.

Most of the region's economic activity is in agriculture. Livestock is important, and the Central West has become a major producer of rice. Beans, corn, manioc, coffee, and sugar are also significant crops in the region. In the field of extractive agriculture, the region is important in babaçu and rubber.

Mining is a small but growing regional activity. Goiás is Brazil's principal producer of tin ore (cassiterita) and rock crystal. Goiás also

[17] For additional information see *Plano de Desenvolvimento Econômico de Goiás: 1961-1965*, Estado de Goiás, Goiânia (1961).

produces mica, chrome, and rutile. Mato Grosso has a small but expanding output of iron ore and manganese ore. In general, however, the mineral resources of this interior region are little known.

The Central West experienced its big economic boom during the first half of the 1950 to 1960 decade, and since that period the region's overall growth has generally approximated the national average. The gains in livestock have been dramatic, and the output of rice has quadrupled over the decade. But population also expanded rapidly and per capita income has fallen back from 77 percent of the national average in 1953 to 62 percent in 1960. However, economic reporting on this vast region is incomplete. The building of Brasília and the accompanying investment in roads, electric power, and other types of infrastructure do not seem to be reflected adequately in the statistics.

Observations on the Geography of Growth

Has Brazil's recent economic expansion followed an irrational or unexpected geographical pattern? Has it been regionally unbalanced—whatever this cliché connotes? From an objective technical point of view the geographical pattern has not been illogical or unexpected. In fact, it is somewhat surprising that greater geographical concentration has not occurred. If regional balance means a narrowing of regional disparities, Brazil has recently begun to move in the direction of balance. But if regional balance means that new jobs and increased income should have been spread evenly over all regions and within regions, Brazil has not achieved balance. But how unreasonable to expect such a phenomenon.

At least five separate but interdependent variables influence geographical patterns concurrently. One factor is the physical resource potential, which varies among regions and with technological developments over time. A second variable is human and institutional resources which spark and nourish development differently in the various areas. A third force is governmental influence in the form of policies or affirmative development programs. A fourth factor is the influence of international markets, foreign investment activities, government to government foreign aid programs, and other similar forces external to a region. And a final variable is the changing composition and level of demand—regional, national, and international—for specific products.

These many variables, independently and in many combinations, influence different areas at different times and in different ways. In a country as large and diverse as Brazil, however, all regions have benefited over the last decade from some of these stimuli and influences. Within the agricultural sector, for example, the most consistent growth factor has been the greatly increased domestic market for meat and other livestock products. This has stimulated most the states of Paraná, Mato Grosso, and Goiás because of their natural resource advantages and proximity to the southern markets. Of the agricultural export crops, the international market has been most favorable over the last decade to cotton, cocoa beans, sugar, sisal fiber, castor bean oil, tobacco, Brazil nuts, and Paraguay tea (*ervamate*). Coffee, of course, has been a highly fluctuating element. The regional "mix" of agricultural crops in the North and Northeast benefited most from the influence of international markets.

Governmental policies and public investment in transportation, communication, electric power, etc. greatly favored and stimulated Brazil's rapid industrialization. And as normally happens in industrializing countries, the already established agricultural and commercial sectors were forced to provide much of the financing, particularly foreign exchange, for the expansion of industry. The bulk of the transfer of resources from agriculture and commerce to industry occurred within the regions of the South and Southeast because these industrializing areas also have large agricultural and commercial operations.

At an early stage of industrialization such as in Brazil, considerable geographical concentration of the new industry being established is inevitable. One reason is technology and the optimum size of producing units. When the size of the market can support only one or two producing units of minimum economic size in a particular field, the productive capacity cannot be scattered throughout the country. But at a later stage, when the market grows, additional units of production may be located in new regions and result in greater dispersal. Second, industrial production requires many services and materials that are not easily available in any location. Once an area begins to industrial-

ize, powerful forces stimulate the area to become better prepared for
more industry. The South and the Southeast regions were best prepared institutionally and with entrepreneurial and other human resources to support industrial expansion in the 1950's.

These generalizations largely explain why Brazil's industrialization
has resulted, and should have been expected to result, in further
concentration of manufacturing activity in the Southeast and the
South, particularly in São Paulo. But it should not be overlooked that
a sizable amount of industrial expansion occurred outside of São
Paulo and Rio de Janeiro. Many resource oriented industries have
been located outside the principal manufacturing centers, and regional markets have stimulated many industries that produce efficiently with small units dispersed throughout the country.

In theory, at least, the government might have forced what it considered to be a more balanced geographical pattern of economic
expansion over the last decade. But a level of government effectiveness, unlikely to exist at Brazil's stage of development, would have
been necessary. Even then, the question would have to be faced
whether a radically different pattern would have created a better
base than now exists for continued growth. As Hirschman has emphasized, "In the geographical sense, growth is necessarily unbalanced," and the unbalances are themselves forces for growth.[18]

[18] Albert O. Hirschman, *The Strategy of Economic Development* (Yale University Press, 1958), p. 184.

3

Recent Economic Trends in Northeast Brazil

THE BRAZILIAN NORTHEAST is the oldest, the poorest, and until recent years the most populous of Brazil's major regions. As presently delineated, the Northeast includes nine states with a total area of about 600,000 square miles and a population of 22.4 million in 1960. The smallest state—Sergipe—has an area slightly larger than the state of Connecticut or the nation of Israel. The largest—Bahia—is close to the size of California. In area, Northeast Brazil is larger than any country in South America, except Argentina. In population, the Northeast is larger than any country in South America.

Over the last decade and particularly since 1955, the Northeast has expanded at a rapid rate. The region's economic progress has not been widely recognized in Brazil.[1] One reason is that the gains in agriculture, which have been heavily responsible for the economic improvement in the region, are by their nature more widely dispersed geographically and less apparent visually than the dramatic and geographically concentrated industrialization of the South. Another major factor is that popular and political emphasis has traditionally been focused on how the Northeast is doing in comparison to São Paulo and the South rather than on absolute progress in the region.

[1] In early 1963, on the basis of the research completed for this study, the Brazilian government officially recognized that the Northeast has been progressing economically. See Brazil's new three year plan for economic and social development 1963-65 prepared under the direction of Celso Furtado, who was serving as Brazil's Minister of Planning. *Plano Trienal de Desenvolvimento Econômico e Social: 1963-65* (Síntese), Presidência da Republica, Brasília (1963), pp. 81-88.

And finally, of course, despite substantial progress, the Northeast is still a very low income area.

During the 1950 to 1955 coffee boom, the Northeast rate of growth lagged behind the rest of Brazil. Coffee production in the Northeast is small and the region did not benefit from the favorable international coffee market. Furthermore, the important agricultural sector of the region was seriously hurt by the droughts of 1951 and 1953. Also, the Northeast did not share greatly in Brazil's accelerated industrialization.

But during the last half of the decade, except for the drought year 1958, total income in the Northeast expanded more rapidly than in any other region of the country. And in 1960, the Northeast's share of Brazil's total income was larger than in any year since 1950. (See Table 2.4.)

In terms of income per person, the Northeast gains were even greater relative to the South and the national average. Due to extensive out-migration from the Northeast to the frontier areas of the central interior, to the urban industrial centers in the South, and to the new capital of Brasília, the Northeast population increased at a significantly lower rate than in other regions. As a consequence, per capita income in the Northeast increased from a low in 1955 of 43 percent of the national average to 51 percent in 1960. Over the same period, the South dropped from 154 to 146 percent of the national average.

Nevertheless, despite encouraging economic gains and a narrowing of regional disparities, the Northeast still remains as the lowest income region of Brazil, and the gap between the Northeast and the industrial South in levels of economic welfare remains large. The best available estimates of Brazil's income in United States dollars indicate a per capita income in 1960 of $140 for the Northeast as compared to $410 in the South and $280 on the average for all of Brazil.[2] But it

[2] *The First Annual Report, 1961,* of the Inter-American Development Bank, shows a domestic per capita product for Brazil of U.S.$332 in 1960 (p. 51). This estimate is based, presumably, on the series "Gross Domestic Product at 1949 Prices" of the Getúlio Vargas Foundation. National income was assumed to equal 85 percent of the gross domestic product based on past trends. The estimate of $140 for the Northeast—50 percent of the national average—compares with Cr.$13,600 for 1960. The basic Getúlio Vargas Foundation estimates imply an exchange rate of Cr.$100 to U.S.$1.00 as compared to the average Free Market exchange rate for 1960 of Cr.$190 to U.S.$1.00. The disparity between the im-

should also be noted that per capita income levels in the Northeast
are not much below those in the North and Central West regions
which in 1960 were 61 percent and 62 percent respectively of the
national average. Furthermore, because of recent economic expansion,

Per Capita Income of Northeast Brazil, 1950-1960

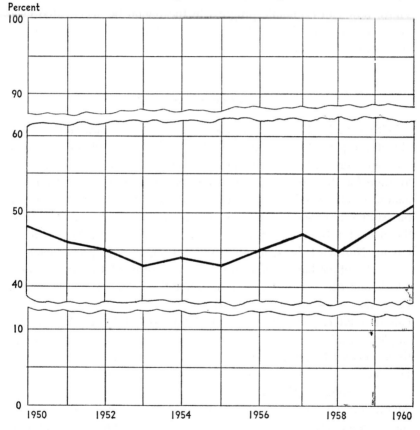

(Percentage of National Average)

Source: Table 2.5

the Northeast no longer ranks as the lowest income area in Latin
America. Paraguay and Bolivia which have not been experiencing
significant growth now have lower income levels than Northeast

plicit rate and the Free Market does not, however, invalidate the estimates. On
the basis of living experience in Brazil during 1960, I feel that the 100 to 1 rate
was a better real income conversion basis than the free rate.

Brazil. And Peru, Guatemala, Honduras, and Ecuador are not far ahead of the Northeast.

The Northeast region, then, is a low income area but with considerable expansion underway. For purposes of guiding future development activities, the situation poses several key questions. First, why are income levels so low in the Northeast? Second, what dynamic sectors or activities have been responsible for recent growth trends? Third, how can economic progress in the region be accelerated even more? Before considering these questions, however, a brief overview of the Northeast economy should be presented.

The Northeast Economy

Within the Northeast significant variations exist in natural resources, climate, types of economic activity, and degree of urbanization. Average per capita income ranges from 29 percent of the national average for the state of Piauí to 60 percent in the more urban Pernambuco. These and many other internal differences suggest considerable caution in generalizing about such a large area. They also point up the need for thorough and objective subarea studies. Not even the famous Northeast droughts are a general region-wide phenomenon.

On the other hand, there are certain features of the region about which one can generalize with substantial confidence. Agriculture is the major economic activity in the Northeast, accounting for almost half of total regional income and about two-thirds of total regional employment. The Northeast is predominantly rural with two of every three persons living outside the rapidly growing urban centers. As a low income area largely dependent on agriculture, and subject to periodic droughts, the Northeast has long experienced sizable out-migration.[3] The population of the region is heavily concentrated in the younger age groups—43 percent of the total population in 1950 was 14 years or under. Levels of illiteracy are high—74 percent of the population 5 years or older in 1950 was unable to read or write. Despite recent progress, both transportation and electric power facilities are still poorly developed.

[3] For the most recent comprehensive study of Northeast out-migration see João Gonçalves de Souza, Migrações Nordestinas, Tese de concurso para provimento efetivo da Cátedra de Economia Rural da ENA, da Universidade Rural, Rio de Janeiro (1957).

TABLE 3.1. *Principal Cultivated Farm Crops of Northeast Brazil, 1960*

Crop	Value of Production (Billion cr.)	Northeast as Share of Brazil	Leading States
Cotton	21.5	50%	Paraíba, Ceará
Sugar	10.4	35	Pernambuco, Alagoas
Manioc	10.2	43	Bahia, Pernambuco
Beans	8.7	22	Bahia, Pernambuco
Cocoa beans	7.8	97	Bahia
Corn	6.1	12	Ceará, Bahia
Bananas	4.4	50	Ceará, Pernambuco
Rice	4.3	8	Maranhão, RGN
Sisal	3.2	100	Bahia, Paraíba
Coconut	3.0	93	Bahia, Pernambuco
Tobacco	2.9	42	Bahia
Coffee	2.1	3	Bahia, Pernambuco
Other	(est.) 11.4	—	—
Total crops	(est.) 97.0		

Source: Instituto Brasileiro de Geografia e Estatística, Conselho Nacional de Estatística, *Anuário Estatístico do Brasil, 1961.*

Agriculture

In Northeast Brazil, cultivated field crops are the major source of farm income (about 70 percent). Livestock and livestock products are next most important (about 24 percent) and extractive agriculture generates the remaining 6 percent of total farm income. The dozen most important crops for the Northeast are shown in Table 3.1.

Other farm crops in order of importance are castor beans, sweet potatoes, oranges, mangos, lima beans, onions, and pineapples. The principal extractive products are babaçu (palm tree nuts from which oil is extracted) and carnauba wax. In 1960, the value of babaçu production was comparable to tobacco, and the value of carnauba wax was about the same as regional production of coffee. Oiticica, a source of tropical oils, and piaçava fiber are also produced in the Northeast, but the value of their output is relatively small.

Bahia, the largest and most populous state of the region, accounts for almost one-third of total Northeast farm income. It has a virtual monopoly of cocoa bean production in Brazil and is the principal tobacco producer for the region. The state also leads in regional food products such as manioc and beans, and has become the top-ranking area for sisal, an expanding export crop. Paraíba and Ceará are the leading cotton states in the region and the humid coastal areas of Pernambuco and Alagoas lead in sugar production. Maranhão is the major producer of rice and babaçu. Ceará and Piauí are the main areas of carnauba production.

Many of the leading Northeast agricultural products are important export items for Brazil. The major share of Brazil's cotton exports comes from the South, but the Northeast produces a long fiber tree cotton that commands premium prices in domestic and export markets.[4] Sugar may come from São Paulo, but in 1960 the bulk of Brazil's sugar exports came from the Northeast. Favorable export conditions will benefit prices in both areas. In 1960 cocoa beans and their subproducts such as butter, cake, and paste were the top-ranking exports from the Northeast, accounting for about one-fourth of the value of Northeast exports. Next in order of importance were sugar, sisal fibers, tobacco, carnauba wax, cotton, and castor oil.[5]

Industry

Compared to the Brazilian South and Southeast, the Northeast industrial sector is small, but it is not insignificant. Any area that has 4,000 manufacturing establishments with five or more workers, almost 17,000 factories with less than five workers, and at least 200,000 workers in manufacturing—as reported for Northeast Brazil in the latest (1958) industrial registration—has made a substantial start on industrialization. The South has been industrializing at a phenomenal rate and has six times as many workers and generates almost ten times as much value added as the Northeast. But another comparison might put the Northeast industrial situation in better perspective.

The Philippines had a population of about 26 million in 1960 as compared to 22 million for Northeast Brazil. The Philippines rank near the top in rate of industrialization for underdeveloped countries and is considered to have a substantial industrial sector. In 1958, the Philippines had 228,000 workers in manufacturing establishments with five or more workers as compared to 163,000 for Northeast Brazil.[6]

[4] Banco do Nordeste do Brasil, *Fibre de Alta Qualidade,* ETENE, Fortaleza, Ceará (November 1959).
[5] Banco do Nordeste do Brasil, *Relatório, 1961,* Fortaleza, Ceará (1962), p. lxxxiii.
[6] Republic of the Philippines, *1958 Annual Survey of Manufactures,* Manila (1962).

Thus, Northeast Brazil with a population equal to 84 percent of that of the Philippines had factory employment equal to 72 percent of that of the Philippines.

However, the manufacturing sector of the Northeast was relatively stagnant until the mid-1950's, and many of its factories have been long established and need rehabilitation. Since 1950 the sizable increase in regional electric power availability from the Paulo Afonso project, the expansion of long-term credit facilities through the Bank of the Northeast, and the special incentives and other industrial development activities of SUDENE, the federal government's planning and development coordination agency for the region, which will be discussed subsequently in greater detail, all have been contributing to a rejuvenation of industrialization of the Northeast. As of 1960, nevertheless, Northeast agriculture was four times as important as industry in terms of regional income and even more significant as a source of employment.

Northeast Brazil was once the principal manufacturing region of Brazil. In 1866 the Northeast had six of Brazil's nine cotton mills, one in Alagoas and five in Bahia. At least one of the Bahia mills was started as early as 1840.[7] But with the transfer of Brazil's capital from Bahia to Rio de Janeiro and with coffee agriculture in the South overshadowing both cotton and sugar over the last half of the nineteenth century, the Northeast's pre-eminence in manufacturing was lost to the South. Plantation agriculture based on slavery dominated the Northeast economy until the abolition of slavery in 1888 and exerted another inhibiting force on industrialization.

In Brazilian statistics, the industry category includes the extractive industries, construction, electric power, and manufacturing. In manufacturing, as of 1958, four industry groups—food, textiles, chemicals, and nonmetallic minerals—accounted for about three-fourths of the Northeast's factory employment and value added by manufacturing. (See Table 3.2.) The sugar mills heavily concentrated in Pernambuco and Alagoas were the region's major food processing activity, but meat packing and flour mills were also of importance. Textile manufacturing is located through all of the states except Piauí, but Pernambuco, Alagoas, and Bahia account for more than 60 percent of total employment in the industry. The re-equipment and modernization of this

---

[7] Stanley J. Stein, *The Brazilian Cotton Manufacture* (Harvard University Press, 1957), pp. 20-24.

TABLE 3.2 *Industry in Northeast Brazil, 1958*

Industry	Establishments with Five or More Workers						Establishments with Less than Five Workers					
	Number Establishments	Employment	Salaries Cr$ (millions)	Value of Product Cr$ (millions)	Value Added Cr$ (millions)	Leading States (Employment)	Number Establishments	Employment	Salaries Cr$ (millions)	Value of Product Cr$ (millions)	Value Added Cr$ (millions)	Leading States (Employment)
All industry	3,922	162,735	5,470	49,566	20,354	Rio Grande Bahia	16,720	31,656	745	6,642	2,709	Maranhão Sergipe
Mining	166	8,529	229	867	684	Pernambuco Alagoas	414	844	8	35	35	Pernambuco Bahia
Food	825	40,292	1,976	16,439	5,973	Pernambuco Alagoas	6,330	18,331	440	4,915	1,676	Piauí Alagoas
Textiles	581	59,929	1,809	13,693	5,070	Pernambuco Bahia	734	1,299	7	82	23	Bahia Pernambuco
Chemicals	269	8,984	461	8,072	3,068	Pernambuco	276	571	13	201	76	Bahia
Non-metallic	544	11,291	372	2,333	1,409	Pernambuco Bahia	2,968	6,446	97	365	301	Ceará Bahia
Apparel	296	4,671	133	755	345	Pernambuco Ceará	951	2,429	39	191	103	Alagoas Bahia
Beverages	170	3,989	157	1,332	680	Pernambuco Bahia	322	765	17	92	59	Pernambuco Bahia
Printing	214	4,254	184	758	406	Pernambuco Bahia	102	301	9	29	16	Pernambuco Bahia
Leather	90	3,409	133	904	419	Pernambuco Bahia	436	956	14	85	41	Pernambuco Bahia
Metals	112	3,347	134	1,020	460	Pernambuco Bahia	65	120	3	15	10	Pernambuco Bahia
Lumber	232	2,839	91	461	248	Pernambuco Bahia	1,241	2,428	31	147	81	Pernambuco Bahia
Furniture	196	2,734	104	438	261	Pernambuco Bahia	422	1,043	26	102	58	Pernambuco Bahia
Paper	23	1,456	50	625	215	Pernambuco Bahia	10	32	1	9	2	Pernambuco

Source: Instituto Brasileiro de Geografia e Estatística, Conselho Nacional de Estatística (1960), *Produção Industrial Brasileira: 1958.*

long-established manufacturing activity has a top priority in SUDENE's development program.[8]

The chemicals and pharmaceuticals industry of the region consists largel of processing vegetable oils and fats from cotton seed, babaçu, castor beans, oiticica, and cocoa butter. Since the 1958 survey, however, the production of petroleum products by the Landulfo Alves refinery in Bahia has expanded rapidly along with the rapid growth in Bahia petroleum production. From 1958 to 1960, the refining of diesel oil and gasoline in the Northeast increased fivefold and kerosene sevenfold.[9] The production of phosphate fertilizers in the Northeast based on the phosphate rock deposits of Pernambuco also expanded rapidly from 1958 to 1960. Consequently, the chemicals industry of the region has recently become more diversified, greatly enlarged, and significantly more dynamic.

Cement production accounted for about half of total output in the nonmetallic minerals category. The production of tiles, bricks, pottery, dinnerware, and sanitary ware is also represented in this industry group. The three states of Pernambuco, Paraíba, and Bahia, which have cement plants, are the most important areas in nonmetallic minerals.

Next in importance after the four major industry groups are apparel, beverages, printing, leather, metals, lumber, furniture, and paper. Pernambuco with its capital of Recife, the third largest city of Brazil, is the trade and manufacturing center of the Northeast region. It accounts for a large share of the minor industry groups as well as the major manufacturing categories. The less industrialized states of Piauí, Maranhão, and Rio Grande do Norte, on the other hand, have a large share of the region's small industry—less than five workers.

The production of minerals and fuels in the Northeast is still relatively small as compared to manufacturing. But the expansion of petroleum output in the Bahia oil fields, Brazil's only significant oil producing area, has greatly enlarged the importance of this sector in recent years. From 1955 to 1960 Bahia petroleum production increased from 2 million to about 29 million barrels. Natural gas output in-

[8] *Plano Quinquenal de Desenvolvimento para o Nordeste 1961-1965*, Presidência da República, Superintendência do Desenvolvimento do Nordeste, Recife (1961), pp. 106-15.

[9] Banco do Nordeste do Brasil, *Relatório 1961*, Fortaleza, Ceará (1962), p. xxxv.

TABLE 3.3. *Northeast Brazil Mineral Production, 1960*

Product	Value Cr.$1,000,000	Percent
Sea salt	796	52.8
Tungsten ore	207	13.7
Rock crystal	93	6.2
Asbestos	86	5.7
Lead	79	5.2
Phosphate rock	49	3.2
Other products	199	13.2
Total	1,509	100.0

Source: Serviço de Estatística da Produção, Ministério da Agricultura.

creased over the same period from 62 to 535 million cubic meters.

In the mining field, the principal Northeast products are shown in Table 3.3. They account for more than 90 percent of the region's total mineral production. But the total value generated by all minerals production in 1960 was less than the small regional production of coffee, only one-half the value of sisal output, and less than one-tenth the value of cotton production.

Electric power capacity and consumption in Northeast Brazil is still unbelievably low despite the phenomenal expansion of recent years. At the end of 1961, the Northeast had an installed power capacity of slightly less than 400,000 kilowatts—which increased by 50 percent in 1962 when the second expansion stage of the Paulo Afonso project came into production—and an estimated consumption of about 1.2 billion kilowatt hours. The Northeast consumption of about 50 kilowatt hours per person in 1961 compares to about 260 per person for Brazil as a whole and 4,300 per capita for the United States. Even the principal city of the region, Recife, consumed only 320 kilowatt hours per capita (1960)—one third of São Paulo consumption. Furthermore, the use of the power capacity in the Northeast was relatively low—only 35 percent—because of a small amount of high load factor demand such as that of the electro-metallurgical industries.

Before the Paulo Afonso project came into production in 1955 and doubled the power capacity of the region, the situation was even worse: from 1955 to 1961 the production of the San Francisco Hydroelectric Company (CHESF) increased fourfold.

Commerce, Services, and Financial Sector

The remaining categories of income, other than agriculture and industry, account for 43 percent of total regional income (see Table 3.4),
about the same proportion as for Brazil as a whole. In the United
States, however, 58 percent of total national income originates outside of agriculture and industry. The financial, property, and government income categories are relatively small in the Northeast as compared to the rest of Brazil and the United States. Commerce, services,
and transportation are of roughly the same, or of slightly more, regional importance than in the country as a whole. However, a lack
of information for the Northeast makes difficult a more profound
understanding of trends in these categories.

TABLE 3.4 *Structure of Income: Northeast Brazil,
Brazil, and United States, 1960*

Economic Activity	Northeast Brazil	Brazil	United States
Agriculture, forestry and fisheries	46%	28%	4%
Industry (mining, construction, manu- facturing, public utilities)	11	26	38
Commerce	15	12	17
Services	12	11	12
Transportation and communications	6	8	6
Finance	2	3	10
Property income	2	4	
Government	6	8	13
	100%	100%	100%

Source: Getúlio Vargas Foundation, Brazilian Institute of Economics and U.S. Bureau of the Census,
Statistical Abstract of the United States, 1961.

Recent Economic Trends

The economic fortunes of the Northeast are still tied largely to
price and production trends in its agriculture sector. Industrial expansion has lagged behind national increases over the entire decade. But
agricultural trends have been more favorable to the region. Since 1955
Northeast farm income has increased threefold as compared to dou-

bling for the country as a whole. The explanation for the relative gains in the Northeast lies in the particular mix of farm crops within the region.

The rapidly expanding crops in Brazil, in order of rates of increase, have been sisal, beans, coconuts, tobacco, sugar, bananas, cotton, corn, and cocoa beans. These are the important crops of the Northeast.

The lagging crops for Brazil as a whole over the period were coffee, rice, manioc, and wheat, only one of which—manioc—is of leading importance in the Northeast. Thus, except for the drought year of 1958, the Northeast farm sector was expanding at a more rapid rate than the rest of the country.

Of the export crops of Brazil, cotton, sugar, and cocoa beans have prospered more in recent years than has coffee. The favorable export situation stimulated income gains through higher prices, but physical production increases have been equally important to the Northeast. Despite the crucial role of several export crops, the bulk of Northeast production has been food crops for domestic consumption.

The livestock and extractive agriculture sectors have not been expanding rapidly, but these lags were more than offset by the gains in farm crops.

But the agricultural sector has not been the only source of rapid growth in the Northeast. Several branches of industry have been significant growth points even though the sector as a whole has been lagging. The expansion of petroleum, natural gas, and electric power has already been mentioned. And the impact of added electric power capacity is only beginning to be felt. Petroleum refining and sugar processing in the manufacturing sector have expanded along with the increased supplies of raw materials. The industrialization of sisal has been initiated in recent years on a large scale. The production of cement, beverages, phosphate fertilizers, and oiticica oil have been other growth factors.

As a result of the growth points in agriculture and industry, the Northeast has gained on the rest of the country over the last five years. It has also exceeded the economic growth rate of 2.5 percent per year per person suggested as a minimum goal in the Alliance for Progress.[10] But this rate of progress has not been sufficient in North-

[10] Organization of American States, "Alliance for Progress," ES-RE-Doc. 145, Rev. 3, Punta del Este, Uruguay, August 17, 1961.

east Brazil to satisfy the social and political pressures generated in the region.

Factors Explaining the Low Income Levels

Future efforts to improve the levels of economic welfare in the Northeast must be based on an accurate understanding of why income levels are low in the region. But before suggesting answers to this question, two qualifications concerning the average per capita income estimates for the Northeast deserve attention.

First, no statistics are available on the distribution of income among individuals. Average per capita income is derived by dividing total estimated regional income by total population. If a small share of the population receives a large portion of the income, the earnings of the large bulk of the population are significantly lower than the average. It is generally accepted in Brazil and elsewhere that income is more unequally distributed in a poorer region like the Northeast than in a richer and more industrialized region like the South. If this is true, the gap in economic levels between most individuals in the Northeast and in the South is greater than indicated by the per capita averages.

On the other hand, for the Northeast as a whole, total income is likely to be understated by the official statistics. Much of the region is not yet operating as a money economy, particularly in agriculture. For this reason, it is much more difficult to secure information on production and incomes in the less developed areas than in the advanced regions like the South. The industrial sectors are more likely than the agricultural sectors to provide reasonably representative data. The significance of these two limitations is that available statistics understate the overall level of economic welfare of the Northeast as well as the regional disparities in individual incomes for the bulk of the population.

The traditional explanation of the Northeast "problem" for many decades has been the droughts. But it is now becoming more widely recognized that the Northeast problem is poverty and that the droughts are only a partial and limited cause of the low income levels of the Northeast. To be sure, the droughts explain the sharp fluctuations in Northeast income, such as occurred in 1958. And it might be argued that the droughts have hindered the Northeast farmers from accumulating capital and from making permanent improvements in their farming operations. But it must also be recognized that the Northeast has gone for long periods without experiencing a drought, and regional poverty still persisted.

A more modern explanation popular among some economists is that low economic levels are a result of insufficient capital investment.[11] The extensive use of "capital-output ratios" symbolizes the idea that low income is a result of low levels of investment. But does this kind of explanation truly reveal basic causal factors? The Furtado report, discussed in greater detail below,[12] demonstrates that public investment in the Northeast has been remarkably high but not very productive. The report also reveals that sizable amounts of private capital have been flowing from the Northeast to the South rather than being reinvested in the region. If the low economic level of the Northeast is to be explained in terms of lack of investment, the appropriate question is why has not the available capital been productively invested in the region?

A third widely accepted explanation is that the Northeast economic situation is largely a result of federal policies which have discriminated against the Northeast. The implication of this argument is that a change in these policies will, within a short period of time, permit the Northeast to accelerate its rate of development and probably equal the economic levels existing in the South. It is true that the federal policy of encouragement to industrialization did in fact benefit other regions of Brazil more than the Northeast. But as previously explained, in an early stage of a country's development it is inevitable that industrial expansion will be concentrated in a small number of areas. Furthermore, the experience of the Northeast over the 1955-60 period shows that external forces such as favorable international markets, as in the case of sugar and cotton, or unfavorable international markets, as in the case of coffee, can be as influential or more influential than domestic government policies in explaining economic successes or failures.

Making discriminatory government policies the "scapegoat" is not

[11] See, for example, *Desenvolvimento e Conjuntura* (April 1959), p. 40.
[12] Conselho de Desenvolvimento do Nordeste, *A Policy for the Economic Development of the Northeast*, Rio de Janeiro (1959).

a satisfactory explanation of low income levels in the Northeast. A more valid, but still only a partial, explanation is that a federal policy toward the Northeast exclusively concerned with fighting the drought was not an effective policy. It is not the same thing to argue that federal policies discriminated against the Northeast as to recognize that federal policies for the Northeast were not appropriate or well designed.

As a basis for future development action, none of the three widely accepted explanations—the droughts, a lack of investment, or discriminatory federal policies—warrants a high priority. Much more meaningful as basic factors explaining the economic poverty of the Northeast are the following:

1. The physical resource endowment of the Northeast, particularly the soils, is not outstanding.
2. The Northeast is specializing in a relatively low income activity—agriculture.
3. A relatively small share of the Northeast population is "economically active" because of inadequate job opportunities and because an unusually large part of the total population is in the lowest age groups.
4. Traditionally, the Northeast has never made substantial investments in its richest resource—its people.
5. Productivity is low in the Northeast due to a serious lag in adopting technological innovations as well as to physical and human resource limitations.

The Physical Resource Base

The North American geographer, Preston James, has concluded: "The Northeast of Brazil is a region of poverty and hardship because of the peculiar association of land quality and land use in that area. . . . The combination of physical and biotic conditions on the one hand with the economic conditions introduced by the Portuguese on the other has produced a region of poverty through the gradual destruction of the resource base."[13]

The Northeast is an old area, well cut-over, that no longer has valuable forest resources. In much of the region, the soils are shallow and the combination of rainfall and tropical climate makes a large

[13] Preston E. James, "Patterns of Land Use in Northeast Brazil," *Annals of the Association of American Geographers*, Vol. 47 (June 1953).

share of the region a semiarid zone. The only major hydraulic potential for electric power is the Paulo Afonso Falls on the San Francisco
River. The Northeast has no known coal resources, but it does have
the principal petroleum production of the country.

Although the resource base of the Northeast has not been thoroughly appraised, the poor quality of much of the land for agricultural purposes is becoming better known and greater skepticism is
developing about the previously accepted romantic evaluations of the
agricultural base of the region. But as Professor James has observed,
"To many Brazilians such skepticism is a form of disloyalty."[14] He also
concludes that the application of modern scientific farming either
to worn-out soils or to soils of low natural fertility can greatly increase
their productivity and lower the cost per unit of food production.

Specialization in Low Income Activities

Statistics on the share of the Northeast's population engaged in
agriculture have not yet become available from the 1960 census. But
in 1950 the Northeast had 71 percent of its labor force engaged in
agriculture—as compared to 52 percent in the rest of Brazil. In most
countries of the world, agriculture has long provided lower income
to workers than they can earn in manufacturing and other nonfarm
activities. This has also been true of the Southeast region of the
United States. A major exception, however, is the highly mechanized
and capital intensive agriculture in some parts of the Middle West
and Far West in the United States.

Within industry, also, certain manufacturing activities, particularly
those that are highly competitive like textiles, provide lower incomes
to workers than other forms of factory employment. The Northeast
industrial sector has a large share of its activity in the low income
manufacturing industries. These industries require lower levels of
worker skills and may not be as capital intensive as the higher wage
industries.

[14] "Brazilian Agricultural Development," Simon Kuznets (ed.), *Economic Growth:
Brazil, India, Japan* (Duke University Press, 1955), p. 78.

Thus, with a large share of its activity in low income agriculture and in low wage industries, it is inevitable that the income per capita in the Northeast is lower than in other regions that specialize in higher wage activities.

Population Characteristics and the Labor Force

The total and per capita income of a country or a region can be low because of the small share of the total population that is economically productive. The difference between developed and underdeveloped countries in this respect can be illustrated by contrasting Northeast Brazil with Western Germany and the United States. In Western Germany almost one-half of the total population is employed. The United States had in 1960 about 40 percent of its total population in the (civilian) labor force. In contrast, Northeast Brazil had only 31 percent of its total population in 1950, the latest year for which such data are available, classified as "economically active."

This means that Northeast Brazil has only one of every three persons contributing to regional production and that the earnings of each employed person must be shared by two others. In Western Germany, there is only one dependent person for each employed worker. This characteristic of the population and labor force means that a worker in Northeast Brazil would have to earn one and a half times the income of a worker in West Germany—and presumably be one and a half times as productive—in order for average per capita incomes of the two areas to be equal.

Both the age composition of the Northeast population and an inadequate expansion of new jobs relative to rapidly growing population explain the small share that is economically active. In 1950, 43 percent of the total Northeast population was fourteen years of age or younger. High and increasing birth rates add greatly to the dependent younger age groups. Inadequate growth in employment possibilities limits the opportunities for the employable group in the region to become economically active and encourages out-migration which is often heaviest in the employable age categories.

Low Regional Investment in Human Resources

The long history of the Northeast as a plantation slave economy probably explains the region's lack of emphasis on education and investment in human resources. Education has been considered a privilege of the rich and a preparation for the "good life." Illiteracy rates are sensationally high in the region—in 1950, 74 percent of the population five years of age and above was classified as unable to read and write. The small number of children in school is another reflection of the region's failure to invest in human resources. In 1959, only 1.5 million of an estimated 5.8 million children of the relevant age group were enrolled in elementary education in the Northeast. Secondary school enrollment in the Northeast as of 1961 totaled only 180,000 from a potential of more than 2 million youngsters.[15] University enrollment after a rapid increase in recent years reached only about 16,000 in 1961.

The expenditures on education in the Northeast have not been analyzed in any great detail and need to be scrutinized as to type of expenditure—buildings versus staff and student scholarships—as well as amounts. As of 1961 the expenditures, or amounts budgeted, in the region by the several levels of government for education and cultural projects have been estimated as follows, in millions of cruzeiros.[16]

	Education	Total
Federal (10 months)	3,330	8,931[17]
State	3,520	28,809
Local governments	787	8,657
Total	7,637	46,397

The indicated expenditures of all units of government in the Northeast are estimated at about Cr.$46 billion for 1961, of which Cr.$29

[15] Instituto Brasileiro de Geografia e Estatística, Conselho Nacional de Estatística, *Anuário Estatístico do Brasil, 1961*, Rio de Janeiro (1962), p. 368.

[16] Banco do Nordeste do Brasil, *Relatório 1961*, Fortaleza, Ceará, pp. C, CV, and CVIII.

[17] Total is incomplete; does not include military expenditures or SUDENE appropriations.

billion was spent by the states and almost Cr.$9 billion by the local governments.

The expenditures for education by state and local governments in Northeast Brazil are about 18 percent of the total as compared to about 35 percent of total expenditures devoted to education by state and local governments in the United States.[18] There are no comparable federal expenditure figures for the United States that can be separated by states. In the case of the Northeast, the public expenditure for education was about 2 percent of regional income.

The low regional investment in human resources means great shortages of the skills necessary for high levels of progress and greater efficiency.

Low Levels of Productivity

The limitations in natural resources, human resources, and institutional factors are all reflected in the low productivity of economic

TABLE 3.5. *Average Yield in Kilograms per Hectare of Selected Crops in Various Countries*

Country or Region	Unmilled Rice	Corn	Beans	Lint Cotton	Cane Sugar (Tons)
Northeast Brazil	1,300	780	550	107	42
Brazil	1,508	1,238	659	140	44
Argentina	3,170	2,090	940	190	37
Mexico	2,080	810	360	490	56
Japan	4,620	2,270	1,250	—	33
India	1,370	730	240	100	35
United States	3,590	3,280	1,320	520	200[a]

Source: Adapted from American International Association for Economic and Social Development, *Agriculture in Brazil*, Rio de Janeiro (March 1961), pp. 11 and 29, and Banco do Nordeste do Brasil, *Relatório 1961*, Fortaleza, Ceará (1962), p.XLV. Statistics based on 1956 to 1958 yields as reported in the *Production Yearbook*, *1959*, Vol. 13, of the U.N. Food and Agriculture Organization, Rome, pp. 33ff.
[a] Hawaii only.

activity in the region. The low levels are particularly conspicuous in agriculture. (See Table 3.5.)

Output in agriculture per worker is even lower than the levels

[18] U. S. Bureau of the Census, *Statistical Abstract of the United States, 1961*, p. 409.

indicated by the comparisons per hectare. Because of the large population in agriculture, the Northeast in 1950 was using an average of only 1.5 hectares of land in cultivation (cropland) per worker in agriculture. This compared with 2 hectares per worker in Brazil as a whole, 3 hectares per worker in the state of São Paulo, and 20 hectares per worker in the United States.

The low levels of agricultural productivity reflect the use of outmoded farming methods, the prevalence of undersized subsistence farming units, and the drought.[19] Farming methods have progressed little since colonial times. For the majority of farmers, the hoe and machete are the only tools. Clearing, planting, cultivating, and harvesting are done by hand. Rarely is animal power used for anything except transportation. Little if any attention is given to soil and water conservation.

Irrigation, frequently considered to be a panacea for the Northeast, will not cure all the ills of the region. The irrigation potential for the region has been estimated at 790,000 hectares,[20] or about 1.4 percent of the area now in cultivation. This estimate, which includes irrigation from rivers, storage reservoirs, lakes and wells, is a theoretical maximum. Thus, only a minor fraction of the area can be irrigated, and exaggeration of irrigation possibilities obscures a more important agricultural solution, better dry-land farming.

Subdivision of the large farms of the region into small units offers little, if any, solution to the problem. On the contrary, in most cases it would only aggravate an already bad situation. In most of the region, the opposite approach—consolidation of small farms into larger, more economical sized units—offers much more hope.

Resettlement of large numbers of people in more favorable farming areas of Brazil should be given a high priority. The Northeast has a higher concentration of population in agriculture than the resources can support at acceptable economic and social standards. Much more emphasis must be given within the Northeast to education, agricultural research and extension, agricultural credit, and adjustment of rural population to available soil and water resources.

[19] American International Association for Economic and Social Development, *Agriculture in Brazil,* Rio de Janeiro (March 1961), pp. 23-36.

[20] J. G. Duque, "Agricultura do Nordeste e o Desenvolvimento Econômico," *Boletim do DNOCS* (May 1959), p. 61.

However, the experience with supervised rural credit in the Northeast has not been too successful thus far.

The levels of productivity in much of manufacturing, particularly the textile industry, are unusually low. As a special study has revealed, "Almost all of the equipment of the textile industry of the Northeast is obsolete, having been in use for more than thirty years. . . . 81 per cent of the looms, for example, were made before 1930. The mills use an excessive amount of labor. Many factories do not have efficient plant layouts. And the administration of the industries is extremely weak."[21]

Future Directions

Future progress toward improving levels of economic and social welfare in Northeast Brazil requires two general lines of action. First, the share of the population employed must be increased so that the large human resources of the region can be economically productive. Second, the productivity of economic activities in the region must be improved.

The physical phenomena of the drought with its drama and misery has for many decades focused popular and political attention on the physical resources of the region and on development programs to combat the physical uncertainties. The idea of investment in human resources has gained little attention in competition with the drought. Yet the ultimate objective of development is to improve the lot of the people.

How can the amount of employment be increased in the region? One possibility is to increase the number of jobs in agriculture. But here the opportunities are not promising. The best judgment of agricultural experts is that the amount of land that can be added to production is limited. There are possibilities, however, through soils research of making certain areas such as the *tabuleiros* more productive, and some properties exist that are not being sufficiently used. At the same time, the best opportunities for increasing productivity in agriculture are to enlarge the size of farm operating units, to in-

[21] SUDENE, *Sumario do Programa de Reequipamento da Indústria Textil Regional*, Recife (1961), pp. 10, 12.

crease the investment in machinery, and to accelerate the adoption of improved technology. The effect of these measures would be to decrease the need for workers in agriculture.

Agricultural experts suggest that family-owned farm units with 120 acres (about 50 hectares) of cropland are necessary for efficient and capital-forming agriculture. This enlarged size will justify shifting from the hoe to machinery and the adoption of improved technology. It will also permit the farmer to accumulate a reasonable share of the capital that should be invested in agriculture. A hypothetical calculation illustrates the drastic effect that a full-scale farm enlargement program would have on employment opportunities in Northeast agriculture. Assuming three workers per family, and using the 1950 ratio of 1.5 hectares per worker, the average size family unit would consist of 4.5 hectares of cropland. With the present land in cultivation, a complete farm enlargement program would displace ten of eleven families in agriculture. Even with a more modest goal for farm size and a substantial increase in cropland, about half of the existing rural population—over 7 million people—would have to be shifted to agricultural areas outside of the Northeast or to nonfarm activities.

One possible future direction, therefore, is to encourage and assist migration from the overpopulated rural areas of the Northeast to the new agricultural frontiers of North Mato Grosso, North Goiás, and South Pará in the Central West of the country. Resettlement in Maranhão and continued out-migration to the North are other possibilities. Dr. Duque, a leading agronomist in the Northeast, has suggested that in drought crises the government relief funds should be used not for emergency projects to provide employment in the area but to assist migration to the Central West.[22]

Such out-migration can be one of the greatest forces for accelerating higher levels of technology in Northeast agriculture. First, it will permit large size agricultural units to be established. Second, it will create pressures for adopting improved technologies because large supplies of cheap labor will no longer be easily available. The experience in other countries, including the Southeast of the United States, demonstrates that it is difficult to persuade farmers to improve their techniques when cheap labor is available. But after excessive

[22] Duque, *op. cit.*, p. 71.

supplies are no longer available, the receptivity to technological progress of those who remain in agriculture is greatly increased.

Land reform, widely accepted in the underdeveloped areas as a new economic panacea, is more a political issue than an economic solution for Northeast Brazil. What is meant by "land reform" and how it will contribute to economic growth has not yet been spelled out in the heat of the political debate. If land reform will reduce the amount of absentee ownership and broaden the ownership base in agriculture so that workers will be motivated to invest in the farm property on which they work, it can stimulate greater productivity. Land tenure and other agrarian problems exist and must be faced. But it is difficult to see how land reform can solve the fundamental problem of too many people in agriculture. If political rather than economic goals are the objective of the land reform movement, a literacy campaign in rural areas might be the most efficient strategy. The ability to read and write is a prerequisite for voting, and because of this requirement millions of peasants are presently disenfranchised.

The need for greatly expanding nonfarm jobs in the region can be met by faster industrialization, and by expansion in construction activities, mining, transportation, and in trades and services. The decentralization of some of the future expansion of industrial activity now concentrated in the South may bring job opportunities in the Northeast, especially in view of the ever increasing market in this region. Activities to encourage industrial and commercial expansion have been accelerated, and prospects are good for absorbing and making productive use of the excess agricultural population and new entrants to the labor market. Fishing and fish processing industries, which are also receiving development attention, may be another significant source of new nonfarm job opportunities.

A third direction that must be mentioned, even though it involves religious factors, is family planning as a means of reducing the region's extremely high birth rate. Although Brazil as a whole is far from being an overpopulated country, Northeast Brazil has a serious over-population problem in relation to its stage of development. A lower birth rate, in addition to reducing the large flow of entrants to the labor market, would change the age structure of the Northeast population so that a smaller share would be in the nonproductive and dependent groups. At the same time, it would mean that the region would find it more feasible to provide education and social services because the financial burden on each worker through taxes or private expenditures would not be so great.

On the other hand, national policies could recognize that the Northeast is a source of population for the rest of Brazil. But then, the federal government should shoulder the financial burden of education and social services. Furthermore, it should have an effective program to assist and guide migration from the Northeast to the interior and other regions of Brazil.

A fourth direction is major improvement in the human and institutional resources of the region. This direction is basic to all other directions mentioned above. The principal limitation on regional development efforts has been the low productivity and efficiency of administration and institutions in achieving development goals. This has been more crucial than the availability of government or private funds. The principal limitation on increasing productivity in agriculture and industry has been the inadequacy of education and training for the human resources. Many experts on United States agriculture have explained its phenomenal productivity almost exclusively in terms of education. The farmers know how to read and write, and many of them have had university levels of education. They are prepared to receive and to act on new technology as it is developed in research stations, and they are equipped to provide the necessary levels of management skills.

These and other questions, such as the short-term steps necessary to implement these long-term goals, will be discussed in greater detail in subsequent chapters in relation to the development activities now underway. But there is virtue in trying to maintain a simplified picture of the complex development situation of the Northeast. This picture is that the ultimate goal of Northeast development is to improve the welfare of the people. This may be accomplished both by improving opportunities in the region and by out-migration. Therefore, development activities for both the short and long term should have two principal goals: to increase the proportion and number of persons making economic contributions to the region; and to increase the productivity of these persons and other factors of production that are being used in the region.

4

Fighting the Drought

DURING DECADES and even centuries, the Northeast "problem" was exclusively perceived as the periodic drought, or the *sêcas*. The published record of the *sêcas* goes as far back as 1614 to the reports of a mining prospector searching for emeralds in the San Francisco Valley.[1] And beginning with the severe drought of 1877, the Brazilian government officially recognized the Northeast *sêcas* as a national problem.

The diagnosis of the Northeast problem and the proposed solutions are changing rapidly and radically. But the seventy-five year campaign—from 1877 to 1952—of "fighting the drought" has left this approach still strongly entrenched. Although a major purpose of this study is to place the Northeast situation in the economic development perspective of the "New Era," it would be remiss to neglect completely the drought issue. More and more, the Northeast is recognizing that it has economic and social problems—overpopulation, low economic productivity, unemployment, and widespread poverty—that are separable from and more basic than the drought. But the drought as a phenomenon of nature is real, and its role is still strong in the struggle of popular and official ideas that guide the economic future of the Northeast.

To be sure, there is no shortage of popular and technical writings on the Northeast drought. The drama of the *sêcas* has for decades been a favorite of the talented and prolific writers and poets of the Northeast. The technical challenges of this physical phenomenon

[1] Miguel Arrojado Ribiero Lisboa, "O Problema das Sêcas," *Boletim,* Ministério da Viação e Obras Publicas, Departmento Nacional de Obras Contra as Sêcas, Vol. 20 (November 1959), p. 4. A reprinting of a speech made in August 1913.

have likewise been a stimulus for thousands of articles by engineers and agronomists. And all professions have been stirred to write about the political aspects of the problem. A recent study modestly entitled a "Contribution to a Bibliography of the Droughts," lists more than 1,000 publications on the subject.[2]

The drought as an inspiration for literary eloquence can be illustrated by a recent book (1955) on Sergipe and the problem of the drought written by a civil engineer who was public works director for the state.

> Sergipe always is absent in the plans for combating the sêcas of the Northeast. Her shouts of anguish and of suffering do not resound in the distance. The large Federal funds destined for the works against the drought are channeled to other states. The Sergipano fights alone, abandoned and almost disillusioned.[3]

> Some think that the Northeast is a cowboy "Sahara" almost all desert, of dried up vegetation, a burning sun, an arid soil, sterile, where inferior humans live, famished and thirsty—taking care of cattle herds also inferior, famished and thirsty—held to that hell by congenital laziness that saps their bodies and souls. Those who think in this way have a "genial" solution for the case: the complete abandonment of the region, a grand exodus of all the people through the desert, having to lead them, a modern Moses, the government, who will transport them to the happy lands of Canaan. The accursed land would be transformed into the "land of no one," the boundaries of the Official Polygon would be the frontiers of Hell, and then, behind the Curtain of Fire, there would be nobody left to create absurd problems. Oversimplified reasoning, infantile solution.[4]

The Drought Phenomenon

Contrary to widespread impressions both within and outside of Brazil, the Nordeste is not a desert. A large coastal area running South from Natal on the "hump" has ample and dependable rainfall averaging over 50 inches per year. The large state of Maranhão near the Amazon region on the North, and officially included as part of the Northeast,

[2] Rui Simões de Menezes, *Contribuição a Bibliografia das Sêcas,* Banco do Nordeste do Brasil, Publicação No. 22, Fortaleza, Ceará (1957).

[3] Jorge de Oliveira Netto, *Sergipe e o Problema da Sêca,* Edição da COTEF, Aracaju (1955), p. 3.

[4] *Ibid.,* p. 9.

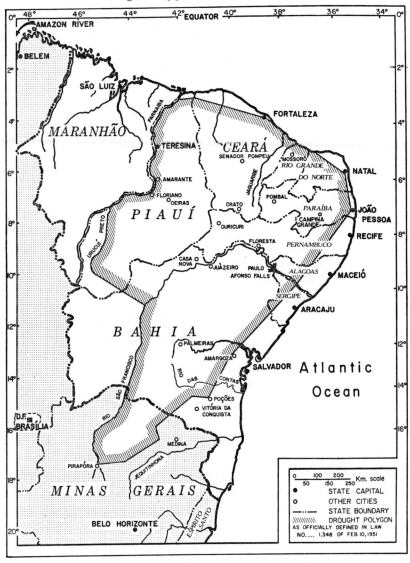

also has plentiful rainfall. A transition zone between the coast and the interior called the *agreste* has fairly reliable rainfall of from 30 to 40 inches. The semiarid interior called the *sertão* has a normal rainfall of from 20 to 30 inches. But rainfall in the *sertão* is highly uncertain and total annual precipitation is heavily concentrated in a short time period.

The so-called Drought Polygon was delineated by law to designate the beneficiaries of special federal programs to fight the drought. At present this official area covers about 940,000 square kilometers or 340,000 square miles—about the size of Texas and Oklahoma combined. Excluding the southern extension of the polygon into Minas Gerais, the official drought area covers about 50 percent of the nine-state Northeast. None of Maranhão is in the drought polygon. In the other states, the drought area ranges from 44 percent of the total area of Alagoas to 98 percent of Paraíba.[5]

But the Drought Polygon is more a political than a physiographic area. The polygon, first defined by law in 1936, was enlarged by legislation in 1947 and again in 1951; the principal motivation being to make more and more political districts eligible for public works projects of the drought agency. As the National Economic Council (NEC) points out, before the 1936 law the problem area was even more restricted—with the droughts being generally referred to as the *sêcas* of Ceará. The current immense size of the area, the NEC emphasizes, is a factor of confusion, creating an erroneous impression concerning the difficulty of the problem.[6]

The Polygon has a variety of climatic areas. The San Francisco River runs through the heart of this region, and its basin accounts for one-third of the Drought Polygon. And this river basin has a vast network of permanent rivers with normal and regular rainfall. The Polygon also has mountainous subareas which average 40 inches of rainfall annually. In general terms, the Polygon has been described as consisting of both semiarid areas and humid areas possessing normal conditions for vegetable and animal life.[7]

---

[5] Instituto Brasileiro de Geografia e Estatística, Conselho Nacional de Estatística, *Anuário Estatístico do Brasil, 1961*, p. 16.

[6] Conselho Nacional de Economia, "O Problema Nacional das Sêcas," *Boletim do DNOCS*, Vol. 19 (February 1959), p. 10.

[7] *Ibid.*, p. 15.

The Polygon also has a variety of soils which, with the exception of the irrigation basins, have not been well studied.[8] In general, much of the soil is shallow and unable to accumulate water. Salinization, therefore, is a widespread problem. The salts dissolved by the rains return to the surface where rapid evaporation caused by the wind and the heat leaves an ever-increasing concentration of salt. Erosion has greatly reduced the quality of the soils, particularly in the caatinga or scrub forest area of the region. Although much of the soil has high natural fertility, its productiveness is limited by salinization, erosion, poor drainage, and inefficient crop patterns.

Agriculture is the predominant economic activity in the drought area, although manufacturing, in the capital cities such as Fortaleza, and mining activities are also important. The major farm crop is cotton. Other significant products are carnauba wax, castor beans, corn, beans, sisal, coffee, manioc, and bananas. About half of the livestock raising of the Northeast is concentrated in the Polygon. The drought area produces a long staple tree cotton (mocó), which rates with the best long staple cotton of the world. This high quality fiber has been consumed mainly within Brazil, but in recent years about 15 percent of the crop has been exported.[9] Fortunately, the Northeast is one of the few areas for raising long staple cotton that has great possibilities for expanding output. Competing countries such as Egypt already engage in intensive cultivation and have limited possibilities for expanding the acreage in long staple cotton.

The Drought Polygon as politically defined embraces the state capital cities of Fortaleza, Natal, João Pessoa, and Teresina, as well as the city of Campina Grande. Including these urban areas, the Polygon has an estimated population of about 12-13 million people. The 1958 drought, considered to be the most severe in many years, affected parts of six states and an estimated 2 million inhabitants. As Dr. Raul Barbosa, President of the Bank of the Northeast (BNB), testified before a special Senate committee in 1958, the number of flagelados, as people affected by the drought area are figuratively called,

[8] A pioneering report on the soils and water conditions of the drought area, and still the classic study, is J. G. Duque, Solo e Agua no Polígono das Sêcas, Ministério da Viação e Obras Publicas, DNOCS, Serviço Agro-Industrial, 3d ed., Fortaleza, Ceará (1953).

[9] Banco do Nordeste do Brasil, Fibra de Alta Qualidade, ETENE, Fortaleza, Ceará (November 1959).

represented about 13 percent of the total population of the Northeast (excluding Maranhão). This compared to 9 percent in 1932, 1 percent in 1942, and between 2 and 3 percent in 1951 and 1953.[10] The BNB also reported that its field survey teams did not encounter, among the people dislocated by the drought, a single case of death by starvation or due to an infectious or contagious disease.[11]

As Professor Hirschman has described the situation:

. . . The problem of the Northeastern *sertão* is . . . less its dryness than the irregularity of the dry spells. It has little in common with such well-known arid lands as Egypt, or the Peruvian Coast or large parts of our Southwest where irrigation is the *sine qua non* of agricultural activity and settlement. . . . In the basic structure of its problems, the region is perhaps best compared, not to other arid zones, but to lands where an unpredictable calamity overhangs pleasant or at least bearable existence, as in Italy or Japan where people make a living on the fertile slopes of occasionally erupting volcanos. . . .[12]

Federal Programs Against the Drought

The federal government's official concern with the Northeast droughts began in 1877 when a severe water shortage after thirty comforting years of abundant rainfall caught the region by surprise. The magnitude and severity of this calamity has been recorded in the history of the *sêcas* with estimates of half of the million inhabitants of the state of Ceará perishing from hunger, thirst, and disease.

Moved by this great tragedy, Emperor Pedro II established an Imperial Commission of Inquiry to look into ways of preventing similar disasters in the future. The commission's principal recommendations were to improve transportation and to build a series of dams. In 1880, a British engineer was brought in to study the dam projects in detail. One of the three dams he recommended was the Cedro dam in the municipality of Quixadá (capacity 128 million cubic meters or about 100,000 acre feet) started in 1884 and finally completed in 1906 after

---

[10] Banco do Nordeste do Brasil, A Sêca de 1958, Informes Complementares, Fortaleza, Ceará (December 1958), pp. 4-5.

[11] Banco do Nordeste do Brasil, A Sêca de 1958: Consequencias da Sêca, Fortaleza, Ceará (August 1958), p. 7.

[12] Albert O. Hirschman, Journeys Toward Progress: Studies of Economic Policy Making in Latin America (Twentieth Century Fund, 1963), p. 16.

many starts and stops. To many Brazilians, the dam stands as a symbol of inefficiency and waste in the fight against the drought.

By 1909, a series of commissions had evolved into a new federal agency, the Inspectoria of Works Against the Drought.[13] With slight changes in name this federal agency has remained in operation ever since. The Inspectoria's duty was to study systematically the physiographic, economic, and social conditions of the drought area and to undertake the construction of works that would prevent or minimize the effects of the "flagellation." The agency had broad powers to build railroads and roads, drill wells, construct dams and reservoirs, and undertake "other works whose utility against the effects of the droughts has been demonstrated by experience."[14]

The Northeast has experienced six major drought periods in the current century—1900, 1915, 1919-20, 1931-32, 1951-52, and 1958. The funds available to the Inspectoria and DNOCS fluctuated greatly with the frequency and intensity of the droughts.[15] Annual expenditures of the Inspectoria, for example, rose from 6 to 95 million cruzeiros from 1919 to 1922 and then dropped to 8 million in 1924. Likewise, expenditures increased from 11 million cruzeiros in 1931 to 125 million in 1932 and then receded to 40 million in 1935.

In an effort to secure stability in the funds available for the Northeast, the 1934 Constitution contained a special provision (Article 177) requiring that no less than 4 percent of the federal tax receipts be allocated for defense against the effects of the drought in the Northeast. The federal Constitution provided also that 4 percent of state and local tax receipts be dedicated to economic assistance of the people in the Drought Polygon. The revolution of 1937 which installed Getúlio Vargas as a dictator disrupted efforts to implement these constitutional provisions, and they were not included in the new Constitution of 1937.

In 1945 the old Inspectoria was transformed into the National Department of Works Against the Drought (DNOCS), and in the following year the constitutional provision for allocating funds to the Northeast was renewed. Article 198 of the 1946 Constitution, which is still

[13] For a more comprehensive history of the "Big Drought" and the creation of the Inspectoria see *ibid.*, pp. 22-37.

[14] Decreto n. 7,619 of 21 October 1909 as reported in Th. Pompeu Sobrinho, *História das Sêcas*, Coleção Instituto do Ceará, Fortaleza, Ceará (1953), p. 215.

[15] See Chart, p. 77.

in force, allocated 3 percent of federal tax revenues for defense against the drought and provided that the states in the Polygon must apply the same percentage of their revenues in construction of reservoirs on a cooperative basis with private landowners and for other services necessary to assist the population. The Constitution also required that one-third of the federal allocation should be deposited in a special emergency relief fund, all or part of which could be used for loans to agriculture and industry in the drought area.

The DNOCS Accomplishments

What were the activities and accomplishments of DNOCS and its predecessor organization? These can be divided into two general categories: (1) the planning and implementation of a hydraulic solution to the drought problem and (2) the emergency measures during prolonged drought periods to employ and assist the people endangered by the calamity.[16]

The key to the hydraulic solution for the drought problem was supposed to be a better utilization of the hydrographic basins of the Polygon. Consequently, a plan was prepared in the 1920's for making use of the valleys of greatest importance to the Northeast economy through the construction of dams, roads, irrigation channels, and power plants. The dams and reservoirs were intended to provided surface water storage. From 1906 to 1959, 190 publicly owned reservoirs with a capacity of 6.6 billion cubic meters or about 5 million acre feet were constructed. About 470 small and medium storage reservoirs with a capacity of almost 1 billion cubic meters were built on a cooperative basis with land owners. For using underground water, DNOCS began a well-drilling program in 1909 and within fifty years drilled 5,124 wells,[17] an average of only one hundred new wells per year for the Polygon.

[16] For the agency's own appraisal of its accomplishments see José Cândido Castro Parente Pessoa (General Director of DNOCS), *Planification and Principal Accomplishments of the DNOCS*, DNOCS, Publication N. 202, Series I.E., Rio de Janeiro (May 1960). For a more objective brief appraisal, see *A Ação Governamental no Nordeste*, Desenvolvimento e Conjuntura (April 1959), pp. 81-88.

[17] National Department of Works Against the Drought, *Relatório de 1959*, No. 194, Series II, M, Rio de Janeiro (March 1960), p. 89.

Resources Consigned in the Federal Budget to Works Against the Drought

(Billions of Cruzeiros of constant purchasing power, 1958)

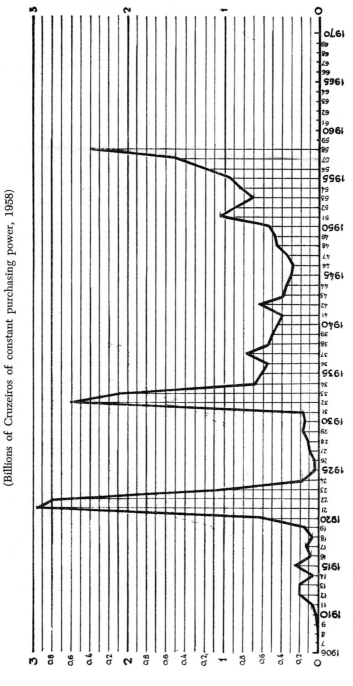

Source: Ministry of Transportation and Public Work, National Department of Works Against the Drought.

77

Extensive transportation and communication facilities were built by DNOCS, which played a significant role in the demographic and economic integration of the region. About 12,000 kilometers of dirt roads were completed in the area, and this program has given the Northeast a road density per square kilometer almost equal to Rio Grande do Sul and double that of Minas Gerais. DNOCS had under construction in 1962 a 2,000 kilometer paved road connecting the Northeast (Fortaleza) to the new capital at Brasília. About sixty airfields for DC 3 type planes were built in the region. A radio-communication system of sixty-five radio stations was established and is operated by DNOCS.

In sharp contrast to the magnitude of the water storage and transportation accomplishments, the irrigation results were small. Up to 1958, DNOCS had constructed about 700 kilometers of main and secondary irrigation canals, which can serve an irrigated area of 6,000 hectares, or 18,000 hectares if the crops of the *vazantes* (dry river beds and receding edges of the reservoirs) and "dry strips" are included.[18] This compares to an estimated 250,000 hectares of land suitable for irrigation with water from the reservoirs (*açudes*)[19] and 3.4 million hectares of cropland cultivated in the drought area.[20]

Agro-industrial and piscicultural research has been a small but long-standing activity of DNOCS. And in recent years, the agency has undertaken the construction of municipal water systems and several relatively small hydroelectric installations and transmission lines.

The drought emergency measures of the Inspectoria and DNOCS have changed greatly over the decades. At the early stage this activity consisted largely of having reception centers outside of the immediate areas affected by the droughts where people could receive first aid before being transferred to emergency work camps. With the construction of roads and other transportation facilities, the emergency relief possibilities have greatly enlarged. In the 1958 drought, for example, DNOCS distributed throughout the area vaccines and other medical supplies, powdered milk, and food cereals. It also made available medical and dental services within the area. Many people

[18] "A Ação Governmental no Nordeste," Desenvolvimento e Conjuntura (April 1959), pp. 87-88.

[19] *Plano Quinquenal de Desenvolvimento para o Nordeste 1961-1965*, Presidência de República, Superintendência do Desenvolvimento do Nordeste, Recife (1961), p. 48.

[20] Duque, *op. cit.*, p. 290.

were employed on the Northeast-Brasília road project and in other activities. The stocks of fish in the public and private reservoirs were made freely available and access to all water storage facilities was granted for domestic water needs.[21]

The Failure of the Hydraulic Approach

In Brazil as in other countries, large public works programs can be vitiated by politics and riddled by scandals, particularly in emergency situations. And much of the criticism and evaluation of the DNOCS works against the drought effort has been in terms of inefficiency and irregularities. Another category of continuing criticism has been of a microtechnical nature which accepts the general validity of the approach but debates the merits of large versus small reservoirs, surface versus underground storage, traditional crops versus xerophilous crops, etc.

Many of the DNOCS leaders were extraordinarily competent professional people such as Vinicius Berredo, Luis Vieira, and J. Guimarães Duque. But even the constitutional allocation of funds did not mean within the Brazilian governmental system that DNOCS had a regular flow of funds. Furthermore, as a traditional governmental agency, it had great difficulty paying adequate salaries to attract and keep professional personnel.

Much of the scandal in the 1951 and 1958 droughts—corrupt handling of funds, padding of payrolls, irregularities in distribution of relief goods, political influence in the selection of projects—was directly related to DNOCS, but prior to that period DNOCS had led a generally honorable existence. Private individuals, pressure groups, and some politicians have had a less impeccable record. Even more significant, the drought has long been an integral part of the political style of the Northeast. For decades, Nordestino politicians have based their urgent claims for increased national attention and resources on exaggerated reports of droughts and famine. And among many Brazilians, this phenomenon has been labeled, "The Industry of the Drought."

But with the development of an extensive transportation network

[21] Luiz Carlos Martins Pinheiro, "Obras Contra os Efeitos das Sêcas (Sêca de 1958)," *Boletim do DNOCS* (February 1959), p. 156.

and reservoir system in the interior, the *sêcas* have become less a period of human suffering and more a political phenomenon. But the traditional "bad" pictures of the Northeast drought as a period of misery, starvation, and death still are dominant. The 1958 drought was serious without question, but the frank comment of one Nordestino congressman to the author is still relevant. "With such large amounts of poverty and unemployment in our vast region," he explained, "politicians can create a drought almost at will. Thousands of eager job seekers are always available for emergency relief projects, and grateful recipients of relief foods are plentiful. Even when rainfall is scarce," he continued, "we now have the roads and transportation facilities to prevent humans and animals from dying of thirst and starvation. When we fail to do so, bad politics, inefficient administration and corruption are usually to blame."

The crucial underlying question, however, is not DNOCS, politics, or scandal—but the basic validity of the hydraulic approach. Given the state of knowledge in the 1880's, the engineering solution was undoubtedly a very "modern" way of trying to handle the problem of the Northeast. Economic development techniques are still new and poorly developed, but, as will be discussed in subsequent chapters, they now seem to provide a much more promising solution for the Northeast situation. The hydraulic approach emphasized physical facilities as a defense against an act of nature. The economic development approach focuses on poverty and low economic productivity as the main problem of the Northeast. It emphasizes the need to strengthen the economy and improve social welfare levels so that the people in the region will become less vulnerable to the effects of the drought. An expansion of mining and industrial employment, as one example, will both increase the income and productivity of the people moving out of agriculture and base their livelihood on activities that are less affected by a shortage of rainfall.

The San Francisco Valley Commission

A transition period in federal programs for Northeast Brazil began in the late 1940's with the establishment of two resource development agencies: the San Francisco Valley Commission (CVSF) and the San

Francisco Hydroelectric Company (CHESF). The 1940's were years without any serious drought emergencies for the Northeast, and the new development activities emerged out of events and policies largely unrelated to the traditional fighting of the drought.

The San Francisco River starts in the southeast of Brazil near Belo Horizonte in the state of Minas Gerais. After flowing northeast for about 1,700 miles, the San Francisco swings sharply to the east and plunges over the Paulo Afonso Falls (192 feet) before continuing to the South Atlantic about 300 miles away. The hook-shaped valley encompasses about 263,000 square miles, as compared to 40,000 square miles for the Tennessee Valley in the United States. The northern half of the river basin, which includes the Paulo Afonso Falls, runs through the center of the Drought Polygon.

The establishment of a multipurpose river basin commission for the San Francisco resulted from Brazil's long-standing desire to populate the interior, from a growing world enthusiasm for integrated river basin development sparked by the Tennessee Valley Authority experience in the United States, and from coastal shipping problems encountered during World War II.

Brazil's continuing desire to develop its interior regions is well articulated by one of the early leaders of the Valley Commission project, Lucas Lopes.[22]

> The problem of the economic valorization of the San Francisco is of the highest political interest to the Nation. The effective occupation of the Valley and its economic development would eliminate the vacuum that separates the Northeast from the Center and the South, giving an objective meaning to the force that we still need to expend to strengthen National Unity.
> Along more than a thousand kilometers of the margins of this great river exist population vacuums. Unlike the great valleys in other regions of the world, the San Francisco Valley lacks the power to attract and keep immigrants and pioneers.

The Tennessee Valley Authority project initiated in 1933 received extensive international publicity and greatly encouraged the idea of an integrated river basin project for the San Francisco. The American Technical Mission to Brazil of 1943, led by the distinguished en-

[22] Lucas Lopes, *O Vale do São Francisco,* Ministerio da Viação E Obras Publicas (1955), pp. 29-30.

gineer Morris L. Cooke, who had been associated with the TVA project, was asked to make a preliminary survey of the San Francisco River basin and the hydroelectric possibilities of the Paulo Afonso Falls. The favorable report of the Cooke Mission gave further impetus to river basin thinking.[23]

Navigation on the San Francisco River is feasible for traffic movements between distant points in the interior. But the Paulo Afonso Falls prevent transportation from the interior to the Atlantic. Nevertheless, the transportation features of the river began to receive increased attention during World War II when coastwise shipping was disrupted by German submarines. And in mid-1944, the government made a special appropriation for improving river navigation on the San Francisco.[24]

Unlike the experience of DNOCS, the source of funds for the Valley Commission was earmarked before either an organization or specific program existed. The 1946 Constitution provided that, for twenty years, 1 percent of the federal tax revenues should be employed in the comprehensive economic development of the San Francisco River and its tributaries. (The Amazon River basin was assigned 3 percent of federal revenues in the same Constitution.) The San Francisco Valley Commission was created in 1948, but work did not begin until 1950 when a general development plan was completed. It is interesting to note that President Dutra in proposing the CVSF to the Congress characterized the San Francisco development problem as one "that surpasses the ambit of regional interests and acquires extraordinary national significance."[25]

A separate stream of developments to be described below preempted the principal source of hydroelectric potential in the lower basin—the Paulo Afonso Falls—for a separate government agency. Thus, electric power development was not a dominant aspect of proposed CVSF activity. The basic plan completed in 1950 included programs of stream regulation and water control, river and port improvement, provision of navigation equipment for the river, irrigation and drainage, roads, airfields, telegraphy and communication facilities, mu-

[23] See Chap. 7, pp. 122-23.

[24] Decree No. 6643 of June 29, 1944.

[25] *Plano Geral para o Aproveitamento do Vale do São Francisco*, Comissão do Vale do São Francisco, Presidência da República, Rio de Janeiro, Brasil (1950), p. 9.

nicipal water and sewage installations, and several hydroelectric projects mainly outside of the Northeast.[26] Few of the proposed activities were new to the region. The novel feature of the project was the concept of one agency being responsible for a wide range of inter-related programs within a natural resource region.

But the new agency created to transform the San Francisco Valley led an undistinguished career.[27] In practice, the commission followed what it called "a great policy of small services." It built access roads, infirmaries, and small hospitals and provided water and power for a number of small towns. Early in its existence, the commission was "captured" by certain political groups. It did not demonstrate initiative and imagination, and it had little contact with DNOCS and the drought problem. When President Kubitschek decided in 1956 to proceed with a major multipurpose dam at the Tres Maria site on the upper reaches of the river outside the Northeast, he entrusted the project to CEMIG, the state owned power company of Minas Gerais, rather than to the San Francisco Valley Commission.

Organized as a traditional government department, CVSF did not have continuity of leadership. It has had many different heads. Also, its future promise was limited in its inception when it did not receive responsibility for the major Paulo Afonso power project. Without its electric power responsibility, the Tennessee Valley Authority undoubtedly would have had much less success.

The San Francisco Hydroelectric Company

The Paulo Afonso Falls, located almost in the center of the Northeast region, had been discussed for decades as a source of hydroelectric power. But nothing happened until Apolônio Sales, as Minister of Agriculture, became interested in a source of electric power for a colonization project he wanted to create at Petrolandia in the state of Pernambuco. A small 1,500 horsepower privately owned power plant had been built at the falls in 1913 to supply a textile plant and Minister Sales' first plan was to purchase this power station.

[26] Ibid.
[27] For a more detailed history and evaluation of CVSF, see Albert O. Hirschman, op. cit.

But technicians in the Division of Water of the Agricultural Department suggested that he begin developing the vast unused potential of Paulo Afonso. Minister Sales became enthusiastic about the idea and had his engineers go ahead with the planning. He also visited the Tennessee Valley in 1944 and explained, "My main purpose in coming to Tennessee was to study TVA's dams and see how they can be applied in Brazil."[28] Various studies, political debates, and campaigns followed and in late 1945, three weeks before being deposed as dictator, Getúlio Vargas signed several decrees which authorized a new "mixed" corporation, the San Francisco Hydroelectric Company (CHESF) to have a power concession for the Paulo Afonso Falls.

Several years were required for CHESF to raise its capital through stock sales and develop its plans. And it became established in 1948 almost concurrently with the new Valley Commission. The original plans were to install 120,000 kilowatts of capacity—almost a doubling of the Northeast electric power capacity. It was not surprising, therefore, that general skepticism prevailed whether such a large increment in power could be marketed. This skepticism was reflected in the Twentieth Century Fund study of Brazil published in 1949.[29]

> The middle San Francisco Valley has long been one of the "problem" areas of Brazil. . . . The need for practical steps to redeem this area is generally recognized. But some observers believe that the Paulo Afonso power project is premature. The construction of transmission lines and receiver systems to serve the coastal cities is expensive in view of the distances involved. Furthermore, the existing and prospective industries of that area are not large consumers of electric power.

But under the leadership of Alves de Sousa, former head of the Department of Mineral Production, the CHESF project went ahead. President Dutra gave strong backing to the four directors of the company as did Getúlio Vargas when he returned through election to the presidency of the Republic. Above all, as one of the directors, General Carlos Berenhauser, explained, "In the early days, President Dutra

---

[28] TVA Technical Library, *TVA-Symbol of Valley Resource Development*, A Digest and Selected Bibliography of Information, Tennessee Valley Authority (June 1961), p. 11.

[29] George Wythe, *Brazil: An Expanding Economy* (Twentieth Century Fund, 1949), p. 157.

made sure that CHESF received funds at the right time. This was crucial to the efficiency and morale of our project."[30]

In 1950, the World Bank granted a $15 million loan to CHESF to cover the cost of imported equipment. And although CHESF had already established a pattern of administrative efficiency and technical competence, the World Bank involvement provided outside support for the integrity of the project. The growing prestige of CHESF was noted in the 1953 report of the Joint Brazil-United States Economic Development Mission which commented:[31]

> It is generally considered that the company (CHESF) has the benefit of competent management. The general design of the project is considered to be well suited to the local conditions of the site. The quality of the construction and the general performance of the organization has in general been satisfactory, particularly when taking into account the remote location and difficulties of transportation and access to the project, as well as the limitations of the labor market.

From the engineering point of view, the Paulo Afonso project was a great success. However, the preoccupation with the engineering and technical problems weakened CHESF's attention to the market side of the problem. The preparation of the distribution systems in Recife and Salvador, owned by subsidiaries of the American and Foreign Power Company, lagged because of the general difficulty faced by foreign utilities in raising capital and uncertainties about expropriation. CHESF made some efforts to get state development commissions started, but it did not undertake extensive industrial development research and promotion. The original plans had been enlarged from 120,000 to 180,000 kilowatts, and for a period of time after 1955, when this power first became available, CHESF was operating at a low level of capacity.

One problem faced by CHESF in selling electric power was the region's possessive attitude toward natural resources. In 1951, the Reynolds Aluminum Company was prepared to locate a large $150 million aluminum plant in the Northeast and CHESF was willing to construct new capacity to supply the 200,000 kilowatt power re-

[30] Interview with General Carlos Berenhauser, February 1962.

[31] Institute of Inter-American Affairs, *The Development of Brazil*, Report of the Joint Brazil-United States Economic Development Commission (1953), p. 220.

quirements. (The Falls have a potential of more than 1 million kilowatts.) Brazil had only a small market for aluminum at the time, and the Reynolds output would have been largely for export. But a coalition of Northeast businessmen, who were financially interested in another aluminum project outside of the region, and nationalists succeeded in killing the Reynolds project on the emotional grounds that the export of aluminum was in effect an export of Brazil's natural resource—hydroelectric power.[32]

Although slow in starting, electric power demand in the Northeast increased rapidly with the expanded availability. And in the late 1950's CHESF began construction on a second powerhouse, to be completed by 1965, which will add 390,000 kilowatts of capacity. SUDENE has given CHESF expanded power responsibility in the Northeast, and the CHESF activities were easily incorporated into the regional coordination effort for the area.

CHESF deserves special attention because it stands in sharp contrast to previous federal projects in the Northeast. It demonstrated that a federal agency could operate efficiently, effectively, and honestly. And the reasons for its success are important. First, the "mixed" corporation approach gave CHESF great administrative flexibility even though the government controlled the agency. Second, its leadership was technically competent and nonpolitical. Third, the competence and determination of the leadership were able to attract the necessary kind of political support and to continue without major change from 1948 to 1960. Fourth, the agency had a specific and well-defined responsibility of an engineering nature and an activity about which adequate know-how was available in the country or from outside consultants. Finally, whereas CVSF had more or less assured funds, CHESF had to augment its financial resources from time to time from domestic and international sources. In the process, CHESF frequently had to demonstrate the technical, administrative, and economic integrity of its project.

Thus, both as an affirmative resource and economic development experiment and as an effective demonstration of the ability of government to contribute to Northeast economic progress, CHESF represented an important transition between "fighting the drought" and the "New Era."

[32] CHESF, *A Indústria do Alumínio no Brasil: Possibilidades de sua Instalação no Nordeste*, Rio de Janeiro (June 1952).

5

The New Era

FOR DECADES after the 1877 drought, the hydraulic solution to the Northeast problem reigned as the undisputed goal of federal policies and actions. Each new drought crisis demonstrated that expensive dams and water storage projects had little improved the economic security of the Nordestinos. But the lack of success was invariably ascribed to politics or deficient technical implementations of the basic policy. Frequent and heated controversies raged over subissues. But the basic philosophy of fighting the drought through water conservation projects persisted unchallenged.

Fundamental policy changes toward the Northeast required more than the apparent failure of long-existing policies. Strongly supported alternative solutions also had to be available and by the early 1950's such alternatives were emerging. New ideas about the economic development and planning role of government were growing in strength and pervading intellectual, political, and governmental circles on the national scene. As a counter force to the long-standing influence of engineers in Brazilian society, *technicos* trained in economics were beginning to flow from recently established faculties of economics. And an increasing number of competent and experienced engineers and lawyers were shifting their professional interests and abilities to economic problems. Thus, when another drought crisis occurred in 1951, accompanied by the usual political scandals and popular disillusionment, new ideas and supporting personnel were on hand to gain a beachhead in the struggle to reshape federal policy toward the Northeast.

The New Era "economic solution" focuses directly on the economic welfare problem rather than the physical drought phenomenon. It emphasizes economic development planning and argues that higher regional levels of income, employment, and production and a greater dependence on activities other than agriculture are the best defenses against the drought. Its basic strategy is to encourage all regional possibilities for economic expansion—mining and manufacturing as well as agriculture, the humid areas as well as the semiarid interior—and thus to increase the economic resistance of the Northeast to the periodic droughts when they occur.

The creation of a regional development bank in 1952, the Bank of the Northeast (BNB), marked the first official government acceptance of the economic solution as federal policy for the Northeast. However, the new policy was adopted as a supplement to rather than a substitute for the hydraulic solution. The National Department of Works Against the Drought (DNOCS) continued to exist and to disburse its constitutionally allocated share of federal revenues for fighting the drought. Nevertheless, from 1954 when it began operations until the major drought of 1958, the BNB made significant progress in preparing regional institutions and personnel for the New Era approach and in educating the region. Thus, when another series of DNOCS failures and drought scandals accompanied the 1958 crisis, the economic development approach make a second major advance: a new federal agency was established to plan and coordinate all development efforts for the region.

Under vigorous leadership, the new Superintendency for Northeast Development (SUDENE) has won political victories against potent political and governmental opposition. It now faces the even more crucial challenge of achieving specific and concrete results in economic development. The transition in philosophies will continue as a stormy period for some time to come. The conflict will be strongly affected by related issues of powerful political and economic vested interests. But the economic solution now seems destined to dominate federal action for several decades at least.

New National Forces

From the beginning of the Vargas era in 1930 until Brazil entered World War II in 1942, the federal government was fully occupied with the political integration of the country. During World War II, however, the economic role of the national government came to the fore in response to military and economic security needs. And in the postwar period, the government's participation in the economic sphere continued and expanded with economic development becoming the goal and responsibility of federal agencies. The major change in Brazilian policy toward the Northeast is directly related to the new national forces for economic planning and development that were increasing in strength in the late 1940's.

Under the Vargas regime the power and influence of the federal government gained greatly over the centrifugal tendencies of the states. But in the economic sphere, the only prewar federal organization that approximated a national economic planning effort was the National Foreign Trade Council established in 1934. Foreign trade problems had gained early acceptance as national responsibilities. The Council's functions, however, were much broader than the name suggests. It made studies of a wide range of economic problems, and its decisions on some matters such as tariffs were given the force of law.[1]

Immediately on Brazil's entry into World War II, Vargas appointed a Coordinator of Economic Mobilization with vast powers for directing the economy. Although aiding the war effort was the primary objective, the experience gained in economic intervention acted as significant preparation for the later development role of the government. In recognition of Brazil's strategic importance to the Allied war efforts, in 1943, the United States sent a high level American Technical Mission (Cooke Mission) to assist Brazil in planning for greater economic self-sufficiency.[2]

Working with one hundred Brazilian counterparts, the Cooke Mission investigated measures to stimulate local production of essential

[1] George Wythe, *Brazil, An Expanding Economy* (Twentieth Century Fund, 1949), p. 342.
[2] Morris L. Cooke, *Brazil On The March—A Study in International Cooperation*, Reflections on the Report of the American Technical Mission to Brazil (McGraw-Hill, 1944).

goods in short supply, to develop substitutes for foreign goods unobtainable in wartime, to expand and maintain Brazil's domestic transportation system, and to establish a sound basis for industrial development. A major result of the mission was to develop a Brazilian confidence in economic planning and provide training and experience for a large number of Brazilian professionals.[3]

An Economic Planning Commission, established in 1944 as a subcommission of the National Security Council, was active for a short period in matters of transportation, industrial expansion, and mineral resource development. By the end of the war, with the overthrow of Vargas and the adoption of a new Constitution in 1946, the responsibility of the government in economic matters had become widely accepted. In Article 146 the new Constitution authorized government economic intervention and created for the first time a National Economic Council (NEC) to work with both executive and legislative branches of government. The NEC did not begin its activities until 1949.

During the Dutra presidency, from 1946 to 1951, the trends toward economic development planning continued with great strength. At the direction of President Dutra a five-year plan for national development, called the SALTE plan, was prepared and submitted to the Congress in 1948. In the same year, the Joint Brazil-United States Technical Commission headed by John Abbink and Dr. Octavio Gouvêa de Bulhões undertook a general survey of the Brazilian economy and its economic and financial problems. As a final official step in the economic field, the Dutra administration signed an agreement in December 1950 with the United States for a more ambitious joint effort in economic development planning, the Joint Brazil-United States Economic Development Commission, which, under the Point Four program, was operational from 1951 to 1953.

The growing governmental initiative in economic development, stimulated and supported by United States technical assistance, was accompanied by two other developments—the expansion of economic research and the training of economists—that strengthened the base for economic planning. The quasi-governmental Getúlio Vargas Foun-

[3] Romulo Almeida, "Experiência Brasileira de Planejamento, Orientação e Contrôle da Economia," *Estudos Econômicos*, Confederação Nacional da Industria, Rio de Janeiro (June 1950), p. 74.

dation established in late 1944 pioneered in both research and training. And its first research publication, written by a trained engineer turned economist and released in 1946, was a strong plea for the planned development of the Brazilian economy.[4] Other significant economic research activities were initiated by the National Confederation of Industries, the São Paulo Federation of Industries and Association of Commerce, and a number of government agencies.

The supply of trained economists, still a critical bottleneck in Brazil, was enlarged by the establishment of faculties of economics at some major Brazilian universities during the 1940's, by the on-the-job-training experience of working with the several foreign assistance missions, and by the initiative of a small number of Brazilians like Roberto Campos and Celso Furtado in pursuing economic studies in foreign universities. By 1950, the United Nations also was beginning to make an impact in the personnel field through foreign fellowships, international seminars for economists like the 1950 Puerto Rico conference attended by Romulo Almeida and Roberto Campos, and by providing technical assistance.

What the economic historian, João Frederico Normano, identified several decades ago as the main problem of Brazil, "to inject an economic substance into the political area,"[5] was well on its way to resolution when the 1951 drought crisis opened up another opportunity for a change in Northeast policy. And the fact that the policy shift resulted from new forces at the national level rather than from stimuli originating in the region explains the continuing conflict of philosophies within the area and the persistent need to expand the regional understanding of the economic development approach.

The 1951 Drought

In 1951 another major drought hit the Northeast—the first since 1942. And Getúlio Vargas, who had won the presidential election of 1950, was faced with a Northeast crisis. Horacio Lafer, Vargas' Minis-

---

[4] Américo L. Barbosa de Oliveira, *O Desenvolvimento Planificado da Economia Brasileira*, Fundação Getúlio Vargas, Rio de Janeiro (June 1946).

[5] J. F. Normano, *Brazil: A Study of Economic Types* (University of North Carolina Press, 1935), p. 222.

ter of Finance and a São Paulo industrialist, visited the Northeast in April 1951 to attend a conference on cotton. Impressed by the discussions of agricultural credit shortages at the meetings and by his close contact with the worsening drought situation, Minister Lafer suggested in a note to the President the establishment of a specialized credit institution for the region.[6]

Minister Lafer was strongly critical of existing programs. "I have the impression," he reported, "that in the combat of the *sêcas* up to the present the preoccupation with engineering or hydraulic works frequently overshadows the economic side of the problem." And he added that the combat against the *sêcas* through large engineering works would be futile unless accompanied by steps to strengthen the regional economy.

With Vargas' approval Minister Lafer drafted a law in mid-1951 to create the Bank of the Northeast. The proposed bank as a "mixed" public-private agency would use the emergency financial reserves for the Northeast provided in the Constitution and give major emphasis to financing agricultural crops, irrigation works, acquisition of farm machinery, construction of silos, and the exploration of economic crops adapted to semiarid regions. The specific proposal represented primarily an attempt to make available in the region less expensive and longer-term agricultural credit.[7]

Vargas had as presidential advisers three Nordestinos who were intimately involved in the New Era thinking on economic planning and development—Romulo Almeida, Jesus Soares Pereira, and Cleantho de Paiva Leite. It was not surprising, therefore, that when Vargas sent his message to the Congress in October 1951 asking for the establishment of the Bank of the Northeast, the project had been broadened into a major regional development institution. The presidential message explicitly argued that federal government policy for defending the Northeast from the drought required a revision in traditional methods. "The title itself, 'Works Against the Drought'," Vargas stated, "expresses a limitation, focusing on the problem above all from the angle of engineering works. In the light of past experience and modern techniques of regional planning, it is time for a definite economic and social di-

---

[6] Banco do Nordeste do Brasil, *Banco do Nordeste, Origens (I)*, Fortaleza, Ceará (1958), pp. 35-38.
[7] *Ibid.*, pp. 42-45.

rection to be impressed upon the solution of the problem."[8] And he called for a general plan to attack the economic and social effects of the phenomena.

Vargas also warned, "We must not through a spirit of unsophisticated egalitarianism or ill advised *distributismo* retard the progress of the most vigorous zones of the country simply to help the others, since that would be to compromise the growth of the country as a whole and thus the actual future of the regions most backward."[9]

In line with the broader thinking, the new bank was given responsibilities far beyond those initially suggested by Minister Lafer. It was required to set up an Advisory Council including the Director of DNOCS, the Superintendent of the San Francisco Valley Commission, a representative of each of the eight states then included in the Drought Polygon, and regional representatives of agriculture, industry, and commerce. The BNB was required to create a technical office of economic studies for the Northeast. The emphasis on industrial financing operations was strong, and the BNB was permitted to act as an underwriter for securities, to build buildings for industries, and to take initiatives and risks of a pioneer nature in stimulating special productive private enterprises.

In July 1952, the law creating the BNB was signed and within about eighteen months the Bank began its initial operations. It followed by one month congressional approval for the National Development Bank (BNDE) and shared with the BNDE common origins—a new national feeling of government's affirmative economic development responsibility.

The Bank of the Northeast

Almost a year passed before an incorporating commission was named to implement the BNB law. One reason for the delay was that the extension of the drought calamity into 1953 absorbed the emergency reserve funds that were supposed to become the financial base for the new regional bank.

By 1954, however, Romulo Almeida, the President's economic ad-

[8] "Mensagem N. 363, de 1951," *Banco do Nordeste, Origens*, p. 145.
[9] *Ibid.*, p. 149.

viser, was named president of the BNB, and the agency began functioning in the region out of its Fortaleza headquarters. Operating within a frequently unstable and restless national political environment, the bank has had significant successes. At the same time, the project has disappointed some of its early supporters who had high expectations for the regional development impact of the new experiment. Two inherent features of the BNB institution—the joining together of commercial and development banking responsibilities and limitations imposed by the source of funds—undoubtedly explain a large share of the disappointment.

The major continuing source of BNB funds has been the 1946 constitutional earmarking of 1 percent of federal tax revenues as a special emergency relief fund for Northeast droughts. By special legislation in 1949 the Congress permitted this emergency fund to be used for agricultural and industrial loans in the Northeast through the Bank of Brazil. (No loans were made by the Bank of Brazil under this authority.) The Congress also stipulated that ready cash be available at all times equal to the previous year's total contribution to the fund. This proviso applied also to the Bank of the Northeast when it became the depository for the emergency funds and resulted in a requirement that at least 30 percent of the Treasury deposits must be used for short-term credit of ninety days or less—obviously a major restriction on long-term development loan activities.

The BNB's commercial banking responsibilities were an even more serious inhibition on development programs during the early period. They were the easiest to get started and for some time consumed most of top management's attention. The law required that the BNB establish in each of the eight states at least one branch for each 400,000 population, or about forty agencies, and the political pressures were strong for implementing this legal requirement. Large numbers of clerical and subprofessional workers were needed for the commercial banking activities, and much effort was expended in recruiting this staff. Furthermore, paternalistic federal laws strictly regulate the working conditions for traditional banking employees. For example, the law limited working hours to thirty-three per week. The numerical predominance of traditional subprofessional banking personnel in the total staff of the bank made it politically difficult to establish high salaries necessary to attract scarce professional personnel for development operations, even though it was recognized that the *technicos* would work on a full-time basis.

In August 1954, an eighteen month series of national crises was triggered by President Vargas' suicide. In Brazilian style, all heads of major government agencies change with the national presidency and the BNB top post was occupied by four different persons during the agency's first year and a half of operations. When Juscelino Kubitschek assumed office in early 1956 as President of the Republic, the BNB entered its first period of stable leadership under the direction of Raul Barbosa, former governor of the state of Ceará.

From 1954 to 1960 the BNB increased its number of branches from 7 to 41, its number of employees from less than 200 to 1,500, and its resources from about 320 million to 6.4 billion cruzeiros, or from about U.S. $6 million to U.S. $33 million converted at prevailing free exchange rates. Commercial operations through the so-called "general credit portfolio" accounted for 80 percent of total loans in the first full year of operation (1955) but declined to 38 percent in 1961.[10] Of major significance, however, the BNB, in all of its operations, determinedly maintained a reputation, almost unprecedented for a government agency in the Northeast, of nonpolitical and businesslike practices.

The BNB development experience deserves special attention, not only because this responsibility represented the principal *raison d'être* of the new institution, but because of the crucial significance of this experience to similar efforts underway in many underdeveloped countries. The difficulties in a democratic setting of shifting from long-established and politically controlled welfare and public works projects to economically viable development programs are formidable. Invariably, such a shift, when imposed from the top, finds an area completely unprepared in terms of technical personnel, well elaborated development projects, necessary economic and technical data and analyses, supporting institutions, and essential public understanding. All of these problems were faced by the BNB in its attempt to fulfill its development responsibility. And foreign technical assistance was one of the BNB's key hopes for overcoming these difficult obstacles.

With the help of a United Nations economic development adviser,

---

[10] *Relatório, Exercício de 1961* (Annual Report, 1961), Banco do Nordeste, Fortaleza, Ceará (1962), p. 7.

the BNB began in 1954 to implement its regional planning and development responsibilities largely through the Bank's economic programming staff, the ETENE (*Escritório Técnico de Estudos Econômicos do Nordeste*), but results were slow in coming.[11] Brazil's relatively few professionals with economic development qualifications, fully occupied with remunerative activities in Rio and the South, were quite uninterested in leaving such expanding opportunities at the economic and political centers of the country for a precarious experiment in the distant Northeast. The only possibility for the BNB, therefore, was to recruit personnel in the region and invest heavily of time and money in extended training.

Shortly after the training approach was implemented, the bank succeeded in recruiting a trained economist from the South, Diogo Gaspar, as director of the ETENE. Sr. Gaspar had recently returned to Brazil from two years of study at Harvard on a United Nations fellowship and was willing to take his chances for professional success through the pioneering venture in the Northeast. He made an important contribution toward the initiation of economic research and planning in the Northeast. In 1957 he returned to the South and subsequently headed the planning office for the state of São Paulo.

The first training experience, a course for "specialists" in economic development, was completed in mid-1955. The significant success of this combined recruitment and training experiment inspired the BNB to follow this pattern in filling other technical positions and to extend the concepts of training and investment in human resources into a major regional program for other private and public agencies. From 1955 to 1960 the BNB sponsored twenty special training programs involving more than 700 trainees in economic analysis, economic development, statistics, industrial project evaluation, administration, and rural credit including training for agronomists and veterinarians. About half of the participants were employees or potential employees of the bank.[12] University professors brought into the programs as both teachers and students, and into contact with advanced training methods, stimulated great changes in the major regional universities. Business-

[11] For a report on this mission see Stefan H. Robock, *Economic Development in Northeast Brazil*, United Nations (TAA/BRA/3), Feb. 7, 1957.

[12] *Programa de Treinamento e Formação do Pessoal*, Banco do Nordeste, Fortaleza, Ceará (November 1959).

men, private consultants, army officers, and employees of other government agencies also enrolled in the courses.

The BNB gave scholarships for bank and other personnel from the Northeast to attend the annual economic development training course in Rio initiated in 1956 by the Economic Commission for Latin America. (In 1959, ECLA was persuaded to offer in the Northeast a training program on the preparation of projects.) Northeast trainees were sent to the Getúlio Vargas public administration school in Rio and the business administration school in São Paulo. The National Economic Council offered a special training course in the region in which one hundred people sponsored by the BNB participated. The BNB sent thirty staff people on foreign fellowships provided by the United Nations, the United States, and the Organization of American States. Direct expenditures of the BNB in training professional and subprofessional personnel increased from 50,000 cruzeiros in 1954 to 12,000,000 in 1959.

A second major preplanning activity of the BNB was in the field of data collection and research through the work of the ETENE. Although the Northeast and Brazil as a whole still face serious problems of statistical and other data deficiencies, the sizable amount of available information on the region's economy had never been assembled prior to 1954. By making use of research completed as part of the first training program, the Annual Report of the BNB for 1955 presented the first general economic analysis of the structure and trends of the Northeast economy. This research project was followed by a basic statistical manual, a handbook on industrial location, subarea studies, technical studies on sisal, and a number of industrial opportunity reports.[13] This flow of economic and technical research formed the foundation for policies and activities of public and private institutions in the region.

The first president of the bank, Romulo Almeida, as a national leader in thinking on economic planning, intended to have a Northeast development plan prepared. And prior to the Vargas suicide a number of government officials had been assigned specific aspects of the Northeast plan for elaboration. But with Romulo's resignation from the BNB in late 1954, this dispersed effort to prepare a regional plan did not

[13] See Stefan H. Robock, *Segunda Visita ao Nordeste Brasileiro*, BNB, Fortaleza, Ceará (1960) for a list of 91 BNB reports released from 1954-1959.

continue. Although representatives of the state governments and several federal agencies active in the Northeast were members of the bank's advisory council, the BNB did not have authority except through bank operations for comprehensive planning activities or full implementation of development plans.

On advice of the United Nations adviser, therefore, emphasis was shifted from preparing a plan document for which adequate technical data and research did not exist to the creation of a continuing planning process. In this way, planning research was implemented as it became available, and a decentralized planning philosophy stimulated a greater degree of implementation than would have been accomplished by a highly centralized planning operation.[14]

As an extension of the training and research activities, the BNB played a major role in changing the regional mentality and the attitudes of regional leaders. Isolated from the growing national interest in economic planning and economic development, the Northeast had persisted in its popular and official attachment to the traditional dialogues on "fighting the drought," "salvation of the Northeast," and "fixing the man to the soil." The universities, in some cases, had gone through the formality of establishing faculties of economics, but the quality of this and other training was poor and unrelated to the needs of a developing society. Within a five-year period, largely due to BNB activities, a remarkable change in regional thinking and regional institutions occurred. Furthermore, a number of regional institutions had become better prepared to support economic development efforts through training and technical assistance provided by the bank.

The development credit operations of the bank had a slow start. The concept of preparing techno-economic projects for loans rather than working through political connections was strange indeed for the region. And for several years, there was no flow of prepared projects for the bank to finance. The bank's first year was consumed in recruiting, training, and implanting its planning and research staff, the ETENE. A second year was required to organize the Industrial Credit Department and staff it with trained engineers and economists. At the same time, the bank was expanding its technical assistance and training activities for potential borrowers.

[14] For a discussion of "Plans versus a Planning Process," see Chap. 4 of the 1957 U.N. report on technical assistance to Northeast Brazil by Robock, *op. cit.*

During the first three and one-half years of operation, the BNB had much more money to lend than loanable projects. At the end of 1958, however, the efforts of previous years began to bear fruit. The logjam was broken and a large flow of projects began to appear. Within the two-year period ending in 1960 industrial development loans expanded almost six-fold and "specialized" rural credit almost four-fold. And the backlog of development loan applications increased even more sharply.

BNB loan activities increased significantly in the late 1950's, and by 1962 the BNB loans outstanding equaled the total for the entire private banking system in the region. This excludes, of course, the banking activities of the Bank of Brazil, which is in effect a government bank with central bank responsibilities.

When compared to other federal activities in the region, the BNB has been a relatively small recipient of federal funds. In 1959, for example, out of 10.5 billion cruzeiros budgeted by the federal government for the Northeast, more than half was for DNOCS and other public works, and the BNB received in new treasury deposits less than 1 billion cruzeiros.[15] This also compares to the annual outlays of 27 billion cruzeiros included in SUDENE's Northeast Plan. Of course, the BNB deals only in repayable loans, mainly to private enterprise, and SUDENE has broad responsibility for public investment in the region.

Regional Coordination Efforts

Not unlike the situation in other countries, each new regional initiative of the federal government resulted in an additional agency operating independently of other federal activities in the region. The need for coordination at the regional level of the many special federal agencies, the regular federal departments, and the state and local governmental activities operating in the Northeast had been recognized for many years. But the political difficulties involved in securing a regionally coordinated effort had been insurmountable.

In his early study on economic planning in Brazil, Américo Barbosa

---

[15] "Recursos Publicos Destinados ao Nordeste," *Desenvolvimento & Conjuntura* (April 1959), p. 107.

placed the need for regional coordination foremost among his recommendations:

> . . . The different governmental departments plan and develop their activities exclusively from the point of view of their own special functions. It is not necessary for them to recognize a priority classification for their activities in relation to other types of projects, nor the complementary projects in different fields. And there is a complete absence of a force for coordinating plans in light of regional social and economic realities.[16]

Romulo Almeida raised the issue in his 1953 report on the drought to President Vargas,[17] recognizing, however, that a separate coordination agency did not appear to be a possibility within the Brazilian administrative environment because it would interfere with the authority of the ministers. He suggested that an interdepartmental committee of federal and state representatives be formed to plan and review on a continuing basis the results of government action in the area. The committee would have a permanent technical secretariat and be a first step toward a comprehensive regional planning and coordination agency.

In fact, a coordinating committee was established in 1954 under the leadership of Minister of Finance, Oswaldo Aranha. The effort was interrupted by the political crisis following Vargas' suicide. But in November of that year a Commission on Northeast Investments was created by President Café Filho, a Nordestino, within the Ministry of Public Works. The commission, which included representatives from thirteen federal agencies, was authorized by presidential decree to study and coordinate government investments in the Drought Polygon. With continuing political crises and consequent changes in personnel, the committee shortly became inactive.

In 1956 the Bank of the Northeast renewed the pressure for a regional planning and coordination effort by requesting President Kubitschek to act on its United Nations adviser's proposal that a global planning group be created.[18] Accepting this proposal with modifications, Kubitschek established a Working Group for Northeast Develop-

---

[16] Américo L. Barbosa de Oliveira, *op. cit.*, p. 116.

[17] *Planejamento do Combate às Sêcas*, Banco do Nordeste do Brasil, Publicação No. 4, Fortaleza, Ceará (November 1953), pp. 22-23.

[18] Stefan H. Robock, *Projeto de Planejamento Global para o Nordeste do Brasil*, Banco do Nordeste do Brasil, ETENE, Fortaleza, Ceará (December 1955).

ment (GTDN) in the executive office of the presidency (Decree 40.554, December 14, 1956). The Working Group was headed by a former director of the BNB and assisted by a United Nations team of advisers. The group had little authority and uncertain financial support. Furthermore, President Kubitschek's interests and energies were being dedicated to the Brasília project. But the Working Group did complete several valuable planning studies in such fields as transportation and mineral resources.[19] It also surveyed for the first time the full range of federal activities and expenditures in the Northeast. For example, a GTDN report identified at least forty separate federal government groups working in the Northeast in agriculture alone.

A nongovernmental initiative by the Northeast bishops of the Catholic Church also played a part in the movement toward coordination. The Catholic bishops became active early in 1956 both as a result of the widespread regional publicity for BNB economic research and the stimulus of Don Helder Camara, a Nordestino stationed in Rio as Archbishop and effective national leader for the church. Don Helder, in his growing concern for the slums, or *favelas*, in Rio related the Rio problem to continued out-migration from the Northeast and the Northeast problem.

A Conference of the Northeast Bishops was held in May 1956 in which President Kubitschek, the BNB, and many other groups participated. The emphasis was on action, and Kubitschek was persuaded to approve a series of action projects to be implemented by different agencies. However, the bishops' wariness of the research and planning emphasis of the GTDN delayed for several months the establishment of this group. In 1959, a second major Bishops' Conference was held which resulted in a series of thirty presidential decrees for another series of action projects.[20] The success of the bishops' activities has not been evaluated, but the educational effect of this involvement by a major leadership group resulted in significant support for various activities such as SUDENE.

The many efforts for regional coordination reached their culmination in the setting of another major drought crisis in 1958. It was an elec-

[19] Some published GTDN planning studies were: *Estudos sôbre Transporte do Nordeste* (1958); *Estrutura Federal do Nordeste* (1958); *Recursos Minerais do Nordeste; Mão-de-obra.*

[20] *II Encontro dos Bispos do Nordeste*, Presidência da República, Rio de Janeiro (1959).

tion year for many Northeast governors, and President Kubitschek was forced by this and drought scandals to direct increased attention to the Northeast. He made federal funds available for emergency relief projects. He also requested assistance from the National Development Bank in his search for "new solutions" to the Northeast problem. Celso Furtado, a native of the Northeast who had returned to Brazil in 1958 as a director of the BNDE after a distinguished career with the Economic Commission for Latin America, was asked to fulfill the President's request.

Assisted by the Working Group and competent BNDE economists who had been trained by the Bank of the Northeast and who had started their professional careers with the ETENE of the BNB, Furtado prepared a comprehensive and forceful report entitled *A Policy for the Economic Development of the Northeast.*[21] Building on the greatly increased amount of economic analysis and planning work available, Furtado emphasized the critical need for a coordinated regional effort placed in the context of Brazilian economic development.

The Furtado proposals when released in early 1959 were well publicized and enthusiastically received. Kubitschek responded by a new decree transforming the GTDN into the interim CODENO agency, the Economic Development Council for the Northeast, and placing Furtado in charge of the Northeast operation. At the same time a proposal was sent to the Congress to establish by law an expanded and powerful development agency for the region. On December 15, 1959, the SUDENE law was passed and signed, and the new institution started to function in March 1960, taking over CODENO's staff and program. Within three months, by May 1960, SUDENE completed and submitted for congressional approval the first plan, a five-year plan for the Northeast. Eighteen months later, on December 14, 1961, after bitter political conflict and a change in national administration, the plan was finally approved by the Congress.

[21] First published in 1959 as a report of the Grupo de Trabalho and later published in English as Document No. 1 of CODENO.

6

The SUDENE Phase

THE SUDENE PHASE of the New Era must run for some time yet before its impact on the economic and social aspirations of the Northeast can be evaluated. A philosophy or ideology that combines key political as well as economic issues has been articulated. A symbolic and operational development plan has been prepared and approved. But during the two and a half years between the Furtado report and congressional approval in December 1961 of a five-year plan for the Northeast, the focus of SUDENE action has been predominantly political. And the political successes achieved, though dramatic and formidable accomplishments, are only the prelude to the even more difficult task of getting concrete development results in a hurry.

"Political Economics"

As Celso Furtado has recently observed, "Economic development must be political-economic development."[1] It follows, therefore, that the philosophy, plans, and performance of SUDENE can only be evaluated in relation to Brazil's political environment and the ultimate need in any development effort for political decisions. This interrelationship has been described by Professor John P. Lewis as follows:

> The first principle to remember is that central economic planning is primarily a political activity. It proposes to tamper, at the most pivotal decision-making points in the society, with a very wide range

[1] Personal interview, Jan. 26, 1962.

of vital decisions. To be effective, it must be done with the full, express, day-to-day consent of the society's political authorities and must be knit into the mainstream of a government's decision-making process.[2]

It is convenient in academic discourse to separate political and economic issues for purposes of research and analysis. However, this is a dangerous procedure; and, in the case of SUDENE becomes virtually impossible because the politician and economist are joined in one person and political and economic strategy are combined in one plan. Three aspects of the political-economic experience of SUDENE are of particular interest to students of economic development: How did a technician succeed in politics? What was the nature of the political opposition to coordinated regional development? And what political decisions were implicit in SUDENE's development strategy?

In the decade prior to his Northeast Brazil responsibility, Furtado had become highly regarded in Latin America as a scholar and an economist's economist, with a theoretical and technical orientation. A priori, he could not have been considered the man most likely to succeed in politics. Furtado's political success, therefore, may be significant for future political patterns in Latin America.

In reflecting on his political experience, Furtado has concluded that: "Economists and other technicians have generally failed in politics because they tried to become party politicians. One must be a politician but not a party one. The political battle must be forced in terms of the technician's strength."

As a nonparty politician, Furtado generated support for the Operation Northeast by the force of technical ideas, a vigorous articulation of them, and an ingenuous merging of modern economic thinking with traditional Northeast folklore. He kept so free of party commitments that both of the 1960 presidential candidates, Jânio Quadros and General Henrique Lott, sent written assurances to Furtado that he would be reappointed after the election as head of the Northeast program.

The opposition to a powerful single federal agency for coordinating and directing regional development in the Northeast did not arise

[2] John P. Lewis, *Notes on the Nurture of Country Planning*, Indiana Business Information Bulletin 47 (1962), p. 7.

out of disagreements over the basic SUDENE development philosophy. It was based on political considerations and was led by federal deputies and senators from the Northeast and heads of many existing federal agencies with major programs in the region. The politicians were unwilling to give up their control over the allocation of federal funds in the region. The bureaucracy did not want to lose its autonomy and be subordinated in status to another agency. It is interesting to note that the same kind of political problem, particularly acute for regional coordination efforts that limit the operations of national governmental agencies, was identified by David Lilienthal as the principal reason the Tennessee Valley Authority pattern has not been expanded in the United States.[3]

Although President Jânio Quadros gave Celso Furtado Cabinet member status, neither Quadros nor his successor, João Goulart, exerted strong political leadership to have Congress approve the Northeast plan. To win the political battle, Furtado and his dedicated associates developed five main sources of political strength: the state governors in the Northeast, federal legislators from the South, university student groups, Brazilian nationalists, and the United States foreign aid program.

Under the old regime the governors had little control over federal funds, but as members of the Deliberative Council of SUDENE they were destined to increase their influence over federal activities in the region. Many federal deputies and senators from the South were convinced that the SUDENE effort would reduce significantly the "waste" of vast federal resources being dedicated to the Northeast. University student groups in the region, a potentially strong "left wing" force, participated in strikes and demonstrations to achieve what they hoped would be an improved future for "their land." Brazilian nationalists, a dispersed but potent force in Brazil, felt philosophically "in tune" with many SUDENE leaders. The United States, largely motivated by its discovery of the Communist threat of the Peasant League in the Northeast, overcame previous political reservations on cooperating with Furtado and SUDENE, and, in various ways, including an invitation for Furtado to visit the United States and meet with President Kennedy, gave the SUDENE campaign the political leverage of prospective large-scale foreign aid.

[3] David E. Lilienthal, *TVA: Democracy on the March* (Harper & Brothers, 1953), pp. XIV-XV.

The colorful and exciting political history of SUDENE arises, how-ever, out of a political strategy implicit in SUDENE's approach to the Northeast problem. By demanding complete and direct authority over all aspects of regional development and by establishing a re-gional plan which, despite a commitment in principle to decentralized planning, was imposed from the top down, the SUDENE movement was destined to evoke the maximum of political resistance. The Tennessee Valley Authority, on the other hand, with a reasonably similar social and regional development responsibility, was not en-dowed with legal authority over the other federal and state agencies and achieved international renown as a planning and coordination agency without ever producing an overall plan or blueprint.[4]

An evaluation, at some later stage, of SUDENE's political strategy in terms of ultimate development results should be productive. The SUDENE choice may prove to be the best for the Brazilian environ-ment, but it has resulted in large expenditures of scarce talent and energy on political battles. Also, the political fight created high ex-pectations for rapid development and forced SUDENE to concentrate in its first year of operations on quick and dramatic actions, leaving many fundamental longer-range needs unmet.

The SUDENE Philosophy

The preparation of a comprehensive development policy for the Northeast represented a major advance in the campaign to replace the hydraulic approach with an economic development approach to the Northeast problem. The Vargas message to Congress in 1952 recommending the establishment of the Bank of the Northeast articulated only the general principles of the economic solution. The BNB and GTDN research and planning greatly expanded the understanding of the Northeast economy. The Furtado report,[5] build-ing on the previous foundation, attempted to analyze the nature and trends of the Northeast economy and to develop concrete recom-mendations for future developmental actions.

[4] Ibid., Chap. 18, "Planning and Planners," pp. 186-95.
[5] Conselho de Desenvolvimento do Nordeste, A Policy for the Economic De-velopment of the Northeast (1959). Cited hereinafter as Furtado report.

The development of a new philosophy invariably begins with an evaluation and rejection of existing philosophies. As Furtado explained at the Seminar for Development of the Northeast held in March-April 1959:

> I am a Nordestino. I suffered the droughts and what we see is that the Brazilian government after 50 years of effort, using competent people, has not succeeded in resolving the problem, and the drought is more serious than 50 years before. Consequently, there was an erroneous diagnosis when the policy of "works against the drought" was established. My initial effort in this work was to know exactly where this error was. From there we went to the idea of considering two grand paths of action in all development policies for the Northeast: to create an economy resistant to the drought, and to restructure the agrarian economy and intensify industrial investments.[6]

The Furtado report was a one hundred page document that attempted to place the Northeast problem "in the broad context of Brazilian economic development." Its goal was to answer three questions: (1) Why is the Northeast a top priority national problem? (2) Why are present development policies aggravating rather than helping the Northeast situation? (3) What new policies should be adopted?

Furtado's argument for Northeast priority, resting basically on social and political grounds, is as follows: A great disparity exists between income levels in the Northeast and the rest of the country, particularly the central and southern regions. Over recent years (from 1948 to 1956) the rate of economic growth in the Northeast has been substantially lower than that in the Central South. Since growing regional disparities are a cumulative process and hardly reversible, this gap is likely to increase with the "possibility of an upsurge of new conflicting points in the interrelations" between the two economic systems.

Furtado's criticism of federal policies as they affect the Northeast focuses particularly on industrialization policies, foreign exchange and import controls, the tax system, the nature of federal expenditures in the region and migration. The criterion used in criticizing these policies is a "regional equity" standard rather than a demonstration that the policies are retarding Brazil's overall growth.

[6] *Seminario para o Desenvolvimento do Nordeste*, 1959-Anais-Vol. II, Confederação Nacional da Indústria, Rio de Janeiro (1959), p. 226.

Brazil's industrialization policy of the previous decade, Furtado argues, favored the Central South which was better prepared for industrialization. The adverse effect on the Northeast has been a large and steady transfer of assets from the region to the Central South through a triangular trade pattern. The Northeast earns large amounts of foreign exchange. But the Central South gets access to most of this foreign exchange because of the priority for industrialization in federal foreign exchange allocation policies. Through foreign exchange policies, Northeast exporters among others do not receive equivalent value in local currency for their exports and, in effect, sell their goods at discount prices. On the other hand, the prices of the manufactured goods purchased from the south are kept artificially high by the protection for manufactured industries through import controls.

Besides the transfers of real assets encouraged by foreign exchange policies and selective import controls, the Furtado report claims the Northeast loses a large amount of private capital which is attracted to the south by the investment opportunities arising out of the rapid industrialization.

From 1948 to 1953, Furtado argues, Brazil's foreign exchange policy was aimed at protecting coffee prices in international markets and, by ignoring peculiarities of the Northeast economy, caused a "near collapse" of Northeast exports other than cocoa and sugar. A new exchange policy prevailing since the last quarter of 1953 afforded some recuperation to prices of Northeast foreign exports, but in comparison to the Central South (the Central West, South, and Southeast combined), the "lost ground" was not recovered until 1956.

Furtado recognizes that the federal government has been spending much more than it collects in the Northeast and that in quantity terms these public sector transfers offset the capital leakage through the private sector. But the public sector expenditures are largely in the nature of assistance and fluctuate from year to year. They do not create the new and permanent jobs for the region that would result from investment in the private sector.

The regressiveness of the federal tax system results in a bigger tax burden on the Northeast than should be expected in view of its income level. The still greater regressiveness in state taxes also contributes "to aggravate trends towards disparities among regional levels of development."[7]

The fight against the drought measures, both the short-term emergency assistance programs and the long-term building of dams and reservoirs, have not altered significantly the course of events. Instead, they have contributed indirectly to maintaining in the area a surplus of population and to aggravating artificially the regional demand for foodstuffs.

Furtado's plan for action "is built around three basic policies." (1) Intensification of industrial investments: to increase regional employment opportunities, reduce the adverse flow of private capital out of the Northeast, and make the region less vulnerable to the drought. (2) Reorganization of agriculture: detailed plans which are to be developed should emphasize greater food production in the humid areas—to stabilize food supplies in drought periods—and a transformation of the semiarid zones to increase productivity and drought resistance. (3) Relocation of population surpluses: the Northeast should be redefined to include the state of Maranhão to the north which, possessed of moist soils, could absorb population surpluses created by a reorganization of the semiarid agricultural economy.

The Furtado report is a skillful political-economic document. It presents the most complete analysis of Northeast economic development available up to that time. Its political argument for revising federal policies and for giving high priority to the Northeast is founded on an economic demonstration of regional inequalities. And its plan of action is a series of measures to reduce the inequities.

In the main, however, Furtado's arguments for Northeast priority on the grounds of regional inequity were not new. The migration of private capital to the South, the transfer of assets out of the region through a triangular trade pattern encouraged by unfavorable foreign exchange and import policies, the regressiveness of the federal tax system, and other arguments had been made by Romulo Almeida in his report to President Getúlio Vargas in 1953[8] and by the Joint Brazil-United States Economic Development Commission report of 1954.[9]

[7] *Ibid.*, p. 4.

[8] *Planejamento do Combate às Sêcas*, Banco do Nordeste do Brasil, Publicação No. 4, Fortaleza, Ceará (November 1953), pp. 7-14.

[9] See Chap. 7, pp. 123-26.

The arguments that the Northeast was a large foreign exchange earner and that Brazil's foreign exchange policies caused a "near collapse" of Northeast exports are not consistent. The economic analysis demonstrating that regional disparities in Brazil are growing does not stand up in light of subsequently available data. (See Chapter 3.) Nor has empirical evidence supported the contention that the natural tendencies causing regional disparities are cumulative.

Moreover, the report claims to relate Northeast Brazil to "the broad context of Brazilian economic development" but limits this effort to a consideration of the economic effect of certain policies on the inequitable situation in the Northeast. And it does not face up to President Vargas' warning in 1951 that the progress of the most vigorous zones of the country should not be retarded through "a spirit of unsophisticated egalitarianism or ill advised *distributismo*."

A "pure" economics approach might place the argument for regional priority and for changes in national development policies within a very different context. Regional inequalities would be recognized as an inherent, rather than evil, characteristic of national development. And widening regional disparities would be expected to occur during certain stages of development. National industrialization policies would not be tested solely in terms of their regional impact or the equitableness of securing foreign exchange and investment for industrialization from the agricultural and minerals sectors. The ultimate criterion would be to secure the maximum economic growth for the nation as a whole rather than for any specific region.

The argument for economic priority for the Northeast would focus on regional development potentials and their relative contribution to national development goals. It might also stress that cumulative forces in the existing growth centers need to be offset by federal policies in order to exploit greater development potentials in new "growth centers."

Even though development policies and programs are primarily political activities, technical economic analyses are indispensable for making enlightened political decisions. But the factual basis for a purely economic argument has not been available in Brazil, and a national planning process that considers regional implications and compares regional contributions does not exist. The economic argument might have been most effective before a technical national planning tribunal. But would it have been more effective than the Furtado approach in the political forum where decisions had to be made? And could regional thinking make the jump forward into new and more sophisticated concepts?

Some years earlier, the limitations of economic analysis in treating regional disequilibriums were emphasized by Roberto Campos. But being in advance of the conventional thinking, his caveat received little attention. Campos said:

> The correction of regional inequalities is a problem of cosmic magnitude—complex and delicate—about which the economist has relatively little to say.
>
> The pure economics approach argues that investments should be concentrated in the area of greatest productivity, in order to obtain the most rapid rate of over-all economic growth. Ultimately, this will create a greater transfer of capital and a greater force of propulsion for the less developed regions. But, "will the regions wait?"
>
> Growing regional disparities can generate intolerable social tensions and a chronic climate of revolt, that might end up with an over-all loss in productivity for the country.[10]

The Furtado report, as a political document cloaked in the authority of technical economic analysis, is an illustration of the strategy to force the political battle in terms of the technician's strength. It accepted the long prevailing and politically attractive regional injustice argument and documented it with statistics and analysis. It affirmed the ineffectiveness of emergency relief and reservoir construction activities of the past and rejected them on economic grounds. It raised to greater prominence the politically explosive issue of out-migration from the Northeast by handling the question within the economic context of employment opportunities, population trends, and availability of adequate agricultural land resources. It provided renewed and increased support, again through economic analysis, for the continuing battle to focus more regional attention on industry and to reduce the almost complete preoccupation with agriculture.

On the other hand, the report does not conform to prevailing technical criteria for economic development. It does not relate the regional interests to national development goals, nor does it demonstrate a priority for Northeast programs in terms of development potentials.

[10] Roberto de Oliveira Campos, "A Crise Econômica Brasileira," *Alguns Problemas Brasileiros*, Vol. 1, Confederação Nacional de Comercio, Rio de Janeiro (1955), pp. 63-65.

The technical economic base for the political argument is narrow and does not recognize institutional, administrative, and trained personnel needs of the region as major barriers to development.

But the timing of the Furtado report was fortuitous, and it did raise significantly the economic quality of popular understanding and political debates on the Northeast. Above all, it served as a springboard for possible great improvement in the effectiveness of federal and regional development efforts in the Northeast. Could a document that satisfied sophisticated economists and economic development experts have achieved these political action results?

The SUDENE Plan

The most logical pattern may be for specific development policies to emerge out of the process of economic planning. But because of the force of events, SUDENE became committed to specific development policies before initiating its development planning. It is not surprising, therefore, that the SUDENE plan deviates from the initial philosophy. The intervening time period permitted afterthoughts and further elaboration. Also, specific projects were not available to implement certain policies. Thus, the philosophy represents the ideology, and the plan a beginning step toward the realities of Northeast development activities.

The SUDENE law (Art. 8) provided that a guiding plan should be legally established to include specific projects and programs for developing the various sectors of the region's economy. By early 1960, only a few months after SUDENE was established, it completed and presented its 300 page first plan to the President and Congress. Limited by the short time available, the SUDENE plan was centrally prepared by SUDENE's staff and shaped by the immediate availability of specific detailed projects.

Both the SUDENE law and Furtado's report suggest a decentralized economic planning process which has not yet been followed. The law provides (Art. 8, par. 1) that the federal agencies shall elaborate annual work plans, with the collaboration and approval of SUDENE, within the policies of the guiding plan. As for the state governments, Furtado stated in his report:

> Unrestricted cooperation from State governments is of vital importance to the success of any plan for the development of the

Northeast. The first step to make this cooperation effective, however, will be to afford technical assistance to State governments, in
order to enable them to make their own plans for economic development . . . within the pattern of the development policy suggested
for the region as a whole in the present Plan of Action.[11]

Only a few of the federal agencies such as the CHESF power company, the Department of Roads, and the Bank of the Northeast had
work plans that could be fitted into a regional plan. Other important
agencies like the National Department of Works Against the Drought
(DNOCS) were not in a mood to cooperate with SUDENE. Of
the state governments, only Bahia, where Romulo Almeida was Sec-
retary of Planning, had an active and effective state planning operation. Despite its emphasis on having state plans, however, SUDENE
was unwilling to incorporate much of the Bahia plan into the guiding
plan. SUDENE's explanation was that the Bahia plan included many
programs not yet elaborated for the region, and by supporting such
an advanced plan, SUDENE would be placing other states at a dis-
advantage. Furthermore, SUDENE seemed to feel that a state plan
that had not been prepared under its supervision might present "in-
flexible" opposition to SUDENE's regional planning objectives. In
practice, therefore, SUDENE was not ready to follow its philosophy
of planning from the bottom up as well as from the top down.

The first plan prepared in May 1960[12] did not secure congressional
approval during the Jucelino Kubitschek administration, which ended
on January 31, 1961. It was not approved during Jânio Quadros'
seven-month presidential term ending in August 1961. But on December 14, 1961 (Law No. 3.995) the Congress acted on the plan and
appropriated the equivalent of the planned outlay for the first two
years.

A more complete version of the first plan, the *Plano Quinquenal*,[13]
became available in early 1961. This document prepared for the
Alliance for Progress meetings at Punte del Este was considerably
more complete than the initial effort. And in October 1962, an official

[11] Furtado report, pp. 95-96.
[12] *Primeiro Plano Diretor de Desenvolvimento do Nordeste,* Presidência da
República, Superintendência do Desenvolvimento do Nordeste, Recife (1960).
[13] *Plano Quinquenal de Desenvolvimento para o Nordeste 1961-1965,* Presidência da República, Superintendência do Desenvolvimento do Nordeste, Recife
(1961).

second plan[14] up-dating the first plan for the period 1963 through 1965 was presented to the Congress.

The SUDENE plans have been criticized as not being comprehensive development plans. But the same criticism can be levied against India's first five-year plan and the first plan in most other underdeveloped countries as well. The amount of technical data and analysis required for a comprehensive plan is tremendous. Even if the technical manpower and data were available in an underdeveloped country—a highly unlikely situation—it is almost impossible to secure the necessary financial resources for preplanning work until a decision is made to undertake economic planning. Having made the decision to plan, pressures have been generated that demand a plan document almost immediately.

The guiding plan theoretically will be revised and extended annually so that a current five-year plan will always exist. The 1961 effort does not claim to be all inclusive. As the *Plano Quinquenal* explains:

> . . . The plan here presented constitutes only a first phase of another plan, possibly more ample, that will be substituted as soon as the expansion of SUDENE's staff and the maturing of studies in process will permit. . . . Some sectors of SUDENE activity such as ports, railroads and mineral development were not included in the present plan because adequate planning has not been completed.

The document also suggests that new laws will eventually be required to "overcome institutional obstacles to an economically more rational and socially more desirable use of the land."[15]

The plans demonstrate that priority in fact for specific development activities depends on the availability of working plans rather than on the merit of political and economic arguments. The SUDENE philosophy gave little if any emphasis to the popular approach of investing in the economic infrastructure as a principal stimulus to investment. Yet the "creation of an economic infrastructure" through road building and electric power expansion, activities for which the Northeast has developed planning competence and specific plans, accounted for

[14] *Plano Diretor do Desenvolvimento do Nordeste (Segunda Etapa) 1963-1965,* SUDENE, Recife (October 1962).
[15] Pp. 16, 10.

70 percent of total planned investment in the first plan and about 76 percent of the first congressional appropriation.[16]

Social development ranked as the second major investment category, accounting for 17 percent of planned investment. But social development consisted almost completely of water and sewage systems projects. Detailed plans were available for specific projects because of almost two decades of public health programs in the area supported by United States technical assistance. The Congress did not support the full request for water and sewage systems, probably in anticipation of receiving substantial foreign aid in this field, but it added a significant appropriation for well drilling. Neither the plan nor the appropriation mentioned housing.

Education projects were completely absent from the first plan, except for a small appropriation to support literacy training by radio that was underway. The lack of emphasis on education, particularly primary and secondary education, which are the legal responsibility of the state and local governments, reflected the nonexistence of specific plans and a prevailing philosophy favoring expenditures for physical projects rather than for people. By the time the *Plano Quinquenal* was released in 1961, SUDENE had initiated special training programs at the professional level as a means of building up its own staff, and had become involved in the efforts to improve regional training at the university level. The second plan of late 1962 contained SUDENE's first recognition of educational needs below the university level—mainly primary education—with an allocation of 1.3 percent of the three-year total to this field. In large part, this was a response to the efforts of the United States to make foreign aid available for primary school needs. In total, the second plan proposes 6 percent of planned investment for human resources development through agricultural and industrial vocational training, the preparation of personnel for states and municipalities, and the university and below-university programs already mentioned.

The third most important area of planned expenditure (about 15 percent of the first plan total) was to "transform the structure of agriculture" and to rationalize food distribution in the area. The agricultural plans, spelled out more fully in the *Plano Quinquenal*, in-

[16] *Plano Diretor Em Execução*, SUDENE, Recife (November 1962), p. 9.

cluded projects to resettle farmers in Maranhão, reorganize agricultural patterns in the humid sugar cane producing areas, make public lands in the humid area available for family farms (25,000 hectares), irrigate 88,000 hectares in the semiarid interior, conclude agronomic-economic planning for the middle San Francisco Valley and complete irrigation projects in the Rio Grande tributary and the lower San Francisco, and prepare river basin development plans for the Parnaiba and Jaguaribe rivers.

Thus, infrastructure, water and sewage projects and agriculture, including food distribution, accounted for 99 percent of total planned expenditures in the first plan. The remaining 1 percent was divided among projects for mapping, minerals, and hydrology research and industrial projects.

But the pattern is changing. In the second plan, infrastructure, water and sewage and agriculture and food projects accounted for only 80 percent of 1963 planned expenditures. Preinvestment research and planning of natural resources, such as mapping, minerals, and hydrologic research and river basin planning were scheduled for 8 percent of total investment. The education and training programs mentioned above accounted for 6 percent, industrial development and assistance to handicraft industries about 3 percent, stimulation of the fishing industry 2 percent, and housing programs were first included with support of slightly more than 1 percent of the programed federal investment. The changing relative emphasis, however, results from a larger total outlay through the addition of programs, rather than any reduction in the absolute levels of outlays for infrastructure, agriculture, and municipal water and sewage systems.

Commerce and industry in the Northeast is almost exclusively in the hands of private enterprise. Therefore, the SUDENE plan, essentially a synthesis of the major federal expenditures in the region, does not reflect fully, on the basis of the share of total expenditures, the industrialization activities of SUDENE. The SUDENE law gave the agency authority to direct the BNB and the National Development Bank to give priority in loans to approved industrial projects and to give the following special inducements to encourage industrial expansion in the region: (1) special foreign exchange allocations or concessions; (2) exemption from import tariffs and taxes; (3) exemption from certain domestic taxes.

Up to December 1961, SUDENE had granted special concessions

for forty-six projects involving an investment of 18 billion cruzeiros and about 10,000 new jobs in direct employment. By September 1962, the number of industrial projects that had received tax or import subsidies for modernization, expansion, or starting new operations had increased to almost one hundred.[17]

To summarize, the SUDENE plans as of 1962 were not comprehensive regional development plans. They include very little of the private sector. They do not embrace total federal, state, and local expenditures. They give little attention to the institutional and administrative needs of the region and do not incorporate a manpower plan. They treat the Northeast as a separate country without relating the region to national development goals and plans. They do not contain development goals of production, income, or employment. But a detailing of these limitations should represent an agenda of planning accomplishments still to come, rather than a criticism of past activities.

Implementation

The ultimate development test of the SUDENE program is, of course, the results it achieves in improving economic and social conditions in the Northeast and in maximizing the contribution of the region to national development goals. As emphasized previously, the project is still in too early a stage for evaluating development performance. Yet several significant aspects have already become apparent and warrant brief comment.

Political-economic development involves three interrelated but separate groups of people—the political decision makers, the economic planners, and the implementers of economic plans. The SUDENE story clearly illustrates that favorable political decisions can be secured while comprehensive planning work is incomplete. Likewise the planning work can be satisfactorily completed without an area becoming adequately prepared for the implementation phase. Each is a necessary but not a sufficient condition for development success. And SUDENE's currently most important challenge is to involve the regional leadership and agencies in planning and to prepare people and institutions for plan implementation.

[17] *Plano Diretor Em Execução*, SUDENE, Recife (November 1962), p. 127.

The most serious limitation of the SUDENE plans is that they represent planning from above, done mainly by SUDENE's own staff. Few of the federal and regional agencies have been involved in the formulation of the plans except to supply information. And few of the institutions and leaders in the region have, through participation in the planning process, become committed and feel a responsibility for the implementation of the plan.

This crucial issue was recognized by Diogo Gaspar, the first Chief Economist for the Bank of the Northeast, in the 1959 series of seminars on Northeast development. He said:

> The alteration of the course of events can be accomplished only with the energetic mobilization of all the leadership and all the other regional resources for the promotion of economic development. The participation of the Federal Government is without doubt a necessary, but much short of a sufficient, condition. The profound disbelief with which the Nordestino receives the palliatives with which successive governments try to mitigate the economic hardships in the region, in my view, originates precisely from the Federal Government's attitude of taking onto itself the exclusive responsibility for solving the problems, when the solutions necessarily have to be founded in the active participation of the regional population.
> The exclusion when policies are formulated of any portion of the socio-economic forces interested in promoting—or not impeding—the process of economic development will have the sole effect of creating centers of resistance and irresponsibility toward the policies the Federal Government has to coordinate.[18]

In an underdeveloped area, the task of preparing personnel and institutions for effective development programs and of securing broad regional participation in implementing plans may well be a bigger challenge requiring more time than the winning of political decisions or the preparation of sound plans. But an impossible dilemma arises when expectations for rapid results are a by-product of a difficult political victory, and when heavy reliance in implementing plans has to be placed on public agencies that have bitterly opposed the campaign.

In early 1962, SUDENE felt that its continued survival and future

[18] Diogo Adolpho Nunes de Gaspar, "Ação dos Órgãos Governamentais e das Entidades Particulares que se Voltam para o Nordeste," *Seminário para o Desenvolvimento do Nordeste, Anais,* Vol. II, Confederação Nacional da Indústria, Rio de Janeiro (1959), p. 473.

political leverage depended on achieving some kind of quick and spectacular results. The agency also concluded that it could not meet this political survival requirement by working through the regular government agencies, many of which it considered to be demoralized, improperly oriented, and technically unprepared. SUDENE, therefore, continued to hire hundreds of people for its own staff, most of whom were bright but inexperienced, to assume direct operational responsibility for many of the programs.

One result is that much essential long-range planning work, which should be directed by SUDENE's senior staff, comprising a major share of the technically prepared planning people in the region, will be greatly delayed. Another result may be that SUDENE will be held responsible for the operational failures that are inevitable during the present stage of regional unpreparedness. But the most serious result may be that the widespread participation of regional institutions and leaders, whose potential force for advancing development far exceeds that of a single agency like SUDENE, will not be forthcoming. And as Diogo Gaspar warned, the needed sources of support will turn into "centers of resistance and irresponsibility."

7

The Vagaries of Foreign Aid

WHAT ROLE HAS foreign assistance played in Northeast development? How have United States bilateral and United Nations multilateral aid patterns differed? What guidance for donors and recipients emerges from more than a decade of experience? The answers to these and other questions relating to the Brazilian Northeast may have great value for foreign aid programs in general as well as for the Northeast and the Alliance for Progress in particular.

During World War II, the Northeast "bulge" won major United States attention as a location for strategic airbases and as a source of critical minerals. But as Brazilians are quick to point out, the United States, after using the Northeast as a war base, did little to help it in peacetime. Latin America as a whole did not receive much foreign aid or attention from the United States during the 1950's. Northeast Brazil, although long recognized as that country's major underdeveloped area, received even less attention in the small but growing United States aid effort for Brazil.

With the rise of Castroism and the launching of the Alliance for Progress, the position of Northeast Brazil in United States foreign assistance was reversed. From a bottom ranking in a low priority area, the Northeast skyrocketed within months to a top position in a now high priority program. In fact, the United States-Brazil agreement signed in April 1962 for large-scale development assistance places the region in the center of the Alliance for Progress stage.

In contrast, the United Nations has since the early 1950's concentrated a major share of its modest resources in Northeast Brazil and played a significant role in the region's development. The United

Nations multilateral program was responsive to the development aspirations of Latin America in part, at least, because the twenty Latin American members until the mid-1950's constituted the largest bloc of less developed countries in this international agency. The United States continued during the 1950's to regard foreign aid as a temporary program whereas the United Nations was in the economic development assistance "business" on a permanent, though small-scale, basis.

The history of foreign assistance to Northeast Brazil can be divided into four periods: the World War II period when activity was high in the region; the immediate postwar period during which the region was completely neglected; the decade of the fifties when the area received considerable help from the United Nations but only spillover effects from United States aid programs in Brazil; and the Alliance for Progress era beginning in the early 1960's in which Northeast Brazil rose from obscurity to international fame in the foreign aid field.

The difficulties encountered by the Northeast in breaking into the "big-league" illustrate some important limitations of past bilateral aid programs and reveal the overwhelming and persistent pressures of short-term time horizons on the part of both receiving and donor countries. Past experience also shows how emphasis on assisting specific projects makes it practically impossible for unprepared areas to qualify for aid. Even today, with a recognition of the need for comprehensive economic planning, the pressures are strong—except for situations like the Peasant League activities—for the rapidly developing regions in a country to secure most of the available foreign aid because they are better prepared.

United States Bilateral Aid before the Alliance for Progress

Bilateral aid from the United States, begun in the war years as a phase of the war effort, was continued in the 1950's under the Joint Brazil-United States Economic Development Commission, the Point Four Program for technical assistance and some loans through the Export-Import Bank. Except for assistance in public health and transportation programs, however, the Northeast received little effective aid until the late 1950's.

The War Years

In 1942, inspired both by wartime food and raw material needs and the strategic importance of antisubmarine patrol and air ferry bases along the Brazilian coast, the United States initiated its first foreign aid activities in Northeast Brazil. Under the leadership of Nelson Rockefeller, the Institute for Inter-American Affairs supported multimillion dollar programs in public health, minerals exploration, rubber growing, and food production. As explained by the Coordinator of Inter-American Affairs in connection with the agricultural program, "While the chief objective is the long-range raising of dietary standards, *the program has immediate repercussions on the war effort.*"[1]

United States assistance in public health (Brazil-United States Agreement of July 17, 1942) was concentrated in the Amazon region and the Northeast. The program, administered through the Special Service of Public Health (SESP) established a network of health posts and provided a wide range of services to the local communities and the surrounding regions. The United States contributed technical assistance, equipment, and commodities and even some of the funds for local expenses. It also supported advanced training in the United States for Brazilian personnel.

In the minerals field, United States geologists cooperated with Brazil in surveys of Northeast resources such as lead, zinc, talc, magnesite, and barite. The wartime attempt to revive rubber production in Brazil was primarily directed to the Amazon region, but the Northeast also participated in this program. With thousands of American military personnel stationed on the "hump" and shipping capacity scarce for moving food supplies to the area, the United States also supported a large-scale effort to expand food production in the Northeast.

Another part of the United States wartime interest in Brazil was the American Technical Commission of 1943, led by Morris L. Cooke. Although its primary responsibility was to assist Brazil in planning for greater self-sufficiency, particularly in industry, the mission's activities did touch on the Northeast in at least two respects. A national

[1] Coordinator of Inter-American Affairs, *Brazil, Introduction to a Neighbor* (1944). (*Italics added.*)

industrial vocational education program initiated in 1946 by the Brazilian-American Commission for Industrial Education (CBAI), following the recommendations of the mission, resulted in a small beginning in the Northeast in this field. Most important, however, was the impetus given by the Cooke Mission to the establishment of a multipurpose river basin project for the San Francisco River and the exploitation of the massive hydroelectric power potential of the Paulo Afonso site.[2]

At this stage of United States policy, technical assistance was looked upon as simply one phase of the war effort. Except for public health activities and an improvement in the regional air transportation facilities, the United States aid programs had little lasting effect on the Northeast. In fact, the war had negative effects on the region. Shipping priorities stopped the export of cash crops such as cocoa beans and cut off access to the important domestic markets for such products as sugar. The military bases caused a temporary upsurge in civilian employment, but these jobs quickly disappeared with the close of the war.

When the war ended, United States appropriations for the Institute for Inter-American Affairs dropped steadily from $10.6 million in 1945 to a low of $4 million in 1949 for all of Latin America.[3] During this immediate postwar period, however, a second general survey mission for Brazil, the so-called Abbink Mission, was active but concerned mainly with overall financial questions and made no direct contribution to the Northeast.[4]

The Joint Commission

In June 1950 the United States Congress passed the Act for International Development, implementing President Truman's Point Four program for technical cooperation. Under this program the Joint

[2] See Morris L. Cooke, *Brazil on the March: A Study in International Cooperation*, Reflections on the American Technical Mission to Brazil (McGraw-Hill, 1944), Chap. 10, "The San Francisco, A Multiple-Purpose River."

[3] Special Policy Committee on Technical Cooperation, *Technical Cooperation in Latin America: Recommendations for the Future* (National Planning Association, June 1956).

[4] *Report of the Joint Brazil-United States Technical Commission*, U. S. Department of State, Publication 3487 (June 1949).

Brazil-United States Economic Development Commission began operating in July 1951 and continued until July 1953 when the Eisenhower administration discontinued the project. Although its program had not been completed, the Joint Commission had accomplished enough in techno-economic research and project preparation to create an invaluable storehouse of economic development know-how and materials, which continued to feed Brazil's subsequent efforts. This was an effective project even though, as was true of the preceding two missions, the Joint Commission almost completely neglected the Northeast.

The broad aim of the Joint Commission was "to create conditions for, and eliminate obstacles to, an increase in the flow of investment, public and private, foreign and domestic, needed to promote development." But its immediate goal was "the preparation of projects for investments in basic fields, soundly conceived, to assure an orderly and balanced growth of the Brazilian economy and technically adapted to the requirements of foreign financing institutions, such as the Export-Import Bank and the International Bank for Reconstruction and Development."[5]

The personnel of the Joint Commission, both American and Brazilian, was outstanding. The chairmanship of the United States section was held successively by Francis Adams Truslow—a career diplomat, J. Burke Knapp—later to become vice president of the World Bank, and Merwyn Bohan—another senior foreign service officer. The mission also included many high-level technical people from United States industry. The Brazilian section was headed by Ary Torres as President, with Valentim Bouças, Roberto Campos, Glycon de Paiva and Lucas Lopes as Counsellors. The commission prepared the general report cited above and a series of technical surveys in the fields of transportation, power, industry, and agriculture.[6] The final report recommended forty-one specific projects calling for an investment of about $1 billion, one-third of which should be in foreign exchange. Transportation projects required 61 percent of the total; power projects, 33 percent; and miscellaneous agricultural and industrial projects, 6 percent.

[5] Joint Brazil-United States Economic Development Commission, *The Development of Brazil* (U. S. Foreign Operations Administration, 1954), p. vi.
[6] U. S. Institute of Inter-American Affairs, *Brazilian Technical Studies* (U. S. Foreign Operations Administration, 1955).

The regional composition of the Joint Commission proposals was summarized as follows for railroads, ports, and power, which constituted 94 percent of total planned investment: "The largest share . . . goes, as might be expected, to the fast growing areas of the south where rapid industrial development and increasing agricultural production have tended to create the most serious transport and power bottlenecks."[7]

Why did the Joint Commission effort neglect the Northeast? The commission recognized that wide regional disparities existed and "are likely to give rise to political and social problems." It identified:

> . . . institutional factors that have worked to the detriment of the less developed areas, particularly the north and the northeast.
>
> Among these factors are the overall regressiveness of the Federal fiscal structure, the unfavorable effects of emigration on the age composition of their active population and, in more recent periods, the adverse trend of their export prices, as compared to their imports from abroad or from other regions of the country.[8]

But the commission explained:

> . . . it was neither feasible nor appropriate to embark on an attempt to correct regional disequilibria. Its terms of reference did not entrust it with responsibility for general planning and coordination of all investments. The limitations of resources, external and domestic, that could realistically be counted upon to finance its program, rendered imperative a concentration of effort on obviously pressing priority problems. Finally, its projects were designed for submission to banking institutions; this eliminated the possibility of recommending some types of economic and social overhead investments, which would require assistance in the form of grants in aid rather than bankable loans.[9]

The Joint Commission experience, admirable as its results were, clearly illustrates some of the important biases that can be inherent in development assistance. Its time limit was relatively short because of the assumed political need in both Brazil and the United States to show specific results in a hurry. It was oriented to financial aid—bankable loans in particular—and the commission's work "was largely geared to the examination of those projects for which the technical

---

[7] Joint Brazil-United States Economic Development Commission, *The Development of Brazil*, pp. 80-81.

[8] *Ibid.*, p. 80, p. 80 n. 5.

[9] *Ibid.*, p. 80.

preparation was advanced enough to be capable of prompt financial implementation."[10] The general priorities had been agreed on in the original Brazil-United States negotiations: namely, transportation and power; and in the establishment of specific priorities, "the extent of technical and financial elaboration of projects under study"[11] was given first consideration.

Thus occurs a vicious circle and a problem of cumulative disequilibrium. The priority test in practice is not development potential but the availability of specific elaborated projects to support. Because the advanced areas are better prepared, they are able to advance even more.

Technical Cooperation in the Fifties

The United States bilateral technical cooperation program in Brazil began in 1951 under the general supervision of the Joint Commission. The United States total contribution averaged slightly above $4 million annually over the seven-year period through 1957 and reached a peak of $8.3 million in 1960.[12] Over the decade the United States spent $56 million on its Brazilian Point Four program, about 40 percent of which was made available in the last three years of the period, plus an additional $8 million in 1958-61 for the Brazilian portion of a special world-wide malaria eradication project.

Throughout the decade, the United States program, as described by a high official associated with it, was both passive and piecemeal. The mission never had a central planning staff to guide its total program, but acted on projects presented to it by Brazilians, on proposals initiated by its own staff in their professional fields, and on Washington-inspired specific projects. During much of the period, another limiting factor on the Brazilian program was poor United States diplomatic representation.

The technical cooperation program began with a commitment to a philosophy of "balanced programs." But no comprehensive process was established nor criteria specified for deciding on program prior-

[10] *Ibid.*, p. 81.
[11] *Ibid.*, p. 73.
[12] See Table 7.1.

TABLE 7.1. *United States Bilateral Technical Cooperation Program in Brazil*

(In thousands of United States Dollars)

Fiscal Year	Health, Sanitation	Education	Agriculture, Natural Resources	Public Administration	Industry, Mining, Labor	Transportation	Community Development	Other	U.S. Total Contributions	Malaria Control
1951–54	10,672[a]	1,143	1,101	773	387	—	112	2,266	16,454[a]	—
1955	790	359	845	308	387	1,585	57	63	4,394	—
1956	823	430	750	804	474	541	192	195	4,209	—
1957	841	810	1,094	458	531	283	148	440	4,605	—
1958	768	936	1,479	478	451	252	39	486	4,889	1,490
1959	748	600	1,646	1,822	658	214	37	475	6,200	2,577
1960	855	850	2,171	2,670	613	242	85	814	8,300	4,000
1961	555	883	1,205	1,707	903	211	314	1,564	7,342	165
	16,052	6,011	10,291	9,020	4,404	3,328	984	6,303	56,393	8,232

Source: Special tabulation by U.S. AID Mission to Brazil, Rio de Janeiro, November 1962.

[a] An earlier report for the 1951–54 period shows only $2.4 for health and sanitation and a total U.S. contribution of $8.5 million. See National Planning Association, *Technical Cooperation in Latin America* (1956), p. 146.

ities. The Joint Commission, however, took the position that: "The concept of priorities in the field of technical assistance had not the same application as in the loan programs." During its regime major emphasis was given to agricultural training, "precisely because in this field more than in almost any other, productivity increases can be brought about through the introduction of more advanced methods that do not necessarily require any large-scale investment"[13]—an interesting but invalid development priority criterion. The earlier programs in public health, industrial vocational training, and minerals investigation had managed to stay alive during the period preceding the technical cooperation program, and, because of inherited commitments and the nonexistence of a process to evaluate competing priorities, the "early comers" secured a high priority along with agriculture in the new program.

A precise classification of United States expenditures and technicians by regions within Brazil is not available. But it is unlikely that more than 5 percent of the United States effort was devoted to programs in Northeast Brazil. The inertia of the past and the lack of comprehensive country planning made it inevitable that the North-

[13] *Ibid.*, p. 82.

east would wait for Fidel Castro and the Peasant Leagues to create the kind of eruption that would break the hardened patterns of the past.

In fairness to United States aid personnel, it should be noted that Northeast Brazil has always been a controversial issue among Brazilians. The counterpart Brazilian coordinator of United States technical assistance appointed in 1954 became so involved in the Brasília project that he did not play a major role in shaping the Point Four program. And many top Brazilian officials who were close to the United States embassy and Point Four personnel sincerely believed that the Northeast was a lost cause and that aid should not be wasted on the region.

Whatever assistance the Northeast received from the United States was mainly in the fields of public health and agriculture. The wartime SESP program with modest United States support expanded its network of health posts, designed and installed twenty-two community water systems, provided training for well drillers and undertook other advisory health work. The United States participation in a special world-wide project beginning in 1958 for malaria eradication had its major Brazilian impact in the Northeast. Agricultural assistance in Brazil was administered on a national basis through a Joint Brazil-United States Agricultural Service (ETA). In the late 1950's some of this aid spilled over into the Northeast in the form of several advisers in extension, home economics, livestock, and horticulture stationed in the region. Again through a national program, ANCAR, a supervised rural credit agency in the Northeast, received some United States assistance. To complete the picture, some intermittent minerals investigation work occurred, and in 1960 and 1961 national programs in public and business administration, audiovisual work and public safety were extended to the area.

The Northeast shared to a small extent in the Point Four fellowship program for foreign training. From 1949 through June 30, 1960 about 140 Brazilians from the Northeast, from a total of 3,000 for Brazil as a whole, were sent to the United States for advanced studies or training under United States auspices. The largest number of trainees were, of course, related to the public health programs in the region.

The project-by-project piecemeal United States assistance was not designed to recognize regional needs. Whatever evolved in the form of technical assistance to agriculture, for example, on a national basis might or might not reach the Northeast.

As will be developed below, the Northeast began to identify its foreign assistance priorities in the middle 1950's with the help of the United Nations. And several requests for specific types of technical assistance that the Brazilians considered most urgent were directed to the United States technical cooperation mission. These requests from the Bank of the Northeast and a later general request from SUDENE in early 1960 did not receive enthusiastic responses from the United States. At one stage, United States officials felt that because the United Nations had already received major credit for working in the region, the United States would not receive adequate recognition. At a later period, the aid requests were not acted on because some United States embassy officials were convinced that the key Northeast officials were Communists or anti-American. Another explanation by a top American official was that the Northeast problem was so large that the small United States program was inadequate to tackle it. On the Brazilian side, the Northeast agencies, after receiving lukewarm receptions from the United States officials, did not continue to exert maximum efforts for aid—in part because of their success in getting assistance from the United Nations.

The public health program, which is widely used to illustrate the success of past technical assistance programs in the Northeast, deserves special comment. An evaluation of this program from an economic development point of view has never been made. The standard criticism of such programs is particularly relevant for the Northeast— that improved health and consequent population increases without concurrent programs to increase the supply of food and other economic goods can hinder rather than help in achieving higher per capita economic and social welfare.

Loans and Surplus Food

Some United States loans of a development nature were made to the Northeast during the 1950's, through the Export-Import Bank and Public Law 480[14] (now known as the Food for Peace Program), which

[14] Agricultural Trade Development and Assistance Act, 1954, 68 Stat. 454.

permits the sale of surplus commodities for local currencies and the lending or granting of the currencies for economic aid. The Development Loan Fund, however, was inactive in the region.

Since 1950, the Export-Import Bank has authorized credits to Brazil of $1.1 billion.[15] Of this total about $20 million was in the form of loans and credits to government and private enterprise in Northeast Brazil. The principal loan, for $15 million, was granted in 1956 for expansion of the Paulo Afonso hydroelectric project. Other loans or credits were for the foreign private utilities, the grain storage warehousing project of the state of Pernambuco, trolley buses for the city of Recife, small diesel generator plants in Bahia, and for the purchase of road equipment by the states of Bahia and Pernambuco. All of the Export-Import Bank loans, of course, were for foreign exchange costs and tied to purchases in the United States.

Under the P.L. 480 program, the cruzeiro equivalent of $150 million was loaned to the National Economic Development Bank of Brazil (BNDE) in 1956 for economic development purposes. As of July 1, 1961 about $113 million of these funds were disbursed. The BNDE on its initiative transferred the equivalent of $3 million to the Bank of the Northeast for loans to private enterprise in the region. The BNDE made two other major loans in the Northeast: one for the cruzeiro equivalent of $5 million to the Paulo Afonso project and the other for about $900,000 to the Pernambuco warehousing project.[16]

United Nations Assistance

In contrast to the patchwork history of United States bilateral foreign aid—"a succession of improvisations for the most part stimulated by hostile Communist initiatives"[17]—United Nations technical assistance was conceived and accepted as a permanent program with an economic development goal.[18] The contrast in aid programs, which is sometimes made between bilateral and multilateral efforts, implies

[15] Export-Import Bank of Washington, *Report to the Congress for the Twelve Months Ending June 30, 1961* (1961).

[16] "P.L. 480 Loan Activity in Brazil," Program Office, U.S. Operation Mission in Brazil, Rio de Janeiro, Dec. 1, 1961 (Mimeo).

[17] Lorna and Felix Morley, *The Patchwork History of Foreign Aid* (American Enterprise Association, April 1961), p. 51.

[18] See Article 55 of the United Nations Charter.

that the number of donors is the principal difference. But as the experience of Northeast Brazil reveals, a more crucial difference than the numbers on the donor side is the extent to which the underdeveloped countries can influence the policies for aid programs.

Bilateral programs can reflect the interests of the recipient countries if the receiver has alternative sources of aid and strong bargaining power in relation to the donor's motivation. As Robert E. Asher has observed:

> The underdeveloped countries have come to regard the UN as a projection and protection of their sovereignty. Individually, they are in a weak position in bargaining with the industrialized nations on economic matters—unless they can convince the United States that they are peculiarly vulnerable to communism. Collectively, they can assume a more self-respecting stance and be more influential. For the underdeveloped countries, the high road to dignity and status is via the UN.[19]

Before Castro, Brazil and Latin America had little bargaining power in determining the size and shape of United States bilateral assistance. United States policies therefore dominated the efforts; and, despite good intentions, the United States did not have the experience or know-how for effective economic development assistance. Furthermore it was unwilling, for what it considered a temporary program, to make the necessary investment in development research and in training United States personnel for the task. As a result, in the case of Brazil, the Brazilians were much better prepared than the Americans to identify development assistance needs, but they were unable to influence to any great extent the bilateral program.

When the United Nations technical assistance program formally began in 1950 with agreement by the member nations to establish a $20 million fund, the Latin American nations were numerically dominant among the underdeveloped nation members of this international organization. They were able, therefore, from the beginning to secure a generous allocation of the small program. In 1952, for example, Latin America received almost $5 million of the $19 million spent by the United Nations Expanded Technical Assistance Program.[20] More important they played a major role in formulating the aid policies,

[19] "Economic Co-operation Under UN Auspices," *International Organization* (Summer 1958), p. 291.
[20] "A Statistical Summary of Activities from July 1950-June 1962," United Nations, *Technical Assistance Newsletter* (August-September 1962), p. 2.

even though the United States was the principal contributor to the United Nations program.

During the first three years of the United Nations program, each of the specialized agencies—the United Nations Educational, Scientific and Cultural Organization (UNESCO), the International Labour Organisation (ILO), the Food and Agriculture Organization (FAO)— operated independently in granting technical assistance, with the coordinating Technical Assistance Board of the United Nations limiting its activities to dividing available funds among the competing agencies. But in 1953 the United Nations moved toward the concept of coordinated country programs by making the governments requesting assistance responsible for formulating annual programs.

In Brazil a National Technical Assistance Commission (CNAT) was created in late 1950 to receive and coordinate all requests for United Nations assistance from Brazilian agencies.[21] Also regional commissions were constituted for nine states and two territories to prepare projects of interest for their areas. The regional commissions were never effective, and the technical requests coming to CNAT were frequently stimulated or "guided" by promotional efforts of the United Nations specialized agencies. Nevertheless, with the assistance of the United Nations resident representative, the Brazilians each year went through the formalities of preparing a country program and establishing priorities among competing demands.

Over the decade ending in 1961, Brazil's annual allocation of United Nations technical funds fluctuated from a low of $370,000 in 1954 to a peak of $900,000 in 1956 and totaled about $6 million for the period. On a money basis, therefore, the United Nations technical assistance program cost about one-tenth of the United States program. The United Nations International Children's Emergency Fund (UNICEF), a child welfare program financed out of other funds, is not included in development assistance.

Although the United Nations had an early mission on rural housing in Northeast Brazil (1951), its sustained attention to the region began with the 1953 Singer Mission.[22] In the following year, although a

[21] *O Brasil e os Programas de Assistência Técnica da ONU e da OEA*, Ministério das Relações Exteriores, Commissão Nacional de Assistência Técnica (1953).

[22] H. W. Singer, *Economic Development of North-Eastern Brazil*, United Nations, Technical Assistance Programme (Nov. 19, 1953).

large share of the United Nations funds were used for support of national projects such as a school of public administration, the Northeast received about 10 percent of the total country allocation. Another regional program—for the Amazon—shared even more heavily than the Northeast. But the Northeast program steadily increased in absolute and relative importance to reach an estimated 44 percent of Brazil's United Nations technical assistance budget in 1961. Including two United Nations Special Fund projects—one of which is in the Northeast—Northeast Brazil has been receiving the major attention of the United Nations program since about 1956.

Why did Northeast Brazil receive top priority in the United Nations program—in contrast to the region's bottom priority in the United States program? The general answer may be two-fold. First, the United Nations was the source most capable of providing what the Northeast wanted and needed—development planning assistance. The United States was unsympathetic to economic planning until 1961. Second, a formal Brazilian country program committee existed within which Northeast Brazil, always a strong domestic political force, had to be considered.

It is a safe generalization, also, that Brazilians preferred United Nations assistance. They were members of the United Nations; many key Brazilians in the economic development field had close professional contacts with the United Nations as a result of working on assignments and participating in conferences of the Organization; and the feeling was inevitable that the United Nations was "on their side" and a more appropriate source for objective economic advisory assistance.

UNICEF

The United Nations International Children's Emergency Fund, although a welfare rather than a technical assistance program, deserves brief mention as the first United Nations program to begin major operations in Northeast Brazil. Since 1950 UNICEF has been aiding in child feeding activities and in maternal and child welfare programs in the Northeastern states. It established a milk pasteurization plant in João Pessoa, Paraíba, distributed milk and cod liver oil capsules, provided basic equipment to more than 60 health posts and to over 360 child welfare and maternity centers, initiated and supported the training of midwives and child care aides, financed scholarships for over two hundred such subprofessional workers to be trained at national centers out of the region, provided training in well-drilling for water, sponsored environmental sanitation programs, and stimulated education in nutrition.

The UNICEF program began in 1950 with $229,000 allocated for milk distribution in Northeast Brazil. The drought of 1951 raised the program to an emergency level, and an additional allocation of $550,000 was made for feeding over 150,000 mothers and children at the peak of the emergency program. The program has continued through the years on a relatively large scale, but with emphasis shifting to environmental sanitation work and an integrated health program carried out through mothers' clubs.

Because of its size and lengthy experience, the UNICEF program warrants evaluation and study as an aid program and as an activity to which other programs should be related. And the same questions raised about the United States public health program are relevant to the UNICEF operation: Does a permanent and humanitarian welfare activity contribute to the long-range development of an area if it is not accompanied by programs to increase food supply and economic output on a permanent basis? Of course, investment in a healthier, better fed population can increase a country's productivity if employment opportunities exist or are created.

Development Assistance

As early as 1951, a United Nations expert advised an agency in the Northeast, the Joaquim Nabuco Institute in Recife, on rural housing problems.[23] But the mainstream of United Nations development assistance began in 1953 with the creation of the Bank of the Northeast. This event was the occasion for a three-month survey mission by Dr. Hans Singer, an internationally famous development economist of the United Nations staff, to appraise the development potentials of the Northeast. This one man survey, short in duration and severely limited by the shortage of basic data and previous economic studies of the

[23] Olen E. Leonard, *Rural Housing in Eastern Pernambuco*, United Nations, Technical Assistance Programme (1952).

Northeast, had two significant results. Singer's report supported the position that the Northeast had reasonable development potential and should not be considered simply as a relief problem. Second, by giving the United Nations headquarters first-hand knowledge of the Northeast, the mission stimulated increased interest of the Organization in technical assistance for the area.

Some aspects of the Singer report, such as the estimates of capital requirements for Northeast development and the measures suggested for increasing the productivity of investment, have been severely criticized and frequently discussed in later years. But the specific technical conclusions of the reconnaissance survey had only a limited influence on Northeast policies. Except for two or three preliminary copies, the report did not become available in Brazil until 1956. In fact, the Accioly critique was published before the final Singer report was officially released.[24]

In 1953 the Northeast also received its first UNESCO and FAO missions. E. Aubert de la Rue, a French geologist, made a preliminary survey of mineral resources under UNESCO sponsorship and presented specific recommendations for the systematic exploration of mineral ores in the area.[25] Given the unpreparedness of the region for technical assistance, this brief four-month mission, which did not have personnel-training and institution-building dimensions, did not serve as a base for continued mineral resource activity. An FAO veterinarian expert completed a nine-month assignment in Brazil during 1953 to advise on the control of brucellosis affecting livestock. Part of his work was with the state of Pernambuco in the Northeast.[26]

As a direct consequence of the Singer Mission, the United Nations recruited the author as economic development adviser for Northeast Brazil on a long-term assignment (1954-56). It was hoped that the adviser, working with the Bank of the Northeast, the National Development Bank, and other government agencies, would prepare a comprehensive regional development plan. Two factors, however, changed the

[24] See Pompeu Accioly Borges, *Análise Crítica do Relatório do Dr. H. W. Singer Sôbre o Nordeste,* Commisão de Desenvolvimento Econômico de Pernambuco, Recife (1954); *Desenvolvimento e Conjuntura,* "A Recuperacão Econômica do Nordeste e o Desenvolvimento Geral do Pais" (April 1959), pp. 28-33.

[25] "Enquete Sur les Ressources Minerales du Nord-Est du Brasil," unpublished report, 1954.

[26] United Nations, Food and Agriculture Organization, *Report to the Government of Brazil on the Control of Brucellosis,* Rome (September 1954).

objective of my mission from that of preparing a plan to creating a continuing planning process. One factor was my conviction that plans prepared by outside consultants are rarely implemented. The second consideration was the complete lack of personnel, technical information, and basic research essential for sound planning. The objective of the mission became, therefore, that of creating an economic programing organization, of recruiting the staff, giving training and orientation to the planning personnel, and outlining and initiating a program of research and planning activities.[27]

The mission, as previously discussed (Chapter 5, pp. 96-97), helped to establish a strong training tradition in the Northeast that has persisted and grown; encouraged a flow of data and analyses on the Northeast economy and its development potential; assisted the Brazilians to program future technical assistance needs of the region; and stimulated the establishment of a comprehensive regional planning and coordination agency for the Northeast.

The general philosophy for technical assistance requests adopted by the Bank of the Northeast was to proceed from the general to the specific. In agriculture, for example, the first request was for a general agricultural economist who could appraise the total agricultural picture and establish priorities within the sector for development programs and additional technical assistance requests. A similar pattern was followed for minerals, industrial development, and transportation. In addition, continuing assistance was requested for administration and training. On all technical assistance projects, the BNB tried to use the outside experts to train and supervise Brazilian staff rather than to prepare independent reports.

The United Nations Northeast program in 1954-55 also included a rural credit adviser for ANCAR, a new supervised rural credit agency for the Northeast, created jointly by the Bank of the Northeast, the Bank of Brazil, and the American International Association of the Rockefeller Brothers, and a UNESCO engineer-geologist who initiated in 1955 a long-term program of hydrologic technical assistance and training. With the help of the UNESCO mission, the first school of geology in the Northeast was opened in 1957. And in the following year, an Institute of Geological Research was established. This insti-

---

[27] Stefan H. Robock, *Economic Development in North-East Brazil*, United Nations Technical Assistance Programme (TAA/BRA/3), February 7, 1957. Mr. Robock was the United Nations expert working with the mission.

tute, attached to the University of Recife, was to specialize in hydro-geology and mineral prospecting.[28]

With the establishment of the Working Group for Northeast Development (GTDN) by President Kubitschek in late 1956, the United Nations attempted to organize its technical assistance to the Northeast under a chief of mission who would also be the counterpart of the Brazilian director of the Working Group. The United Nations agreed to a team of six experts to work with the task force—a general economist, administration adviser, regional planning economist, industrial development expert, water policy adviser, and a minerals economist—and thereby to increase its total Northeast mission to thirteen experts as compared to two in 1954.

The hope of the United Nations and others that the task force would become a strong factor in coordinating Northeast development did not materialize. Nevertheless, the number of United Nations experts in the region increased to eleven in 1957 and remained at about that level until 1960. The experts were dispersed among the BNB, the GTDN, the UNESCO geology project, and ANCAR. In the absence of a strong Brazilian institutional framework for coordinating Northeast technical assistance, the United Nations might conceivably have become that coordinating force. But it did so only to a minor extent.

The establishment of SUDENE in early 1960 created for the first time a regional agency with specific legal authority to coordinate all technical assistance for the Northeast. But this SUDENE responsibility had not been implemented by early 1962. SUDENE initiated in 1961, with support from the United Nations Special Fund, a major five-year project to survey the physical and economic feasibility of introducing large-scale irrigation in the middle reaches of the San Francisco River. For this and other projects SUDENE had fourteen United Nations experts working with its staff as of early 1962. Five other experts were assigned to Northeast projects, making a total Northeast complement of nineteen. The SUDENE team includes seven people on the Special Fund project, a group of four UNESCO geologists assigned to the School of Geology and the Institute of Geological Research, and advisers on transportation, industrial development, and agriculture.

[28] Etienne J. P. Stretta, "The Training of Arid Zone Specialists in Brazil," *Arid Zone*, No. 6, UNESCO, Paris, France (December 1959).

The United Nations and its specialized agencies have also made a number of foreign training fellowships available to the Northeast. Since 1955, twelve engineers attached to various organizations working in the Northeast have been sent abroad on UNESCO fellowships for periods ranging from eight to fifteen months, after "internships" with the UNESCO geology team. About a dozen United Nations and Food and Agriculture Organization advanced foreign study fellowships were also granted during this period.

Loans

The only development loan assistance to the Northeast from an international agency prior to 1960 was a $15 million twenty-five year loan by the World Bank to CHESF made in 1950 for financing the Paulo Afonso project.

The United Nations program with ten to twenty experts, although the principal technical assistance effort in the Northeast during the fifties, was still a small effort for a region of more than 20 million people. Furthermore, the missions were not all successful—as is inevitable in technical assistance work. An objective evaluation might classify one-third of the missions as excellent, one-third as passing, and one-third as poor in terms of performance. In some cases, the failure resulted from professional or personal limitations of the experts. In other cases, the failure was on the Brazilian side. But in comparison to results from a comparable allocation of United Nations technical assistance resources in other countries and in United States bilateral programs, the United Nations accomplishment in Northeast Brazil appears to be above average. The Brazilian evaluation of past United Nations technical assistance runs the gamut from "not very effective" (Celso Furtado) to "of grand importance" (Raul Barbosa).

The Alliance for Progress Period

By mid 1960 the total of all United States and United Nations technical assistance to Northeast Brazil, the most extensive area of poverty in the Western Hemisphere, had increased to the level of about fifteen technical experts and an annual expenditure of about $500,000. Development loan programs were not active in the Northeast, but the area was receiving a small number of United States and United Nations fellowships for foreign training. SUDENE, newly created, made a general request for increased United States aid. But with a small aid budget for Brazil, and many continuing commitments, and with some United States embassy personnel convinced that the SUDENE leadership was either Communist or anti-American, the prospects for much greater United States help continued dim.

A Sharp Turn in Inter-American Relations

A series of events forced a sharp turn in United States policy toward Latin America and within eighteen months the Northeast rose from obscurity to fame in the foreign aid picture. The United States "awakening" began with the violently antagonistic reception Vice President Nixon encountered on his Latin American good will tour in June 1958. Following this event, President Kubitschek of Brazil proposed to the United States and the other American states his "Operation Pan America," "a mutual effort to formulate new measures for economic cooperation." A first response to the new situation by the United States in September 1958 was to concur in the plan for a new Inter-American financial institution, a project which the United States had previously opposed. A second response of the United States was to participate more actively in the late 1958 and early 1959 meetings of the Organization of American States Committee of 21, a special group established to develop further the "Operation Pan America" proposal. The United States, however, did not yet feel a sense of urgency. Fidel Castro had come to power in Cuba on January 1, 1959, but United States disillusionment with Castro did not begin until early 1960. In fact, after his February 1960 visit to Brazil, Argentina, Chile, and Uruguay, President Eisenhower declared that United States relations with Latin America were at an all-time high.

By June 1960, however, United States patience had become exhausted by Castro's violently anti-United States policies and ever-closer relations with the Soviet-bloc nations. In that month, the United States brought charges against Cuba in the Organization of American States for a campaign of distortion and falsehoods. Castro responded immediately by expropriating an estimated $800 million worth of American property in Cuba. And in July 1960, President Eisenhower announced in his "Declaration of Newport" that the United States was willing to cooperate with the countries of Latin America in efforts to accelerate the economic and social progress of their peoples. He also announced that he was asking the Congress for a $500 million fund to fulfill the purposes set forth in the Declaration of Newport.

The tempo of United States activity then picked up sharply. In September 1960, the Congress approved in principle the proposed fund. In the same month, the OAS Special Committee reconvened and by early October had adopted fifty important resolutions and recommendations as the Act of Bogotá "for social improvement and economic development within the framework of Operation Pan America." The radical shift in inter-American policy continued with the change in administration and received more definitive orientation through the "Alliance for Progress" formulated by the new president of the United States, John F. Kennedy. In March 1961, President Kennedy proposed the Alliance in a White House speech to represent-atives of the Latin American countries. The Inter-American Economic and Social Council was again called to a special meeting in August 1961 at Punte del Este, Uruguay, and, for the first time, the American governments fixed collective goals of economic progress and social well-being to be attained in the next ten years through the concerted efforts of the American peoples. The United States pledged itself to provide a major part of the minimum of $20 billion, principally in public funds, which Latin America was expected to need over the next ten years from external sources.

The United States Discovers Northeast Brazil

Within this rapidly changing environment of growing United States sensitivity to the Castro threat throughout Latin America, Northeast Brazil, almost by chance, became a "cause celebre." With the United States embassy, New York Times, and the National Broadcasting Company discovery of "Marxist" Francisco Julião and the Peasant League land reform movement in the Northeast, the stage was set by late 1960 for Northeast Brazil to receive prompt and high level atten-tion from the new administration. Almost immediately after President

Kennedy took office a series of urgent visits were made to the Northeast by White House officials, Adlai Stevenson, and others. Celso Furtado, the head of SUDENE, was invited to Washington to confer with President Kennedy and others. And in late 1961 the United States dispatched a special mission to the Northeast led by retired ambassador Merwyn Bohan, erstwhile head of the Joint Commission, to review Brazilian development plans and make recommendations for a major United States aid commitment to the area.[29]

President Goulart of Brazil was invited to visit the United States in April 1962, and the highlight event scheduled for his visit was the signing of the agreement between the United States and Brazil on April 13, 1962 to assist development in Northeast Brazil. The specific United States commitment was $131 million over two years for "making a fast start on some of the most critical problems of the impoverished region." Of the United States commitment, more than one-third was Brazilian currency derived from past sales of United States surplus food. Brazil committed the equivalent of $145 million. The joint program for "immediate action as well as for the beginning phase of a long-range development program" was proclaimed by the United States news release as "one of the most ambitious actions yet taken under the Alliance for Progress."[30]

The program for immediate action was intended to do such things as putting pure water into cities, towns, and villages; electric light into rural communities; sending mobile dispensaries through the area and building elementary and vocational schools. The United States committed $33 million for the immediate action program, of which more than half was in local currency from the sale of surplus food to Brazil.

It is highly questionable whether the allocation of local currencies for the Northeast program can be considered as new and additional United States foreign aid for Brazil. The United States parted with a real physical resource—agricultural commodities—when the agricultural commodities were "sold" to Brazil under Public Law 480. At that time Brazil received the benefit of saving scarce foreign exchange in importing essential goods through transferring local currency to the account of the United States. The cruzeiros, by agreement, are inconvertible; they can-

[29] U. S. Department of State, "Northeast Brazil Survey Team Report," February 1962 (mimeo).

[30] Agency for International Development, Press Release, April 13, 1962.

not be used by the United States for buying Brazilian exports; they cannot be used in Brazil except for purposes and projects to which the Brazilian government agrees; and their contribution to such purposes obviously represents no fresh or additional commitment of American resources to Brazilian development, over and above the original assistance that gave rise to the cruzeiro funds.[31]

The long-term program support of the United States stresses such measures as irrigation, road improvement, electric power development, primary and vocational education, and better methods of farm production and marketing. The agreement states, however, that "the decisions as to actual use of the funds committed will be made on a project-by-project basis—with each project subject to agreement between United States and Brazilian experts in the field."

The United States has stationed a high level representative of the Agency for International Development (AID) in Northeast Brazil to manage its part of the program. And as future events unfold, the implementation of the joint agreement will undoubtedly vary significantly from the patterns originally outlined. Except in the fields of agriculture and public health, the United States has had limited experience and familiarity with Northeast Brazil. The Bohan Mission was restricted by time and the availability of information largely to a review of the planning work SUDENE had available. In education, for example, where the United States had shown a strong interest in supporting projects, the foundation needed on which to base foreign assistance had not been prepared. Consequently, as SUDENE's planning work evolves and the United States develops more expertise in the area, the implementation of the joint agreement will be affected.

Nevertheless, as will be discussed in the final chapter, a number of serious problems confront both parties because of the high expectations created in both the United States and Brazil for quick and dramatic results and because of the abrupt and sharp increase in United States aid to Northeast Brazil—from about $250,000 to $65 million per year. Some of the issues are: the inconsistency of the United States action—in relation to its own AID criteria and the Alli-

[31] For further discussion of this subject see John P. Lewis, *Quiet Crisis in India* (Brookings Institution, 1962), Chap. 12, "Foreign Aid's Financial Vehicles"; and Robert E. Asher, *Grants, Loans, and Local Currencies: Their Role in Foreign Aid* (Brookings Institution, 1962).

ance for Progress agreements—in supporting a regional program that is not an integral part of a national comprehensive development plan; the great emphasis on projects that will have short-term impact; the suitability of aid in the form of surplus food and money rather than in trained personnel and administrative talent; the adequacy of United States preparation in terms of experience, technical know-how, and personnel for meeting its part of the bargain; and the relationship of social and political reform to economic aid.

By the end of 1962, the AID program had negotiated projects for the Northeast which will require an estimated $20 million in assistance from the United States. The major share of the financing will be in local currency available from surplus wheat sales to Brazil. It should be noted, however, that the dollar equivalents are overstated. They have been calculated on the basis of 318 cruzeiros to the dollar, the rate at which the United States accepted the local currency at the time of the sale, whereas continuing domestic inflation has forced the free market rate to above 600 cruzeiros to the dollar in mid-1963.

The first projects to be negotiated follow a pattern of financial aid rather than technical assistance, of social welfare and social overhead programs rather than activities to expand regional output, and of emphasis on the rural-agricultural sector in preference to industrial and nonfarming activities. The specific projects will expand rural health clinics, municipal water supply systems, small community electrification, primary education facilities in Pernambuco and Rio Grande do Norte, and resettle the tenants on a large sugar plantation acquired by the state of Pernambuco. A small agreement for $32,000 with SUDENE has also been signed to provide assistance by several reclamation engineers on the irrigation and power aspects of a river basin project.

Loans and Other Programs

Coincidental with the Alliance for Progress, a number of sources of foreign aid have opened to Northeast Brazil. The Inter-American Development Bank granted a long-term $10 million loan in April 1961 to the Bank of the Northeast for relending to private enterprise, a direct private enterprise loan of $615,000 in October 1961 to BRAS-QUIP, a new manufacturing project in Bahia that will produce tool joints and bits for the petroleum industry, and in July 1962, a $3.6 million loan to finance a synthetic rubber factory in Recife. Out of the Social Progress Trust Fund, the Development Bank loaned slightly more than $4 million in November 1961 to expand Salvador's community water system.

A housing loan to help finance 8,500 units for low-income families in Northeast Brazil was announced by the Inter-American Development Bank in late August 1962. But the $3,850,000 loan had not been finally negotiated by the end of the year. In fact, the Bank of the Northeast, the prospective borrower, doubted whether the loan would be finally negotiated because it was unwilling to accept certain conditions being insisted upon by the Development Bank.

The Ford Foundation had extended its overseas development program to Brazil in 1959 and by September 1960 had made a grant of $140,000 to SUDENE for a fellowship program to train forty technicians over a period of four years through field work, observation, and academic courses abroad.

The French government became interested in the Northeast about 1959 and has provided several scholarships for training in France in various scientific and technical fields, a short survey mission to study industrial possibilities of Northeast vegetable oils, a technical mission that advised on food supply programs for the city of Recife, and the organization of market information services. Northeast Brazil has become the major foreign aid activity of France in Latin America; and a major project for the survey and development of the Jaguaribe Valley, to which the French would supply a number of technicians and multimillion dollar financial support, was being negotiated in early 1962.

Japan, Italy, Israel, and the Netherlands are also giving aid to the Northeast or have made firm commitments to do so. In connection with the SUDENE project to rehabilitate the Northeast textile industry, the Japanese are staffing a textile training school in the region. The Italian government has offered a loan of up to $20 million to PETROBRAS, the government oil monopoly agency, to be supplemented by contractual services to drill for oil in Brazil. Virtually all of Brazil's oil production is in the Northeast. The Israeli minister of agriculture, an expert on irrigation of dry areas, visited the Northeast in 1961 and developed with the Brazilians a project for establishing an experiment station for irrigation in the region. The Dutch have for several years provided foreign training fellowships to Nordestinos and are continuing with this program.

Two additional United Nations programs were at advanced negotiation stages in 1962. The United Nations Special Fund has approved a $1.3 million allocation for a survey of rock salt deposits in the state of Sergipe to determine their suitability for the manufacture of caustic soda. The plan of operation, however, has not yet been completed. The Food and Agriculture Organization in late 1961 selected Northeast Brazil as a demonstration area for its new world campaign against hunger.

The Soviet Bloc nations have also become active, according to a report prepared by the United States embassy. The Polish government has offered to send technicians to Brazil and to assist a research institute in Recife to produce vitamins from agricultural waste products. A group of Hungarian engineers are reported to have arrived in August 1961 to study water problems in the Northeast and to drill about 2,000 wells. In fact, the State of Rio Grande do Norte negotiated a contract with the Hungarian government for $147,000 to cover the cost of equipment and technical services for geologic and hydrologic research. But as of the end of 1962, the project had not been officially endorsed by SUDENE and the contract lacked a repayment guarantee from the federal government. The Bank of the Northeast had been asked to guarantee the contract, but under its legal authority could not guarantee obligations of state governments.

8

Development Issues for Brazil

BY THE EARLY 1960's, Brazil had not only accepted in principle the New Era philosophy toward Northeast development but had created significant new institutions for carrying into effect the radical shift in federal policy. A growing number of programs and plans with an economic development tenor are emerging. But many crucial development issues for the future still remain to be identified and resolved.

One issue involves the possible strengthening of national economic planning and the concomitant need for basing regional priorities on development potentials rather than on equity grounds. A second issue concerns the basic planning strategy for the region, both in regard to the planning process and the identification of the major bottlenecks to development. A third problem is the need for greatly improved detailed plans in such key sectors as industrialization and human resources in order to expand programs in these fields. A final issue relates to the implementation philosophy and the region's capacity for implementing development plans.

National Planning and Regional Development

In principle the desirability of comprehensive national planning has been accepted in Brazil for many years. But in practice Brazil has not yet succeeded in establishing a continuing and efficient comprehensive planning process. Many factors explain the gap between acceptance in principle and practice. Brazil has made exceptional economic progress without comprehensive national planning and, there-

146

fore, has not felt a keen need for the broader use of professional technical insights and for the greater discipline and precision of comprehensive planning. In addition, Brazil has had a severe shortage of the technically trained and experienced personnel required for comprehensive planning. And finally, a number of attempts at national planning were vitiated by recurring political crises.

At the same time, Brazil has produced many sectoral and regional plans. The phenomenal expansion of the automobile industry, for example, was a planned development. National plans have been prepared for electrification, highways, shipbuilding, and many other fields. Regional plans of varying quality have been completed for the Amazon, the Northeast, and for many states such as São Paulo and Bahia. But in the absence of a continuing national planning process, the various sector and area plans have not been related to each other; nor have national policies been comprehensively evaluated in terms of their full effects on planned development.

President Kubitschek in his 1956 message to the National Congress recommended a special "studies and surveys" service whose results would serve as a base for a National Plan of Planned Regional Development which he hoped to complete during his term of office.[1] But this political aim never became a reality.

Growing forces for comprehensive national planning, including pressures from the United States and the Alliance for Progress, may push Brazil toward following in practice what it has long accepted in principle. In late 1962, President Goulart initiated another attempt at national planning and appointed Celso Furtado to head the national planning work, as Minister without Portfolio, in addition to his responsibilities as Superintendent of SUDENE. And in January 1963, the office of the President released a Three Year Plan for Economic and Social Development (1963-65).[2]

Comprehensive national planning, if soundly established, will have at least three major implications for the Northeast. First, national policies such as minimum wage legislation, education, land reform, internal migration, foreign exchange and foreign trade controls, and

[1] Juscelino Kubitschek de Oliveira, *Mensagem Ao Congresso Nacional*, Rio de Janeiro (1956), p. 468.
[2] *Plano Trienal de Desenvolvimento Econômico e Social: 1963-65*, Presidência da Republica, Departmento de Imprensa Nacional (1963).

banking and fiscal regulation are likely to be evaluated more thoroughly in regard to their regional impacts. Regional political pressures to influence such national policies, therefore, will have to be guided more by technical economic considerations. Second, development planning in different regions can be interrelated. Third, the competition among the regions for federal development resources will shift significantly toward a criterion of comparative regional development potentials. All of these events will impose a much greater burden on the regions for technical and economic data and analyses.

Regional Dimensions of National Policies

The Northeast has made a start in evaluating the impact of national fiscal, foreign exchange, and foreign trade policies on the region. But, as previously noted, the emphasis has been on regional equity rather than the effect of such policies on national development. In many other fields, not even this much of a beginning has been made.

The effect of minimum wage regulation on regional industrialization goals has not received attention. Political and welfare pressures have resulted in narrow regional differentials in minimum wages—the actual wage many factory workers in Brazil receive. This narrow regional differential may, from an economic point of view, be greatly inhibiting business and manufacturing development in the region. For example, the minimum wage as of October 1961 for Recife and Salvador in the Northeast was 78 and 80 percent respectively of the legal minimum for São Paulo and Rio de Janeiro in the South.[3]

A large supply of untrained surplus labor is a principal development resource of the Northeast region. Are entrepreneurs being inhibited from utilizing fully this comparative advantage of the Northeast by the artificial and restrictive pricing of labor? The choice is not simply higher or lower individual worker incomes. It is also between a small number of jobs at higher wages and a potentially large number of jobs at lower wages. Furthermore, as the demand and supply situation comes into closer balance, and as the skills of Northeast workers improve through the opportunity for working experience and through training programs, the welfare of the workers of the region

[3] Instituto Brasileiro de Geografia e Estatística, Conselho Nacional de Estatística, *Anuário Estatístico do Brasil*, 1961, p. 264.

may rather quickly improve. At the current stage of development greater differentials in minimum wage rates may be necessary for the workers to secure their initial nonagricultural working opportunity.

Basic revisions in Brazil's tax system also deserve much greater attention in terms of their impact on regional development. A key issue here is the distribution of taxing powers between the states and the federal government. The principal source of revenue for state governments is the turnover tax—a gross sales tax on the transfer of goods at every stage of the business process. The first sale of agricultural commodities, however, is frequently exempted.

The state of São Paulo is the most economically advanced area, the major producer of manufactured goods for the nation and the principal importer of raw materials and semifinished goods used for manufacturing. As a gateway and processing center, São Paulo collects for its exclusive state use more in turnover tax revenues than all of the other twenty states in Brazil combined.

Thus, the tax system creates a cumulative disequilibrating force. By exacting a tax toll from much of the business activity of the entire nation, rapidly developing São Paulo continues to receive ever-increasing tax revenues for state development. This is a structural issue of crucial importance to the regional pattern of Brazil that must be considered at the level of national policy.

So little is known about the regional impact of many national policies, such as in banking, that it is impossible at this stage to be reasonably specific about the issues. A few comments can be made, however, about internal migration questions. Brazil has long cherished and articulated its aspirations for increasing the population in the vast interior, but this goal has not been specifically related in plans and actions to regional development situations such as that of the Northeast. Brazil needs comprehensive studies and plans of internal migration as it relates to the national development goals—developing Brasília, settling the interior and the Amazon basin, and reducing overpopulation in the Northeast. Such national planning should also identify future geographical population trends for which the nation should prepare. For example, the normal pattern of economic progress involves a relative shift of population out of agriculture into manufacturing and trades and services, which in turn means a strong urbanization trend.

A better understanding of past and future internal migration trends can also influence policies on financing education and training. If the foreseeable development of Brazil involves continued migration of Nordestinos to the industrializing South, should national policies encourage the receiving areas to contribute to the investment in human resources? Or can the overpopulated Northeast be expected to finance the education and training of large numbers of people who will carry their skills to other regions?

National Coordination of Regional Plans

Regional plans may be complementary as well as competitive. And frequently activities outside of the Northeast can have a greater impact than programs within the region on specific development goals. An important example of this is in agriculture. In the United States a key factor in stimulating the reorganization of southern agriculture toward greatly increased levels of productivity was the draining off of surplus labor by employment opportunities after World War II in the East, North, and West of the United States. Labor became scarce for traditional farming patterns, and farmers became receptive to adopting improved technologies. Much of the technology was not capital intensive and had been long available to southern agriculture. But the motivations to change farming practices were not strong so long as large supplies of cheap labor were readily available.

One of the most feasible steps to assist the reorganization of Northeast agriculture is by means of agricultural development programs for north Mato Grosso, north Goiás and south Pará to accelerate the out-migration of farmers from the overpopulated agricultural sector of the Northeast. The migrating workers can have larger farm units in the central interior, and the workers remaining in the Northeast will also have larger farms because the pressure of population on scarce land resources will be reduced. At the same time, the total contribution to national production will be increased. Therefore, Northeast programs need to be coordinated with development programs of other regions. Furthermore, it must be recognized that a given investment outside of the Northeast might contribute more to the Northeast than the same investment within the region.

Industrialization plans also require coordination. The Northeast is giving high priority to the rehabilitation of the regional textile industry. As a heavily labor intensive industry requiring small numbers of highly skilled workers, the textile industry appears to have comparative advantages for the Northeast. But much of the textile industry is located in the South, and the success of Northeast efforts will depend on a coordination of its industrial development activities with those in other regions.

Regional Competition for National Investment Resources

Comprehensive national planning as it evolves in Brazil will be shaped by special characteristics of the Brazilian situation. One such factor is the weakness of the federal government relative to the states, particularly São Paulo, in control over public revenues. In Brazil, the states collect almost the same amount in total taxes as does the federal government, 211 versus 233 billion cruzeiros in 1960; and the states and local governments together collect more than the national government.[4] The state of São Paulo alone collected state revenues of 95 billion cruzeiros in 1960, or 40 percent of federal revenue receipts. In the United States the federal government collects four times as much as the states and double the total collections of the state and local governments.[5]

Another weakness of the federal government in influencing development plans is the strong tradition of earmarking federal tax revenues by constitutional amendment and by law for specific purposes such as roads and electrification. The Constitution now earmarks 3 percent of total tax revenues for the Amazon, 3 percent for the Northeast (shared by DNOCS and the BNB) and 1 percent for the San Francisco Valley. In addition, the SUDENE law grants the Northeast an additional 2 percent of total federal revenues. In practice the finance minister may influence the amounts and the timing in releasing ear-

[4] *Ibid.*, p. 418. Tax collections of the local governments (*municípios*) for 1960 were not available. In 1959, however, total collections for federal, state, and local governments respectively were 158, 146, and 34 billion cruzeiros. *II Plano de Ação do Govêrno: 1963-66*, Estado de São Paulo (1962), p. 309.

[5] U. S. Bureau of the Census, *Statistical Abstract of the United States, 1961*, p. 403. In 1959 total governmental tax revenue was $99.6 billion of which the federal, state, and local governments respectively accounted for $67.3, $15.8, and $16.5 billion.

marked funds. But even after administrative modifications are made, a large share of the federal revenue goes directly to legally prescribed uses without becoming part of the federal government's control over national development patterns.

When the earmarked commitments, the national defense expenditures (60 billion out of a federal budget of 300 billion cruzeiros in 1961), and the necessary operational expenses of the federal government are excluded from total available funds, the weakness of the federal government in controlling total development expenditures in the country is even more starkly apparent. The federal government does gain some additional financial strength, however, through its ability to borrow from the Bank of Brazil. In 1960, for example, the Bank of Brazil increased its "loans outstanding" to the national treasury and federal entities by 80 billion cruzeiros.[6] The general flotation of government bonds has not been possible because of the long-standing inflationary situation.

One possibility for the federal government to increase its relative financial power may lie in its exclusive prerogative to collect income taxes. In 1960, income taxes accounted for about 30 percent of federal tax collections, as compared to about 40 percent flowing from consumption taxes. Probably, with higher levels of development and a gradual improvement in the complex administration of income tax collection, this source of public revenue may increase relative to other sources so as to give the federal government greater relative financial power.

Foreign aid conditional on comprehensive national planning can be a strong force for increasing federal control and financial power over economic development activities. Conversely, foreign aid given directly in support of regional or state plans, particularly when such subarea plans have not been integrated within national development goals and plans, can seriously weaken the already weak position of the federal government in trying to influence and coordinate development activities from a national point of view.

Assuming, however, that national economic planning that integrates regional development is eventually strengthened and that the regions will have to compete increasingly for federal development resources and policies on the basis of comparative development potentials, the

[6] Banco do Brasil, S.A., *Relatório 1961*, Brasília (1962), p. 151.

Northeast will be seriously disadvantaged unless its activities in pre-investment studies and project formulation are greatly accelerated. It will have to undertake studies of natural resources potentials, of the potential employment and income gains to the individuals and the region from specific projects in irrigation and agriculture, of foreign market potentials for export commodities of the region and of regional markets for particular manufactured goods, and locational advantages for establishing specific industries in the Northeast. Aside from their utility in competing for federal resources, such research can directly contribute to regional development by improving the quality of current activities and by identifying new development possibilities.

Even more important, a change in the Northeast "posture" from that of pleading for help because of poverty and inequities to one of documenting and publicizing existing opportunities will greatly encourage increased private investment from within and outside the Northeast. Current patterns of exaggerating and accenting the negative economic, political, and social features of the region may (or may not) succeed in securing more government help. But they are a major reason for private investment being chary about the Northeast. It is hard to think of a better way to scare off private investment than through continued propagandizing of the traditional inaccurate and unbalanced image of the Northeast's misery.

Regional Planning Strategy: Basic Issues

The development and planning strategy being followed by SU-DENE in Northeast Brazil has not been explicitly articulated. But implicit in the Northeast experience to date are several issues that may threaten the success of development activities. One is a possible confusion in regard to development goals. A second relates to the choice of criteria for determining development priorities.

Development Goals

The impulses that actuate the establishment of economic planning activities in a region or a country are likely to generate an inverted set of goals and priorities. Circumstances, typically those of an emergency, create an urgent demand for new and quick solutions to crisis problems that threaten the economy. The Northeast emergency was the drought and its dramatic demonstration of the weakness of current policies and practices. The urgent demand has been to solve quickly the problems of food shortages, unemployment, low agricultural productivity and inadequate social conditions.

Political realities require that a reasonable amount of effort be allocated to finding the "right" answers for the problems of the moment. But the long-range development aspirations of an area can usually be better served by a steady and lasting improvement in the decision-making and program implementation institutions of a region. As Professor Lewis has emphasized,[7] "The production of a good set of substantive economic decisions—that is, a good 'plan'—for the next one, five, or seven years seldom is as important as even a modest gain in the rationality of the planning process that may be authoring decisions for decades to come."

Obviously, it is not an either/or choice between good decisions on pressing problems and an improved decision-making process. Scarce resources must be allocated to both objectives. The common danger, however—and one being faced in the Northeast—is that the more urgent immediate problems rather than the more important basic needs will absorb most of the attention of the scarce planning talent. "Almost never are the current problems really so urgent compared with the cumulative urgency of the economic issues with which the government is going to have to grapple over the years ahead."[8]

Reinforcing the distortion in development goals resulting from the actuating circumstances are similar forces generated by the standard procedure of development planning. After preparing specific production and income targets for a country, planners have often convinced themselves that the goals of development are to achieve the specific targets of the plan. The subtle but crucial difference is between the dynamic objective of accelerating the momentum of a system and the static objective of achieving specific targets. Population is always increasing and levels of expectations are rising. Specific plan targets, therefore, are never an end in themselves. But the fulfillment of such targets on a continuing basis may be a strong indication that the

[7] John P. Lewis, *Notes on the Nurture of Country Planning* (Indiana University, 1962), p. 10.
[8] *Ibid.*, p. 10.

efficiency, productivity, and momentum of the economic system are improving.

Several examples may help to illustrate the contrast between momentum and targets as ultimate development goals. A specific target may be to influence farmers to use improved hybrid corn seed or more phosphatic fertilizer in order to achieve a designated production level. But the basic objective is to create conditions which make farmers constantly and continuously receptive to new technologies. It is desirable to secure a one-shot increase in production. But it is imperative for economic development, that agricultural output be continuously increasing.

A specific target may be to create a designated number of new housing units within a certain time period. But the basic development objective must be to stimulate on a continuing basis the performance of the housing industry. Even with the help of foreign aid, the maximum feasible targets, if fulfilled, could satisfy only a small proportion of potential housing need. Furthermore, in the Northeast as in most other underdeveloped areas, prevailing political patterns would cause the new housing units to end up exclusively in the hands of political supporters—what the Brazilians call *clientelismo*. Unless the new housing units are part of a general acceleration of housing activity on a continuing basis, they may actually have the negative result of generating increased skepticism and opposition to development efforts.

When economic development is recognized as a problem in momentum and expectations, the content and strategy of economic development programs may have to change radically. As will be discussed below, the issue has great relevance to the choice of implementation philosophies. It is basic to the arguments for institution building and for investment in human resources. And it stands as a reminder that specific target accomplishments may not mean development success unless they are clear products of a significant and lasting improvement in the institutional processes of a developing area.

Priority Criteria and Development Bottlenecks

A principal contribution that comprehensive planning can make toward accelerating Northeast development is by improving the allocation of scarce resources. But it must not be assumed that the critical scarcities in the Northeast and in other underdeveloped areas are the same. There is a strong tendency among development economists to believe that the most critical obstacle to development in backward economies is the scarcity of capital. And this belief seems to have been accepted uncritically in Northeast planning as the criterion for establishing program and project priorities.

But is capital the most critical Northeast scarcity at its present stage of development? Obviously the Northeast needs much more investment to achieve the higher economic levels to which it aspires. But relative to regional capacity—administrative and institutional—to use funds efficiently, the Northeast has had available an excess of financial resources for many decades. The Bank of the Northeast experience with development loans is only one of many illustrations that reveal the region's inadequate preparation of technical personnel and private and public institutions to make effective use of increased amounts of capital.

If the critical bottleneck is the scarcity of administrative personnel and the low efficiency of regional institutions rather than capital, Northeast development programs must be evaluated for priorities in terms of maximizing the returns from the use of this scarce administrative resource. This means that every project being considered must contain an estimate of the personnel and administrative needs for its successful completion. Such a step might reveal, for example, that the Maranhão resettlement project is costly in terms of scarce administrative resources and that the same number of new jobs for underemployed workers in agriculture could be created through industrial development programs, with a significant saving in the scarce resource.

By recognizing scarce administrative resources as the true development bottleneck, SUDENE may have to change significantly its choice of programs. At the same time, it should give top priority to steps necessary for eliminating the bottleneck, through training programs and importing technicians from other regions or foreign countries. The regional administrative capacity is relatively high in certain fields, such as electric power and highway construction, and the pressures to produce results quickly may lead to overemphasis of such programs. On the other hand, the scarcity of administrative capacity for programs in education and industrialization may operate as a bias against giving priority to relatively more productive activities in these fields.

Investment in human resources, to be discussed below, is one means of increasing the administrative capacity of the region. However, other complementary actions will be needed. One of these would be to remove the uncertainties that all government agencies experience regarding receipt of appropriated funds. Also, technical assistance and foreign aid plans should recognize the high priority that must be given to improving the administrative capacity of the region.

A Stronger Industrialization Effort

A major field in which the policy commitment is strong but the action program weak is industrialization. The Furtado report places an "intensification of industrial investments" at the head of the list of basic policies to be followed. The SUDENE plan, however, allocates to industrialization only a minute share of total resources and places almost complete reliance on passive programs of special inducements and financial assistance. This weakness in industrialization efforts is undoubtedly explained by such factors as strong regional pressures for SUDENE to become preoccupied with agriculture and fighting the drought, the greater availability of specific plans and experienced technicians for irrigation, water system, agricultural, and infrastructure programs, and the relative inexperience within the region with industrial development programs.

Nevertheless, the Northeast employment problem emphasizes the urgent necessity for a significant strengthening of industrialization activities. If population trends of the last decade continue—a 25 percent gain from 1950 to 1960—an average increase can be expected of 550,000 persons per year in total population and from 150,000 to 175,000 per year in new entrants to the labor force. Northeast agriculture holds little promise, particularly with the adoption of improved technology, of providing additional jobs for the new workers who choose to remain in the region rather than migrate. In fact, the present level of employment in Northeast agriculture will decline as agricultural productivity increases.

The principal source for new jobs, therefore, will be in nonagricultural fields such as manufacturing, mining, construction, trade, services, and government. Assuming that each new job in manufacturing will create an additional two to three new jobs in trades and services, the Northeast needs from 40,000 to 50,000 new industrial jobs per year to accommodate only the new entrants to the labor force. To the extent that improved agricultural productivity reduces farm employment opportunities, an even greater number of new nonfarm jobs will be required.

An equally important justification for giving more attention to industrialization—and an aspect of the total regional development problem that has not been duly recognized in the Northeast—is the dynamic stimulus that industry can give to increased efficiency and output in the agricultural sector. A recent survey of the phenomenal industrialization success of the Philippines over the last decade reveals that the expansion of agricultural processing industries and the technical assistance given to farmers by industry—under the natural business motivation of increasing the quantity and quality of its supplies of raw materials—has been a major if not *the* major force in stimulating higher levels of agricultural production in rubber, cattle, cacao, coffee, and other major farm products.[9] The Northeast has its own example of this phenomenon in the impact on farm production of the tomato processing activities of Pesqueira in the interior of Pernambuco. Given the limited capacity of the governmental administrative apparatus to stimulate improved agriculture in the Northeast, proper emphasis on encouraging business activities in food processing, fertilizer, and other farm supplies may turn out to be one of the most effective means of achieving regional development goals in agriculture.

An annual increase of 40,000 to 50,000 new industrial jobs may be difficult if not impossible for Northeast Brazil to achieve. But several favorable factors for industrialization, aside from improved transport facilities and electric power availability, have generally been overlooked. One of these is the large and growing internal market of the Northeast, which is protected from the competition of industries in the South by high transportation costs. Even with present low levels of

[9] Stefan H. Robock, "Manufacturing in the Philippines," an unpublished report of the World Bank Mission to the Philippines, 1961.

income, the Northeast population of 25 million offers a large enough market to warrant the expansion of many marketed-oriented industries in the region.[10]

Another favorable factor is a present pattern of transport costs that gives Northeast manufacturers privileged access to the large markets of the South. The Northeast receives much more in traffic movements from the South than it ships. And in order to stimulate return trip traffic, transport rates for shipments from the Northeast to the South are about half the level for shipments from the South to the Northeast. Transport differentials may eventually disappear. But until this occurs the favorable export conditions can permit many new plants to operate profitably in the Northeast while the regional market is growing to optimum scale.

Still another reason for optimism regarding industrialization is the new, vigorous entrepreneurial spirit in the region and the potential growth nuclei the Northeast has in its 4,000 manufacturing establishments with five or more workers and almost 300,000 smaller factory units.

SUDENE's Industrialization Program

In a recent speech, the head of SUDENE's industry staff outlined the agency's industrialization program as consisting of four types of activities:[11] (1) administration of special inducements; (2) financial assistance; (3) technical assistance; and (4) improved regional environment.

SPECIAL INDUCEMENTS. SUDENE has legal authority to allocate foreign exchange at special fixed exchange rates or grant import authorization without foreign exchange cover for "equipment, including farm implements, considered essential to development of the region." Fifty percent of foreign exchange earnings from Northeast exports are by

[10] For a demonstration of the major role that market-oriented industries can play in the industrialization of an underdeveloped region, see Glenn E. McLaughlin and Stefan Robock, *Why Industry Moves South* (National Planning Association, 1949).

[11] Juarez Faria, "Notes Sôbre a Politica de Industrialização do Nordeste," lecture at the training course of the Rio Grande do Norte State Development Commission, January 1962.

law placed at SUDENE's disposition. SUDENE also has power to exempt equipment from import duties and taxes, with priority for basic industries and food industries. However, machines and equipment that are used or reconditioned or whose prototypes are produced and available within Brazil do not qualify for the exemption. SUDENE can grant reductions of from 50 to 100 percent in income taxes up to 1968 for regional industries that process local agricultural and mineral raw materials.

FINANCIAL ASSISTANCE. Under its basic legislation, SUDENE can recommend to the National Development Bank and the Bank of the Northeast the granting of development loans to industrial projects considered to have priority for regional development. SUDENE has no specific legal provision for soliciting and receiving loans from international agencies or foreign sources, but it participated in obtaining a $10 million line of credit from the Inter-American Development Bank to the Bank of the Northeast for financing the foreign exchange requirements of Northeast industrial projects. The 1961 law approving the guiding plan provided a new source of financial assistance for SUDENE which may become very important. Article 34 grants a 50 percent reduction in income taxes to any Brazilian corporation where twice the amount of the tax saving is reinvested or applied in industries considered by SUDENE to be of interest for the development of the Northeast. This special exemption for investment in Northeast projects is open to all companies in Brazil, 100 percent Brazilian owned.

TECHNICAL ASSISTANCE. SUDENE's first direct action industrial program is a cooperative program with the Bank of the Northeast to strengthen and reequip the regional textile industry. Based on detailed techno-economic studies, the program is directed toward (a) improving the technical and administrative patterns of the textile factories through training of workers and administrators, (b) technical reequipment of the industry by providing credit assistance for replacing obsolete equipment, and (c) financial strengthening of textile companies by making increased working capital available. This program affects sixty-one factories with about 32,000 workers and may involve investments totaling more than 10 billion cruzeiros.

IMPROVED REGIONAL ENVIRONMENT. SUDENE expects to improve the overall regional environment for efficient industrial operation through its programs to improve transportation, to increase the supply and lower the cost of electric energy, to expand the availability of agricultural raw materials, to stabilize and lower food costs, to train manpower, to improve municipal and industrial water supplies, and to develop better technical information on mineral resources.

The SUDENE industrialization programs sound impressive and represent a major expansion of previous regional efforts in this field. The BNB in particular has been working for several years to create better preconditions for industrialization through technical assistance to businessmen, training courses in project preparation, and educational programs to change entrepreneurial attitudes in the region. But the urgency of the problem requires even greater and more aggressive action. Fortunately, several of the additional steps suggested below are not costly in terms of scarce administrative resources, and others can be greatly advanced through inexpensive foreign technical assistance.

Special inducements and financial aids for industry are passive measures because their effectiveness depends ultimately on the existence and initiative of entrepreneurs, the identification of specific industrial opportunities, and the elaboration of industrial projects. Contrary to the traditional pessimism of economic development technicians on the entrepreneurial potential of underdeveloped areas, the Northeast has experienced a phenomenal surge of entrepreneurial interest and competence in recent years. Yet the entrepreneurial situation needs to be nurtured and strengthened.

Identifying Industrial Opportunities

Progress has also been made in identifying industrial opportunities and in elaborating industrial projects through the efforts of the Bank of the Northeast, the Economic Development Commission of Pernambuco, and the Economic Planning Commission of Bahia. The BNB prepared industrial opportunity studies—for the manufacture of such products as safety matches, beer, spark plugs, and candy in the Northeast—which sparked the establishment of several such industries in the region. Bahia has had the most ambitious and effective industrialization program in the Northeast. It has prepared projects for shipbuilding, fruit processing, vegetable oils, oilpalm (*dende*), tin cans, and caustic soda, all of which are in process of being executed. Other specific projects being elaborated are for nitrogen fertilizers, aluminum utensils, beryllium oxide, screws, lubricating oil, jute sacks, and even iron and steel.[12] Pernambuco pioneered in planning a synthetic rubber factory using molasses alcohol, a by-product of the region's sugar industry, as the raw material; and in July 1962, the Inter-American Development Bank approved a loan of $3.6 million to help finance the synthetic rubber factory at Recife. In September 1962, the United States Agency for International Development followed with an additional $3.4 million loan.

But much more of the techno-economic project elaboration work needs to be done. Surprising as it may seem, the Bank of the Northeast has had numerous inquiries from potential entrepreneurs in the region who are looking for specific opportunities to exploit. All the Northeast agencies, however, are severely limited by the shortage of technical personnel and know-how for conducting such techno-economic studies. A predominantly agricultural region is inevitably lacking in personnel and experience to discover business opportunities. Yet many such undiscovered opportunities exist.

Industrial Promotion

In addition to expanding regional industrial development research, the Northeast can benefit greatly from following the industrial promotion techniques used successfully in Puerto Rico, Western Europe, and the United States. Researchers may have to expend considerable effort and time to identify a specific industry opportunity. But a businessman on the basis of his industry experience can usually make a sound preliminary identification of an opportunity in his field by spending only a few days in an area. This kind of "short-cut research" technique needs to be exploited. Brazil has a large industrial sector in the South that should be encouraged to survey the Northeast through an organized and efficient industrial promotion program. Supported by a research staff that can supply technical information to interested outside industrialists, industrial promotion efforts could produce a siz-

[12] *Plano de Desenvolvimento da Bahia: 1960-1963*, "Contribuição ao Plano Diretor do Desenvolvimento do Nordeste da SUDENE," Governo do Estado da Bahia, 1961.

able and significant spur to Northeast industrialization. Special incentives are effective only to the extent that the number of new industry prospects is greatly increased.

The Northeast has received virtually no attention from foreign private investment. Nationalistic forces that succeeded in restricting the special income tax reduction to 100 percent nationally owned industries may or may not be representative of regional attitudes toward foreign investment. Yet the extreme nature of provisions of the law prevent even Brazilian companies with a minority foreign interest from taking advantage of the incentives.

As a sovereign government, Brazil is free to follow whatever policies it chooses regarding foreign investment in the Northeast. Nevertheless, it should be pointed out that Brazil's general policy, so successful in industrializing the South, has been one of aggressively encouraging foreign private capital; that Brazilian interests can be controlling in joint enterprises without having 100 percent control; and that foreign private investment even with minority interests can be a tremendous resource for identifying industrial opportunities and for providing entrepreneurial experience and industrial know-how for the Northeast.

Nurturing Regional Entrepreneurship

Another series of affirmative programs should be undertaken to improve the quality and quantity of regional entrepreneurship. With the exception of a modest attempt in Bahia supported by the United States aid program, the Northeast has virtually no training facilities in business administration. The higher education development plans of SUDENE are oriented toward agriculture and give no attention to the need for making modern advanced technical business training available. Subprofessional training for clerical staff is very weak in the region. Some progress is being made in vocational training, but the entire field of manpower requirements for an industrializing society has been only lightly touched.

In industrial finance, the regional situation for long-term industrial loans has greatly improved over the last decade. Nevertheless, the region also needs to develop security markets to provide equity capital for new and existing industries. The lack of institutional machinery to assist industry in securing equity capital is a severe limitation on the success of improved lending facilities, for in order to be eligible for loans the business entrepreneurs must have a reasonable amount of ownership money in the enterprise. The success in the Northeast of recent national stock flotations, such as the sale of Willys Overland do Brasil securities, strongly supports the view that a large supply of savings exists in the region that can be interested in risk ventures. One way of implementing equity financing activities is through the Bank of the Northeast. It has legal authority to underwrite stock and to create an investment company.

A general condition for greater success in industrialization in the Northeast is the recurring issue of the regional image. In attracting new industry and encouraging private investment in the Northeast, probably more so than in any other development effort, the Northeast must present an image of growth and potential for development. The recent industrialization experience of the region can support a favorable image. But the political tradition of pleading for government aid on grounds of drought and misery still has the upper hand.

Importance of Human Resources

> The country which commits itself to accelerated growth . . . must invest wisely both in things and in people. A country's capacity to utilize effectively physical capital is dependent upon the availability of human capital, and vice versa. And it is essential for politicians and planners to understand that any development plan which does not give high priority to human capital formation is simply unrealistic and almost certainly destined to fail, for experience has shown that skilled manpower does not appear automatically or magically.[13]

Is the Northeast investing adequately and wisely in human capital formation? Is it accumulating at a high rate the kinds of skilled people and institutions that are indispensable for the modernization process? Unfortunately, the answers are "no." Furthermore, this critical weakness appears to arise not only out of the strong political pressures for short-range programs with immediate results, but from a failure

[13] Frederick Harbison, *The Strategy of Human Resource Development in Modernizing Economies*, Organization for European Economic Cooperation (September 1961), pp. 4-5.

of government officials and the public to recognize or accept the role of investment in human resources, with a consequent lack of specific plans.

Yet human capital formation is needed to break the critical bottleneck in the Northeast. Increased literacy and better education are essential for improved productivity both in agriculture and industry. Training and education improve the employment opportunities in other regions for Nordestinos who migrate. Most important of all, education is the ideal means of "sharing the wealth" and of countering the widespread claims that too few people in the underdeveloped areas share in the rewards of economic progress. As one outstanding educational leader in Brazil has urged, "Education always presents itself as an alternative for revolution and catastrophe, but, for this, it is necessary that it is not made a road for the privileged or for the maintenance of privilege."[14]

The Northeast has made a valiant beginning in the case of technical and professional manpower needs. However, it does not have plans for increasing the quantity and quality of primary and secondary education so that an adequate supply of properly trained personnel is available for high level training. It has not researched and planned for solving the formidable regional surplus labor problem—a situation which cannot be assumed to disappear with development. In fact, planned reorganization of agriculture and modernization of key industries like textile manufacturing are likely to reduce manpower requirements and further aggravate the unemployment and underemployment problem. The Northeast is not adequately exploiting the potentialities for on-the-job training by using government agencies, private employers, expatriate firms, and foreign technical experts, and thereby economizing on the scarce resources of education administrators.

The Education Situation in the Northeast

One proof of the limited attention manpower planning has received is the almost complete lack of manpower and education studies on the region. A number of scattered facts, however, provide clear indications of the poor educational situation in the Northeast.

[14] Anísio Teixeira, "A Escola Brasileira e a Estabilidade Social," *Revista Brasileira de Estudos Pedagógicos* (Julho-Setembro, 1957), p. 23.

The high levels of Northeast illiteracy are evidence that education has traditionally had a low regional priority. The 1950 census revealed that 74 percent of the population five years of age and above were classified as unable to read and write. It is safe to conclude, moreover, that illiteracy is even higher because of the flexible interpretation in Brazilian census taking of "being able to read and write". Furthermore, over the decade from 1940 to 1950 the official rate of illiteracy dropped only from 76 to 74 percent.

The number of students in school, disregarding for a moment the quality of education, is equally discouraging. In 1958, for example, official government statistics show that almost two-thirds of the children of primary school age in the Northeast did not have access to primary schools.[15] An unofficial estimate for 1957 is that 77 percent of the children of primary school age in the Northeast were not in school.[16]

Secondary education, largely provided by private schools, is even more limited. Only 6 percent of the student potential for secondary education in the Northeast was enrolled in secondary schools (*colegios e ginasios*) in 1959.[17]

The enrollment statistics, however, show only part of the picture. The high rate of dropouts and the selective nature of the system further aggravate the situation. Educational statistics in Brazil are poor, particularly on a regional basis, but a recent estimate has been made of the share of Brazilian students entering the first school year who complete primary, secondary, and university education. In Brazil as a whole, for every 1000 students enrolled in the first school year, only 66 are still enrolled in the fifth or terminal year of primary education, only 16 in the eleventh or final year of secondary training and only 7 in the final year of the university.[18]

In contrast to Brazil's retention rate of 66 per 1000 for primary education—a dropout of 93 percent—the ratio for the Philippines is

[15] Ministério da Educação e Cultura, *Comentários: Ensino Primário, 1959*, Rio de Janeiro (1961), p. 55.

[16] J. G. Duque, "Instrução e Educação," Fortaleza, Ceará, unpublished paper, 1962, p. 6.

[17] *Ibid.*, p. 7.

[18] Américo Barbosa de Oliveira and José Zacarias Sá Carvalho, *A Formação de Pessoal de Nivel Superior e o Desenvolvimento Econômico*, CAPES, Rio de Janeiro (1960), p. 30.

381 per 1000, for Liberia 300 per 1000, and for the United States 830 per 1000. In the case of secondary education, the Brazilian ratio is 16 per 1000; Liberian, 33; Philippine, 120; and the United States, 460. The educational pyramid in Brazil shows only 7 of the 1000 students who began primary education "surviving" at the final year of university training. This compares to 30 per 1000 in the Philippines and 130 per 1000 in the United States.[19]

The Northeast situation is, in general, much worse than the average for Brazil. A rough estimate suggests that in the Northeast for every 1000 students entering primary schools, only 46 conclude the primary course and only 2 finish university.

Explains a recent report by the special federal agency concerned with higher education (CAPES):

> The whole system, beginning in primary school, has a marked selective character. A progressive reduction in number of students is carried out by a system of examinations. . . . Since these examinations are based primarily on catalogs of memorized facts, it cannot be said that they select the more highly endowed, except perhaps within the type of intelligence most apt at this kind of learning.
>
> At the same time, such examinations perhaps explain why public opinion remains unmoved at the great waste of intelligence taking place in Brazil. The general impression is that the tests assure promotion of the most apt; this is based on the generally accepted idea that "academic" studies are really difficult, and that the restrictive demands of the examinations are therefore inherent to the nature of such studies. To this may be added the fact that all those who have passed the tests become enthusiastic defenders of the system, because they have gained prestige—they belong to the privileged group.[20]

In another commentary on the quality of Brazilian primary education Anísio Teixeira described it as: "somewhat shapeless and disordered, including at present congested state schools functioning in

---

[19] For the Philippines: Bureau of Public and Private Schools, *Statistical Bulletins*, Manila, and Bureau of the Census and Statistics, *Handbook Philippine Statistics* (Manila, 1960). For Liberia: *Our President Speaks*, Special Report on Education, Liberian Information Services (Monrovia, 1961). For the United States: U. S. Department of Health, Education and Welfare, *Digest of Educational Statistics* (Washington, 1962).

[20] CAPES, *Admissions to Universities and Higher Education, Isolated Institutions in Brazil*, A report prepared for the International Study of University Admissions by UNESCO, Brazilian Center of Educational Research, Rio de Janeiro (February 1962), p. 54.

two, three and even four sessions, municipal schools with generally
inadequate installations and unprepared professors, and independent
private schools—all simply teaching reading of a selective character.[21]

Formal Education: An Economic Approach

The reform of formal education in Brazil has been receiving growing attention in recent years. But the public and political debate,
mainly in terms of social welfare and state versus church schools, has
not been placed in an economic development framework. Educators
are leading the fight, and few of Brazil's economic development technicians have become actively interested in the human resource issue.
As a result, the ambitious social justice goals of the reform campaigns
are consistently being undercut by the harsh realities of scarce financial and personnel resources.

From an economic development point of view, it is not an easy
task to decide how much of scarce resources should go to education
and what should be the time schedule for programs of improved education. It is equally difficult to allocate educational resources efficiently among the needs for primary education, secondary education,
college and university training, vocational schools, professional
schools, and among teachers' salaries, school buildings, supplies, and
equipment. And the educators are frequently not too helpful in these
tasks. Unwilling to make difficult choices and assign priorities and
erroneously believing that everything can be done at once, educators
in many countries are responsible for wasting scarce resources under
the label of education.

Neither Brazil nor the Northeast can yet afford universal education.
Yet both need a greatly accelerated investment in human resources.
The answer to how much and where resources can be allocated can
come in large part from long-range manpower planning. Especially in
the Northeast, with its more serious educational problem and scarce
resources, such guidance and stimulus are critically needed for educational and training activities.

Northeast Brazil is underinvesting in primary and secondary education in relation to the greatly expanded capacity of its higher educa-

[21] Anísio Teixeira, *op. cit.*, p. 6.

tional institutions. (See Chapter 3, pp. 62-63.) The first steps to correct this situation appear to be a reduction in the primary school dropouts and a major expansion in secondary education, a field now left predominantly to privately owned facilities. Action at this level may be the most effective way of increasing the regional output of technical personnel from the higher educational institutions. It will relieve, also, the serious regional need for primary and secondary school graduates, who do not go on for university training, as supporting personnel in public and private agencies.

For its present stage of development, the Northeast might increase somewhat the share of secondary school graduates who continue with university training. Also, the proportion of primary school graduates who complete secondary training probably can be improved. The real challenge, nevertheless, is to increase the number of primary school completions and enlarge secondary level enrollment. These are the kinds of issues on which research and planning are urgently needed.

SUDENE and Other Programs

The Furtado report makes no mention of investment in human resources or education. Its discussion of surplus manpower and the need to enlarge the agricultural boundaries of the Northeastern economy is the closest the report comes to the subject. SUDENE's *Plano Quinquenal* touches on the question in its section on "Investments of a Social and Cultural Character." The plan concedes, however, that although classified as nonproductive social expenditures, investments in the educational sector can have an economic justification. The law of December 1961 approving SUDENE's plan contains no specific appropriations for manpower programs or human resources investment except for a "basic education" (*educação de base*) pilot project—an experiment in popular literacy training and health education.

The action proposed in the plan focuses almost exclusively on the problem of technical and scientific personnel and the universities. SUDENE plans to increase university enrollments for agronomists and engineers through scholarships and a special preparatory or cram course for university admission examinations. SUDENE also expects to play a continuing role, through its membership in GRUNE—a federally created coordinating committee for Northeast universities—in restructuring technical and scientific education in the region. The plan includes a project to strengthen the Rural University near Rio so that it can train professional staff for Northeast schools of agronomy and middle level personnel for the regional agro-technical schools. Another project is to expand the technical institute at João Pessoa where instructors will be prepared for other technical institutes.

A number of new universities have been opened recently in the Northeast and federal aid to the universities of Recife, Bahia, and Ceará has been greatly increased. But university enrollment has not been growing proportionately, and university facilities are greatly underused. As a result, the average cost per university student in the Northeast is more than double the national average. The SUDENE scholarship program hopes to increase the use of facilities by providing financial support for 300 agronomists and 200 engineers annually. Through this action, SUDENE projects an increase of 544 new agronomists and 384 engineers for the region by 1967.

The plan for restructuring the universities establishes priorities for the different types of professional training. It proposes to avoid duplication in postgraduate work by having the major universities specialize in different fields, to change the *catedratica* career and tenure system for professors, and to reform the curriculum. To facilitate the broad long-range plan, one immediate step will be to bring a number of foreign professors of international reputation to each of the three major universities to work in the postgraduate institutes. Foreign assistance in the basic sciences—physics, chemistry, and mathematics—is given a high priority.

SUDENE's program for scholarship assistance and for entrance examination coaching may increase temporarily the flow of students. But unless the basic supply of students going through the primary and secondary schools is increased, the permanent problem of an ever-increasing flow of professional, subprofessional, and literate personnel will not be touched.

A comparison of the restructuring goals and training priorities for the universities with the allocation of funds proposed for the institutions suggests that old rather than new patterns are still prevailing. Of the proposed expenditures for the 1961-65 period, programs in administration will receive about 4 percent as compared to 13 percent for odontology and pharmacy programs. Medicine, odontology, and pharmacy although placed in second priority—after agronomy, engineering, geology, veterinary sciences, and economics—end up with 40 percent of the total expenditures.[22]

The primary school situation received its first official attention from SUDENE in the second plan of October 1962. The state of Bahia had included an expansion program for education in its 1960 development plan. The state of Pernambuco and United States aid personnel had been working on a program for expanding primary school facilities which culminated in August 1962 in an AID project to finance 1,200 classrooms to be completed in 1962 and 1963. Incorporating the work underway and responding to the possibilities for foreign aid in this field, SUDENE established in its second plan a goal of 7,000 additional classrooms in primary schools by 1966 and the training of 6,000 additional school teachers.[23]

The secondary school situation, however, has thus far been neglected by both SUDENE and the United States aid program. Also, in the case of primary schools, SUDENE has emphasized that it will not become involved in questions of pedagogy and administration. It has limited its role to financing physical facilities up to 10 percent of the total cost of approved projects.

Primary and secondary schools, of course, are the legal responsibility of the state and local governments. And the distorted state and local tax potentials within Brazil previously discussed will be a major limitation on the improvement of primary and secondary education in the Northeast. With its great taxing potential, the state of São Paulo was able to budget for education expenditures in 1961 almost as much as all of the rest of the states in Brazil combined. And the local governments in the state of São Paulo budgeted for 1960 more than all the rest of the local governments in Brazil combined.

Vocational and In-Service Training

The Northeast must place heavy reliance for short- and medium-term manpower development on special training programs. It cannot

[22] *Plano Quinquenal de Desenvolvimento para o Nordeste 1961-1965*, Presidência de República, Superintendência do Desenvolvimento do Nordeste, Recife (1961) p. 176.

[23] *Plano Diretor do Desenvolvimento do Nordeste (Segunda Etapa) 1963-1965*, SUDENE, Recife (October 1962), pp. 31-33.

wait for the graduates of expanded primary schools to grow up. Therefore, the extent and type of training provided for employed manpower
is an important phase of the human resource issue. As Professor
Harbison explains:

> Training and education are quite different processes and planners
> should draw a sharp distinction between them. Training involves the
> development of specific skills which are needed to perform a par-
> ticular job or series of jobs. Education involves the acquisition of
> general knowledge and development of basic mental ability. Both
> training and education are involved in human capital formation.[24]

In the Northeast, the training facilities of vocational schools are
limited, and the training is not necessarily directed toward specific job
opportunities or the kinds of jobs hardest to fill. SUDENE's second
plan includes an ambitious program for improving and enlarging the
region's network of vocational schools. But a more effective strategy
might be that recommended by Harbison, namely, to shift as much
responsibility as possible for training to the major employing institutions rather than relying on costly vocational schools.

The Northeast has made some training progress through activities
of such agencies as the Bank of the Northeast and SUDENE. But
most federal agencies working in the area are not providing in-service
training, and virtually none of the state and local governments have
assumed this kind of responsibility. Furthermore, there is no official
pressure on business, industry, and agriculture to contribute to human
capital formation through training programs.

A Note on Agriculture

The traditional development approach for low income agriculture
like that of Northeast Brazil is to increase agricultural research and
to expand the availability of farm extension services, rural credit, improved seeds, subsidized fertilizer, and farm machinery. The objective
of these activities is to assist the farmer to improve his farming practices and to raise productivity in agriculture. This kind of a direct
approach has been tried to varying degrees in the Northeast and still
receives considerable popular and official support in the region.

[24] Frederick Harbison, *op. cit.*, p. 19.

In contrast to the traditional direct approach, this study suggests that key solutions to low productivity and poverty in Northeast agriculture lie in actions that must be taken outside of agriculture. The land and water resources of the Northeast are not adequate under conditions of efficient farming techniques to support or use effectively the region's large rural population. Agricultural progress, therefore, requires that a large share of present workers in agriculture be attracted into nonfarm employment in the Northeast or into the less densely populated farming areas of the country.

The SUDENE program gives emphasis to enlarging the land and water base for Northeast agriculture through irrigation projects in the San Francisco Valley, integrated development of the Jaguaribe and Alto-Piranhas river basins, improved exploitation of underground water resources, more intensive agricultural use of public lands, and soil conservation activities. Leaving aside the important question of costs versus benefits for specific projects, these activities are moving in a valid direction.

But assuming that the SUDENE projects are economically justified and successful, can they make a significant impact on the massive imbalance between people and resources in Northeast agriculture? With an estimated maximum irrigation potential of only 790,000 hectares for the Northeast and with half or three-fourths of the present farm population becoming redundant under conditions of enlarged family farm units of efficient and capital forming size, the potentials of present programs for improving significantly the agricultural situation of the region appear to be highly inadequate.

These kinds of activities should be continued and even enlarged if the specific projects are economically feasible and if they warrant a high priority in terms of their use of scarce resources in relation to their contribution to total development. But if they are sold to the region as the salvation of Northeast agriculture, they will encourage people to remain in farming and aggravate and retard the eventual solution of the agricultural problem. The most important step is to make the long-run solution of moving people out of agriculture well understood, widely accepted, and reasonably attractive. The implementation of this approach requires a rapid and sizable expansion of nonfarm jobs and assistance and encouragement for out-migration.

But even after the population pressure on limited agricultural re-

sources is relieved, the difficult problem of improving farming practices and levels of productivity is likely to persist. The traditional
approach of increasing the supply of technology and lowering the cost
of farm inputs through government programs has not had great success
in the Northeast and in many other low income agricultural areas of
the world. The principal bottleneck in stagnant rural areas has not
been the unavailability of assistance but the lack of demand, or even
willingness, to adopt new methods.

There is a story told in the South of the United States about the
farm extension worker who visited the old farmer to give him technical advice on the newest farming practices recently developed by
the agricultural research stations. "Why do you waste your time and
mine telling me about these new ideas," the farmer complained, "I
already know better than I do."

The absorption of technology and the creation of incentives for improving productivity in agriculture are difficult problems for which
easy answers are not available. Two approaches, however, hold out
great promise. Elementary and specialized education when made available to the peasants and their children can stimulate a greater receptivity or, hopefully, a greater demand, for improved technology.
Also, the expansion of profit-motivated agricultural processing industries and of factories producing fertilizers, insecticides, and other agricultural inputs can create economic incentives and stimulate the adoption of improved farm technology. In many countries, where the administrative capacity of government is not great for dealing with a
gigantic and dispersed agricultural sector, private industry with a
vested interest in increasing its supply of agricultural raw materials
or in selling its production to the farmers has been very effective in
stimulating agricultural progress.

SUDENE's Implementation Philosophy

The future issue selected for final comment—SUDENE's implementation philosophy—is clearly the most crucial. As Brazilians are well
aware, they have no shortage of plans—good and bad. But the implementation of plans is the real problem. To meet this challenge,
SUDENE has, for reasons of political expediency, followed a cen-

tralized approach and assumed direct operating responsibility for its major programs. For the future, SUDENE may rely heavily in executing its plans on new independent mixed corporations, which it has legal authority to create. The mixed corporation approach will permit SUDENE and private banks to lend money to the operating agencies to keep their work going, instead of annually interrupting their activities while waiting for government appropriations to be released.

The implementation issue is intimately related to the decentralized versus centralized planning approach. And in both cases the pragmatic question is not either/or but what combination of the extremes will be adopted.

The case for decentralized planning as an aid to implementation is strong. First, the technical results of the planning will be better. The operating personnel can contribute to the planning work their intimate knowledge of various situations and their judgments and suggestions regarding feasibility. Economic planning is such a complex responsibility that a central staff can rarely command sufficient knowledge and experience on all aspects of the problems it has to deal with. Also good planning personnel must have imagination and broad vision, but these necessary qualities can lead to "ivory tower" planning unless there is close contact with practical personnel.

Second, the personnel responsible for supporting and implementing the planning will be better informed on the problems, the proposed solutions, and the purposes of the plans when they participate in the planning. The educational process will contribute to better acceptance and more efficient execution of the planning work.

Finally, there will be a commitment by the operations personnel to the results of the planning process. The people responsible for the implementation at all levels will consider the planning programs as their own work. Highly centralized planning, on the other hand, may be received unsympathetically as the proposals of outsiders who do not know the real situation.

SUDENE, by devoting much of its own staff to direct operating responsibilities, might improve the chances for some of its plans being implemented. But such a policy would leave too few staff resources dedicated to the additional research and planning so urgently needed for the region. Moreover, it is not enough to prove that SUDENE with its large resources and selected talent can succeed in implementing selected projects. Instead, the test is whether the institutional capacity of the region can be raised to a more efficient level on a continuing basis. The potential for successful results thus becomes greatly enlarged beyond SUDENE's still limited operational capacity.

Many barriers confront a policy of decentralized planning and implementation, and many deviations will be forced by political and other pressures. But the prospects are by no means hopeless if there is a will to decentralize. One requirement will be to change the political commitment so that the political pressures are directly on the operating agencies rather than on SUDENE, as is now the case. Within such a setting, SUDENE can set up competition among the states and federal agencies by giving priority, for example, to the agricultural department of a state that is willing and reasonably competent to implement certain plans. This should stimulate other states to improve their administrative structure and competence in order to participate in these plans.

Another implication of a decentralized philosophy is that SUDENE will be working more with the least efficient agencies in order to increase their contribution to the regional effort. The tendency at present is to become most closely associated or to assume responsibility in the field where the best administrative jobs are already being done in order that SUDENE can share the success achieved in these fields.

In brief, a philosophy that does not encourage the use of all regional resources for planning and implementation is an unwarranted restriction on development prospects. SUDENE needs the know-how, experience, and administrative resources of many agencies in the region in order to fulfill Brazil's aspirations for Northeast development.

9

The Future of the Northeast and Foreign Aid

WITHIN THE ALLIANCE for Progress setting, Northeast Brazil has become a key testing ground for the validity and viability of this joint effort to "bring a better life to all the peoples of the continent." The tests will be threefold. Will the development results satisfy Brazil's minimum expectations? Will future events represent significant progress in terms of United States goals? And will the specific results and the way in which they are achieved be relevant to the aspirations of other Latin American areas?

In attempting to answer these questions, several points must be kept in mind. First, the Alliance is still predominantly a bilateral program between the United States and each of the Latin American countries, even though multilateral machinery such as the Inter-American Development Bank and the Organization of American States are used. The action being implemented will generally be the result of agreement between the United States and the specific recipient of foreign assistance.

Second, although foreign assistance under the Alliance for Progress represents mutual donor-recipient agreement on many aspects of development activities, the actuating circumstances and the goals to be satisfied by each of the parties are usually significantly different. The giver and the receiver must each secure consent, and account for his actions, in a different political forum. Each is subjected to a different set of political and time pressures. Each has different limitations for giving or receiving specific kinds of aid. The foreign assistance process, therefore, involves many potential conflicts between the parties.

Third, Northeast Brazil was singled out for special attention both by Brazil and the United States not because of promising development potentials, but because the area has serious social problems and because development progress was not considered satisfactory. The selection of the area for priority on a need basis creates inevitable biases toward welfare assistance programs rather than affirmative development assistance. And past events have given overemphasis to the bad features of the area, and little attention to a realistic evaluation of development potentials.

Finally, the goals of Brazil and the United States are reasonably clear at a high level of generality, such as to accelerate economic and social development. But a much greater degree of specificity is essential for guiding development efforts and, above all, for periodic evaluations of progress or success. The Northeast problem is particularly difficult because it brings to the fore the little explored question of regional factors in national development.

Unfortunately, the crucial questions of specific goals, realistic expectations, and the potential role of foreign assistance cannot be answered, as this final chapter will demonstrate, to the satisfaction of policy makers in either Brazil or the United States or of students of development. And the indecisive nature of the answers now available suggests a great urgency for giving additional attention to these matters. Can progress be measured without further clarification and rethinking of goals? Can programs be improved without a more accurate awareness of the limitations inherent in the situation? Can the effectiveness of foreign assistance be steadily increased without a better identification of the kinds of foreign aid most urgently needed? Above all, are current expectations realistic in terms of the magnitude and complexity of the task, the limitations confronting outside assistance efforts, and the inadequate current state of knowledge in the development field?

Northeast Development Prospects

In Northeast Brazil, as in most other underdeveloped areas, there is a serious shortage of objective technical information on resource potentials and development prospects. In the absence of adequate factual information, two sharply opposed points of view exist in Brazil regarding the Northeast. Many people are romantically and hopefully persuaded that the region has phenomenal resources, yet undiscovered, and dramatic development possibilities still unexploited. Many others, mainly from outside the region, are convinced that the resource endowment and expansion prospects are poor. Nordestino leaders use either the optimistic-opportunity or pessimistic-need position to ask for more assistance. The outsiders argue, instead, that the region should be abandoned.

Having committed themselves to Northeast development, both Brazil and the United States must give high priority to securing an accurate and comprehensive evaluation of the region's development prospects. In general, reasonable optimism is justified. And there should be no doubt that the Northeast has adequate potential for a level of development far beyond the stage it has reached.

The development possibilities of the Northeast must not be related solely or principally to physical resource potentials as is frequently done. The development success of Japan, for example, clearly illustrates that physical resources are only part of the picture. Development prospects also depend on human and institutional resources, as well as on external forces such as world commodity markets.

In most of these respects, the Northeast has favorable though incomplete indications of expansion possibilities. In the physical resources field there is the known hydroelectric potential of the Paulo Afonso project, at least 1,500,000 kilowatts, that is only partially used. The recently discovered phosphate rock deposits can support considerable additional fertilizer production. Petroleum production has expanded rapidly in the Northeast and prospects appear promising for further development.

The success of recent training programs and expanded educational facilities is evidence of favorable human resource potentials. The availability of surplus labor in the Northeast is both a problem and an opportunity for growth. The remarkable strengthening of entrepreneurship that has recently occurred is another encouraging sign. Growing regional markets have undoubtedly created many new opportunities for market-oriented manufacturing. The international markets for cotton, sugar, and sisal in particular, also appear reasonably promising for Northeast production.

The strongest argument supporting an optimistic assumption concerning Northeast prospects is the economic progress achieved in the recent past. The gains in agriculture, mining, industry, and trade are persuasive evidence that the region has accelerated its expansion momentum. Although past successes are not positive guarantees for the future, they are significant proof that the area can grow.

This reasonable optimism, however, should be qualified by two known factors. First, the Northeast as a region within a larger political unit will be much affected by policies and programs at the national level. The issue of inflation and price stability, for example, can greatly influence the prospects for economic expansion in the Northeast. The agencies responsible for Northeast development may have only limited control over such crucial factors. A second qualification is that the Northeast is largely a semiarid area and its agricultural situation must be adjusted accordingly. The soils are not rich, the periodic droughts will persist, and a continued high rate of population increase appears certain. The area cannot support its present population in agriculture at a reasonable level, let alone an increased population.

Brazil's Goals for the Northeast

To Brazil, the challenge of the Northeast is to accelerate economic and social development in the nation's most backward region, and thereby reduce actual and potential social and political disorder. As Roberto Campos prophetically warned in the mid-fifties: "Regional disparities can generate intolerable social tensions and a chronic climate of revolt."[1]

But these goals are too general to be operational and too vague to be used as measures of success at some future point of time. Unfortunately, the processes of planning, of popular education, and of political debate have not yet produced reasonably specific and generally accepted development goals. Economic goals are undoubtedly easier to agree on than political and social objectives. But even in this relatively easy field, the task is difficult and largely incomplete.

[1] Roberto de Oliveira Campos, "A Crise Econômica Brasileira," *Alguns Problemas Brasileiros*, Vol. II, Confederaçáo Nacional de Commercio, Rio de Janeiro (1955), p. 64.

Will a reduction in regional disparities within Brazil be considered success? If so, the Northeast was well on the road to success before the latest "big push" started. Contrary to the general belief in Brazil, the relative economic position of the Northeast has steadily improved in recent years.

Is the rate of economic growth a principal test, for example, the 2.5 percent per capita per year agreed on at Punte del Este as a minimum target? If so, the Northeast is probably already a success.

Is an "improved" distribution of income a condition for success? And if so, what kind of a redistribution is the target? This widely accepted goal is based on the assumption, rather than fact, that the gains of economic progress are not being distributed among the people in the underdeveloped countries, and the rich are becoming richer and the poor poorer. Yet no studies of income distribution exist in the Northeast nor has there been any effort to research this important issue.

This author's observations in the Northeast over the last eight years strongly persuade him that the lower and middle classes in the urban areas are sharing in economic progress. In all urban areas, including the "Mocambo" slums of Recife, people have become better dressed, better housed, better fed, and better transported. The rural areas seem least changed. But in view of the rapid rate of increase of the already excessive rural population, the rural sector of the Northeast has had on a per capita basis only limited economic progress to share.

The specific point at issue is not the greater validity of casual personal observations over the widely accepted conventional wisdom, but the need for greatly improved factual information as a foundation for setting valid and realistic economic goals. For decades, the Northeast was convinced that the federal government was collecting more in taxes from the region than it was spending in the region. Yet when the subject was eventually studied, the facts turned out to be the opposite of the accepted regional folklore.

In social and political development, Brazil's specific goals for the Northeast are even less crystallized than in the economic area. Celso Furtado recently attempted to outline some of these goals in his "Reflections on the Brazilian Pre-Revolution."[2] Much of the discussion for

[2] A Pré-Revolução Brasileira, Editôra Fundo de Cultura, Rio de Janeiro (1962), Chap. 1.

obvious reasons does not separate national and regional goals. Also, although Furtado's position as an intellectual leader has strong support in the Northeast, particularly among university students, it is difficult to know the extent to which his ideas represent a regional consensus on social and political objectives.

The ultimate goals of development are humanist, Furtado argues, but these human objectives "can only be achieved if we organize ourselves to attain and maintain a high rate of economic development." To avoid the alternative of revolution, he continues, "we need a plan of economic and social development equal to our possibilities and in harmony with the desires of our people." At a somewhat more specific level, he makes a number of recommendations. The agrarian structure of the country must be modified—by constitutional measures. The governmental administrative machinery, the fiscal system, and the banking structure must be basically changed. Governmental action must be subordinated to a clear definition of the objectives of economic and social development. The parliament should establish policies, but local politicians must be deprived of the power to allocate public moneys. The government needs means to punish those who mismanage public funds, to control superfluous consumption, and to dignify government service. Brazil needs legal authority to discipline foreign capital and subordinate its action to Brazil's development objectives and political independence. Finally, Furtado emphasizes that a major goal of development is to "bring back within the country, its centers of decision," that is, to increase Brazil's control over its own destiny.

Although the process of formulating goals has picked up momentum and become an important phase of the development process itself, it is apparent that Brazil has not yet decided specific development objectives for the Northeast. Nor has a consensus emerged regarding what can be reasonably expected for the region. Many of the social and political goals mentioned by Furtado will require both decision and action at the national level. And for some time to come, a clear picture of what will constitute success in the Northeast project from the Brazilian standpoint is unlikely to emerge. In fact, it is safe to conclude that this indeterminate and changing situation concerning goals and expectations will be the normal working environment for foreign aid efforts in Northeast Brazil during the foreseeable future.

The Brazilian viewpoint on the appropriate role that foreign assistance can play is also unclear. SUDENE has legal authority to coordinate all foreign assistance to Northeast Brazil, but it has not yet
shown much interest in using this authority to develop comprehensive
long-range plans on foreign assistance needs. Furtado's observations
that development should bring the decision centers within the country
and that foreign capital must subordinate itself to Brazil's development objectives and political independence are unmistakable hints that
whatever assistance the Northeast receives will be on Brazil's terms
and in a way that leaves Brazil with the maximum control over its own
destiny.

Even more foreboding is the "unofficial" position recently articulated by the deputy head of SUDENE, Francisco Oliveira.[3] In his
view, foreign aid is not at present an effective development tool for the
underdeveloped countries. Multilateral aid has many defects, among
which is the lack of a specialized United Nations agency dedicated
to technical assistance for industrialization. Bilateral aid is basically
motivated by the cold war and the desire to transform the aid-receiving country into an example of the merits of the donor country's system. Foreign aid, he adds, is too often used as "insurance against
revolutions" with the undesirable effect of frustrating the dynamics of
the social process and causing stagnation. Many foreign aid experts
have urged that the aid program needs a "mystique" that can capture
for it popular support in the aid-receiving countries. But the only help
that makes sense is that which reinforces legitimate and authentic national programs for development and that does not impose from the
outside a "mystique" or any other goals that are not of a national
character.

Such attitudes toward foreign aid portend some bitter conflicts between SUDENE, when and if it begins to exercise its authority in the
foreign field, and the suppliers of foreign aid. The United States, for
example, has not channeled all of its Northeast assistance through this
group, which has legal responsibility for coordinating foreign assistance. A growing amount of United States technical assistance in agriculture has been coming to the region through ETA, the United States-

[3] Francisco Oliveira, "O Nordeste e a Cooperação Internacional," SUDENE,
Recife, November 1962, a speech presented to the Center for International
Studies of the University of Recife and the Pernambuco Student Union.

Brazil service operating on a national basis, and without any coordination with SUDENE plans or priorities. SUDENE's thinking in the housing field is to rely heavily, but not exclusively, on the administrative capacity of private enterprise, which can act with great flexibility and free from political pressures. The specific plan is to stimulate the construction of workers' housing projects as a complement to industrial expansion projects through special loans to the industrial enterprises. Yet, without working through SUDENE, officials of the Inter-American Development Bank have been negotiating directly with public agencies in the region, such as the city of Recife, on loans to expand government housing activities.

SUDENE officials have not requested any Peace Corps assistance on the grounds that a more urgent need is for high level technical experts. Through other channels, the United States has promoted and approved Peace Corps projects for the Northeast. In primary education, also, the United States has developed its projects directly with the state governments, and SUDENE has been brought in only at the final contract signing stage.

In the case of primary education, the United States has explained that this field is the legal responsibility of the state and local governments, that a number of state governors in the Northeast are dissatisfied with SUDENE and that primary education has been neglected in SUDENE development plans. These points are true, but a more fundamental issue is involved. The Alliance for Progress and the United States Agency for International Development are committed to working within comprehensive regional and national planning that assigns priorities among competing demands for scarce resources. If circumvented by aid donors, the institutions established by the aid-recipient countries to implement comprehensive planning can be fatally weakened.

The Goals of Foreign Aid Contributors

What do the foreign aid contributors expect to see accomplished in Northeast Brazil? And, more specifically, what would the United States as the principal donor consider as success from its foreign aid efforts? In part, Northeast Brazil is recognized as a challenge to the welfare and humanitarian urges of the United States. More important, however, given the background of the United States commitment in Northeast Brazil and the United States political realities of securing resources for foreign aid activities, the Northeast represents a political security challenge—a major Castro-Communist "threat" to the Western Hemisphere. As one top Brazilian official observed, "When we discussed our development problems in Washington during 1961, one senior United States senator, after listening for several hours, made his one and only comment as follows: 'You mean that aid to the Northeast will stop Communism?'" And the Brazilian added, "That's all he wanted to know."

With political goals being so important, the United States needs a clear picture of the specific kinds of political developments in Northeast Brazil that would be considered successful foreign aid results. The development of such criteria requires, of course, a thorough knowledge of Brazil's political system and political styles, including a sophisticated and objective understanding of communism, left wing movements, nationalism, anti-Americanism, and the roles of the church and the military within the Brazilian setting. To interpret Brazilian political events within the context of United States political standards and characteristics, for example, will result both in ineffective guidance for foreign aid actions and in erroneous evaluations of the results.

The problem of understanding and evaluating political development in Northeast Brazil is very difficult. The general Brazilian situation is not conducive to careful and unemotional judgments. The explosive pressures for change have generated a Communist hysteria in Brazil. A strong tendency exists, on the part of apparently responsible leaders, to label all social reform leaders as Communists. Celso Furtado, for example, has been so labeled by some leading government officials.

Northeast Brazil has a long tradition of political turbulence, and the growing hemispheric social and political ferment has fallen on fertile ground in this region. But the Communist–anti-Communist dichotomy is not appropriate for interpreting the Northeast. The current governor of Pernambuco, who has been frequently labeled a Communist, has observed, "Left and Right have little meaning in a country like Brazil. It only makes sense if one speaks of those who want to maintain the old structure and those who do not." The Peasant League, for example, is a social reform movement with Communist support. But it also has widespread support from priests, university professors, and even government officials, who are not Communists.

Political science as a field for professional training and research is not well developed in Brazil.[4] There are no scientific studies available on political parties, philosophies, and history. Furthermore, the United States has little experience and has not developed adequate background for understanding and evaluating political development in the Northeast. If political issues continue to be of supreme importance in foreign aid efforts, as is almost certain in the case of Northeast Brazil, the United States needs to make a major commitment of highly qualified personnel to this problem.

Although the Communist party is legally banned in Brazil, Communist groups are not in fact prevented from being politically active. This situation suggests a radically different set of attitudes on the Communist question in Brazil than prevails in the United States. Many who are not Communists in Brazil do not object to working with Communists toward social reform goals and think that the Communist party should be legalized. Some who are not Communists even believe that the party can be a useful safety valve and a maturing experience for politically active young people. This point of view would probably interpret an increase in the number of Communists and Communist organizations as a stage of political development rather than as political failure.

Basic changes in the Northeast's rural structure are inevitable. The shocking feudal and sharecropper conditions of millions of Nordestino peasants have to improve radically. In order to avoid revolution, the frightened and short-sighted vested interests in agriculture and industry need to understand and become associated with necessary and inevitable reforms. And to achieve its own political objectives, the United States must not accept the indiscriminate labeling of social reformers as Communists and thereby preclude cooperating with the inexorable reform movements—even the Peasant Leagues.

[4] Through the influence of Professor Orlando M. Carvalho of the University of Minas Gerais and his *Revista Brasileira de Estudos Politicos,* however, political science is more advanced in Brazil than elsewhere in Latin America.

Foreign Aid Issues

A counterpart of the previous discussion of goals and future development issues is the role that foreign assistance can play in the development of Northeast Brazil. A simplified approach to this question would recognize that foreign aid is a two-sided operation; that Brazil will be guided by a determination of the regional development needs that cannot be supplied by Brazil in the relatively near future; that the United States and other donors will emphasize the kinds of assistance that promise to achieve their goals; and that chances for success increase directly with the size of the mutually agreed upon outside help.

In practice, however, the problem is much more complex and difficult. Foreign assistance can hinder as well as help in development. It may have limited potential for achieving the donor's goals. The donor may not have easily available or may be restricted in giving the types of aid that are needed, whereas what is easiest for the donor to give may not be what is needed or desired. Furthermore, even where assistance is given that is mutually acceptable and consistent with priority needs, the degree of success that can be realistically expected is relatively low.

For Good or for Bad

How can foreign donors hinder development efforts? Simply by giving the wrong kind of assistance, the wrong amount, and in the wrong way. Foreign assistance does not come at "no cost" to the recipient. Invariably, he must consume scarce domestic resources—personnel, administrative and financial—as counterpart matching or simply to participate in the transaction. It is difficult for a country to refuse offers of assistance, particularly when virtually all kinds of help are needed. But when scarce resources are employed to receive and properly use one type of aid, there is an "opportunity cost" in administrative talent, and counterpart requirements are not available for other activities which may have much higher priority at the particular stage of development. In some situations, however, where domestic resources may not be easily transferred from one type of project to another, the opportunity cost is very low.

The United Nations Special Fund project for the San Francisco Valley, for example, was virtually impossible for the Brazilians to refuse because of domestic political considerations. In early 1962, this one project was consuming the full time of about 10 percent of the total SUDENE technical staff. The objectives of determining the physical and economic feasibility of introducing large-scale irrigation in the lower middle reaches of the basin are commendable in themselves and as a training experience for regional personnel. But even if the evaluations are favorable—a highly uncertain assumption—the potential contribution to employment and regional production from a successful project are relatively small compared to other possible activities that are not proceeding.

The wrong kind of aid can also have the negative effect of discouraging domestic economic expansion. Surplus food may give significant short-term benefits to the consumer, but it may also reduce the price incentives of the market for expanded domestic production. Easy access to foreign exchange for importing foreign machinery may make the textile manufacturer happy by reducing his outlays, but it may also frustrate the expansion possibilities for an incipient domestic machinery industry.

An excessive amount of aid, in relation to the recipient's capacity to absorb and use it effectively, can also hinder development and result in great disillusionment and frustration. An increase in United States aid to Northeast Brazil from an annual level of about $250,000 to $65,000,000 sounds like fabulous progress. But unless the kinds and amount of aid have been carefully related to the quality and quantity of the recipient's aid-receiving capacity, many activities are doomed to failure merely by the overwhelming size of the task. Again, it should be emphasized that it is almost impossible for foreign help to be turned down.

Aid, even for priority activities, given in the wrong way can also be harmful to economic, social, and political development. The housing field is one that may become an example of the wrong way of providing outside assistance. As discussed in Chapter 8, primary emphasis on short-term results, in the form of a specified number of housing units created within a given time period, rather than on the permanent improvement of the domestic housing industry, can have a negative impact on economic and social goals. The development of an effective regional coordination agency, considered as a necessary political step by both donors and the recipient of foreign aid, can be seriously retarded by the channeling of foreign assistance through the state and local governments, which may be the most friendly to the donor but which do not have the capacity to implement programs. The most promising forces for political and social development such as SUDENE may not be the most compatible groups with which the donors of foreign aid can work. But the strengthening of the more compatible groups, by making them the channels for foreign assistance, may harden the resistance to essential basic reforms.

The Donor's Potential for Achieving His Goals

Probably the weakest link in the donor's rationalization for offering foreign aid is the assumption that he has a promising potential for achieving his goals—particularly those of a political security nature. This is a crucial assumption that remains to be proved in the case of the Alliance for Progress. The strong and inevitable anti-Americanism and nationalism in Latin America are important limitations on the donor. The lack of an effective set of foreign aid tools is another limitation. And the nature of the task—trying to achieve certain preferred political patterns—is such that the process must be participated in and accomplished by domestic forces.

The Alliance for Progress gives heavy emphasis to improvement in health, education, and housing. But how valid is the implicit assumption that improved social conditions will result in more stable and more democratic political systems? Argentina and Venezuela have the highest per capita incomes in Latin America, yet for some years they have been the most unstable. Is political maturity and orientation a goal that can be guaranteed by the construction of a given number of houses, water systems, or school buildings? And isn't it the momentum of an economy rather than its level that is most important as a necessary but not sufficient condition for social and political development? It is the lack of momentum in Argentina and Venezuela that has contributed to the crises and instabilities rather than the low absolute level of economic welfare.

Another serious problem is the conflicting needs of the donor and the recipient to receive credit for development results. Given the long-standing and persistent anti-Americanism and growing nationalism in Latin America, what "respectable" Latin American politician can press for social reform because it is a condition of receiving aid from the United States? Realistically, he must take credit for reforms and he must demonstrate his political independence from the "Yankee imperialists." On the other hand, the United States foreign aid agencies must persuade their political forum, as a condition of continued support, that they have been responsible for achieving a significant amount of social and political progress in Latin America. Can these conflicting needs be resolved?

What foreign assistance tools exist for achieving social and political goals such as land and tax reform? The donor might be able to supply technical advice and specific plans for accomplishing these goals. The donor might also have leverage to coerce the recipient by withholding or cutting off outside assistance. But the recipient must have the will and the domestic political power to take tangible steps. Can coercion or technical plans supply the domestic political capacity to undertake the reforms?

There are situations, of course, where the promise of foreign assistance will motivate recipient countries to fulfill certain conditions, such as preparing a long-range plan, or will give decisive support to existing reform movements. But if the long-term plan is a special effort of the moment or the social reform is only possible when outside support comes into the picture, are these results really significant? If comprehensive planning is a desirable goal, it must be on a continuous basis and well integrated with the machinery of implementation. A plan document is relatively easy to produce, but it is not evidence that a planning process has been created. Specific social reforms may be highly desirable, but more important is a permanent improvement in the capacity of a country through its political machinery to continually and ever more effectively meet the desires of the people. This is a domestic process that must be improved by domestic performance.

Available Assistance Versus Needed Assistance

The giver and the receiver frequently encounter conflicting situations related to their different political forums. For example, the expansion of petroleum production in Brazil—an activity centered in the Northeast—has a top priority within Brazil as a means of conserving foreign exchange. The United States aid program, however, has not been able to assist the nationalized petroleum industry in Brazil because of the influence of private interests on the United States political scene. It did go so far in May 1962, however, as to offer assistance in developing Brazil's oil shale deposits as an energy source.

On the other hand, it is easy for the United States to supply surplus food items because of its domestic farm situation. In certain cases, surplus food has aided development greatly by financing the use of surplus labor on high priority and labor intensive construction projects. But, insofar as surplus food becomes a charity program and thereby violates the sensitivities of the Latin Americans, or affects the price incentives for encouraging local agricultural production, or appears to be an effort to export a United States domestic problem, the recipient countries are reluctant to accept this aid.

A related problem arises out of the over-all shortage of experts who are prepared to give the most necessary types of technical assistance. By emphasizing comprehensive country planning, agrarian reform, revision of tax systems, and by agreeing to help finance technical assistance in these fields, the United States has created an effective demand for experienced and trained experts far beyond the capacity of the United States and other countries to supply. The United States has long supported training programs for nationals of the underdeveloped countries, but it has been slow to recognize the need for preparing an adequate number of United States personnel to meet the demands for outside help. Nor has the United States yet tackled the problem of making it easier for experienced executives in government and private industry to undertake foreign assignments without sacrificing or risking their domestic careers. Many kinds of high priority expertise are not easily available in the United States—advisers on national planning, for example—and the shortage of experts is likely to persist unless positive steps are taken.

Realistic Expectations for Project Successes

Even when competent experts or appropriate financial aid is available for foreign assistance projects, the realistic chances for success are generally much lower than the expectations of the donor and the receiver. It would be miraculous if between one-third and one-half of the projects were successful.

Great political instability is characteristic of most recipient countries. How can continuity in foreign aid or even domestic projects be expected when Brazil has five presidents in less than eighteen months, as occurred in 1954-56, or when the president resigns after only seven months in office as Jânio Quadros did in August 1961? How fast can results be expected when formidable pressures exist for dramatic accomplishments within unprecedentedly short periods of time? How efficient can programs be when one of the crucial problems of the underdeveloped countries is the shortage of trained and experienced personnel and seasoned institutions? How honest can administration be when unusually large amounts of money are expended quickly in an unprepared environment?

Given the problems of recruiting top-level experts, of their adaptation to a strange environment, of mobilizing counterpart personnel, and many other serious difficulties inherent in the entire process of foreign assistance, is it reasonable to expect quick and satisfactory results to flow from more than a minority of aid projects?

Foreign Aid Suggestions for Northeast Brazil

Although the specific economic, social, and political goals of Brazil and the United States still have not been formulated, and although development programing for the region is still in an early stage, a major joint development program has been launched and is underway in Northeast Brazil. Realistically, therefore, the further tasks of goal formulation and development programing will have to proceed along side of, rather than in advance of, domestic and foreign aid commitments to specific activities. Hopefully, a reasonable share of the on-going effort will eventually contribute to a successful development pattern, the precise nature of which is still unknown.

Within this changing setting, and recognizing the many limitations discussed above, foreign assistance can play an important role in the economic and social development of Northeast Brazil. It can help in the task of goal formulation, and it can accelerate the momentum and improve the efficiency of development activities that clearly merit priority attention. But it should also be remembered that the assumption that foreign assistance, through economic and social welfare accomplishments, can have much influence on political trends is conjectural and remains to be confirmed.

Foreign assistance opportunities will change, of course, as the Northeast progresses and as the foreign aid donors better prepare themselves for the role they have accepted. At this early stage of events, however, the Northeast offers much greater opportunities for technical assistance, in the form of high level manpower on extended assignments, than for financial aid.

National Development Planning

The establishment of national comprehensive development planning which incorporates regional factors is a top priority need for the Northeast project and a leading opportunity for foreign assistance. Both the Alliance for Progress and the United States emphasize comprehensive *national* plans as a basis for the granting of foreign assistance. The United States deviated from this cardinal principle in its initial commitments to Northeast Brazil, but an agreement was signed in July 1962 for United States aid to improve effective planning on national and regional levels, through Brazil's recently established National Planning Council.

Brazil has long accepted in principle the desirability of national planning but its central government has had great difficulty implementing the idea. Foreign aid donors can help the federal government follow a direction it would like to follow by insisting that regional plans be integrated into the national planning process and by supplying outside experts who can supplement Brazil's still limited professional talent in the economic programing field. Such outside help should, of course, work under the direction of and be responsible to the Brazilian government.

It is attractive politically, and superficially it appears logical, to concentrate development activities for the Northeast within the Northeast. But the best available evidence, such as the case of the Southeast in the United States and even Southern Italy, strongly indicates that forces at the national level and in outside regions may be among the most effective means of reducing regional disparities and stimulating growth in the poorer regions.

Development Research and Planning for the Northeast

The first Northeast plan, as explained previously, was predominantly a collection of projects that were available when the plan was prepared rather than the projects most necessary for Northeast development. The subsequent plans still do not embrace the funds and activities of state and local governments nor integrate several federal activities in the Northeast such as PETROBRAS, nor include the private sector and its potential for regional development. Furthermore, SUDENE has deferred much of the additional planning work needed in favor of direct operations by the SUDENE staff. And the SUDENE organization contains most of the experienced planning and research personnel of the region.

Foreign assistance has an unusual opportunity to enlarge and strengthen development research and planning because many of the needs are of a type in which Northeast know-how and personnel are scarce. Technical assistance in manpower planning, including education, in industrial development research and planning, and in basic investigations of physical resources such as soils and minerals, should receive high priority in foreign aid programs. Some of the assistance can be in the form of physical research equipment, but most of the help should consist of technical experts.

Assistance in Implementation and Administration

Foreign assistance can do much to improve public and private administration in Brazil and to strengthen the implementation of high priority programs in fields, such as industrial development and educational reform, where Brazilian resources are weak. Experts in government administration who are prepared to spend one or two years working within Brazilian institutions can help to improve the situation on a practical and day-by-day basis. Executive training programs for businessmen, a field in which the United States has great experience, can be adapted to the Brazilian environment and have an excellent potential for improving levels of administration.

The Private Sector

As Celso Furtado has emphasized: "It would not be possible to solve the problem of the Northeast by limiting our preoccupations to the public sector."[5] Yet only a small start has been made in examining the potentials and stimulating expansion in the private sector. Foreign assistance can be extremely valuable in preparing specific new industry opportunity studies, in helping to establish affirmative industrial promotion programs, in developing financial institutions to meet the growing needs of business and in stimulating a rapid expansion in such an important field as the housing industry.

From an economic development rather than social welfare point of view, housing may warrant high priority as a source of increased employment and a major stimulus to industrial expansion. The production of housing materials generally requires little in the way of foreign exchange. It is labor intensive and exploits local raw materials. Capital requirements for factories producing housing materials are relatively modest. The necessary technical and management know-how is relatively easy to find in the area or to develop—in contrast to the requirements for more complex industries such as steel and chemicals. Moreover, specialized financial institutions when established in the region can generate additional savings to finance consumer demand so that the housing field is not competing for the scarce capital already available. The critical type of outside help needed in the housing field is technical assistance.

Financial Aid

The above proposals have given little emphasis to outside financial aid because the personnel, administrative, and institutional development problems are clearly the principal limitations on Northeast development at this stage. Private capital is available according to SUDENE, but it is flowing out of the region to the South. It is well known that large amounts of foreign exchange are being hoarded or

[5] Celso Furtado, "A Luta pela Nordeste e a Estratégia da SUDENE," January 1962 (mimeo.).

invested overseas by Brazilians. Isn't it more important to reverse these
flows by creating an atmosphere of opportunity in the Northeast and
by restoring confidence in Brazil at the national level than to substitute
foreign aid for Brazilian funds that are flowing out of the region and
the country?

The principal foreign exchange needs identified under current
Northeast development programs are for electrical power facilities, the
rehabilitation of the textile industry, and other industrial expansion.
But even in these cases, the best form of aid may be for the expansion
of Brazilian industries to produce previously imported products. Where
foreign exchange is needed, it can be supplied from the special allocation of foreign exchange earnings available to SUDENE and by
international loans for specific private and public projects. Probably
the foreign exchange component of the Northeast development program will increase greatly over time, but at the early stages the need
for direct foreign exchange assistance does not appear to be large.

The general argument can be made for hard currency or dollar aid
to the Northeast, even though the foreign exchange is used for projects
that are not in the Northeast, that this will permit the national government to make more local currency available to the region. This then
becomes a question whether aid to the Northeast is a desirable technique for solving a national foreign exchange problem.

The United States has control over substantial amounts of Brazilian
currency through the sale of surplus agricultural products to Brazil
and a significant share of these resources has recently been made
available to the Northeast under the United States aid program. But in
the absence of national planning, it has not been demonstrated that
this is the best allocation of these funds from either the national or
regional point of view. The same funds might give more help to the
Northeast if they were applied to resettlement projects in Mato Grosso
and Goiás.

United States Agricultural Surpluses

The role United States surplus food can play in Northeast development deserves careful attention, in part because of the strong pressures within the United States for including a large surplus food component in foreign assistance programs. Surplus food can be effectively

used in the Northeast as emergency reserves for drought periods as soon as a network of storage facilities is available in the region. School lunch programs and food as payment to redundant labor working on new public works projects may be justified. Some food to support charitable activities by religious and other private organizations may also be useful.

The use of agricultural surpluses, however, requires great caution and considerable imagination because the possibilities are very real for retarding overall development through large-scale food grants. The general resentment evoked by charitable activities and the widespread awareness that the program results from a United States domestic problem have already been mentioned. The likelihood that outside food surpluses will reduce incentives for increased production has also been emphasized. Another grave danger is that a large amount of scarce Brazilian administrative talent will be consumed on such projects and not be available for activities that permanently increase the productive capacity of the region. Finally, the United States pressures are such that surplus food aid is likely to be made available on a continuing basis, an approach which makes any foreign assistance for development purposes self-defeating.

Short-Term Versus Long-Term Projects

Probably the most difficult question in the development and foreign assistance field is the appropriate mix of short-term projects that produce immediate visible results and longer-range programs that are more fundamental. If the short-term projects do not consume scarce resources, such as administrative talent needed on the long-range projects, there is no dilemma. And if the short-term projects are integral parts of the long-range efforts, there is little problem. But frequently this is not the case. From the political standpoint, both foreign aid donors and development officials of the recipient countries, through unrealistic promises, have placed themselves in a position where they must show results in a very short time. Thus the battle cry of both parties easily becomes, "We must show some dramatic results in a hurry." The projects selected are generally not consistent with the time sequences and activity priorities essential for development success.

To disagree with both Brazilian and United States officials on the current emphasis given to short-term impact projects in Northeast Brazil, can result in charges that the author is too academic or too distant from the political realities. But on the basis of several years of intimate involvement in Northeast political economic development and additional years as a close observer, the author seriously questions the judgments and analysis which give such heavy emphasis to quick and dramatic impact projects.

The first objection to most impact projects is that they don't work. It is inconceivable that enough school buildings, electric light installations, water systems, and new housing units can be built in a short period of time to satisfy more than a minute share of total needs. Therefore, the assumption must be that if the "have-not" sees the new physical facilities, he will be convinced that the development program he is being asked to support is eventually going to help him. The basic goal, therefore, involves expectations rather than immediate fulfillment. And the Nordestino is cynical enough after many years of promised panaceas to need more than the sight of Señor X—who generally has good political connections—getting new facilities to persuade him that his future is brighter.

A second objection is that the short-term projects generally do not tackle the fundamental problems and have only transitory results. The fundamental economic challenge in the Northeast is to enlarge employment opportunities and increase regional productivity. Improved welfare services are important as investments in human beings, but if they are not accompanied by progress on the employment and production fronts they cannot create a permanent change in expectations. The most persuasive type of activity is one that promises to make development self-sustaining.

A third question involves a likely misconception regarding the political goal of development and foreign assistance programs. The Alliance for Progress is not a popularity contest nor a popular crusade. How relevant are the newspaper reports that few people have heard of the Alliance, that few Latin Americans love the United States, and that the Alliance has failed to spark the imagination and stir the emotions of the masses? The problem instead is one of reducing political explosions and political resistance to necessary development activities. The latter goal may well be accomplished without popularity and crusade tests of success.

But the foreign aid administrator will argue that he needs immediate results to get appropriations from the United States Congress, and the local politician will argue that he needs the impact projects to get re-elected. Generally overlooked in the debate is the fact that the foreign aid administrators and the local politicians have been largely responsible for creating the short-time horizon within which they claim to be imprisoned. This author is strongly convinced from personal experience that the time horizons can be made more realistic in Brazil by sincere and widespread efforts to educate people concerning the complexities of development and by involving large numbers of private and public officials in the development effort, as one form of education. A similar extension of the time horizon needs to be secured from the United States public and the United States Congress. It is encouraging that a growing awareness of the long-range nature of the foreign assistance effort seems to be developing.

Foreign Assistance Planning and Preparation

Foreign assistance, like the process of development itself, requires long-range planning, advance preparation, and the assignment of priorities. The availability of local resources for absorbing and using outside assistance is a separate question from that of the overall availability of resources for development. And the scarcity of the former requires that the matter of foreign assistance priorities be constantly under review and that difficult choices be made among alternative types and amounts of foreign assistance.

Over time, the receiver can improve his ability to absorb assistance, and the giver can enlarge his supply of high priority and scarce types of aid. Long-range planning of foreign assistance can greatly improve the chances that the necessary steps will be undertaken.

Implications for the Alliance for Progress

The Northeast Brazil project was proclaimed in 1962 by the United States as "one of the most ambitious projects yet taken under the Alliance for Progress." The project, however, does not follow in many respects the pattern laid out in the Alliance agreements. It is not based on a national development plan, and the regional plan does not contain many elements of development programs that were considered essential, such as "the establishment of mutually consistent targets," and an identification of "the basic fiscal and monetary policies to be followed in order to permit implementation of the program within a framework of price stability." It does not include certain reform programs such as the reform of the tax structure. And it does not emphasize, as does the Alliance agreement, "the improvement of human resources."

Nevertheless, the successes and failures in Northeast Brazil will have important implications for the broad hemispheric program. A crucial question, then, is whether the Northeast program will be undertaken in such a way that the results can be considered transferable to other areas. In other words, the accomplishments in Northeast Brazil must be predominantly those of the Brazilians and be achieved under foreign assistance conditions that other areas can reasonably expect to duplicate.

United States expectations for the Alliance have been swinging in extreme cycles. Optimism was high when the program was announced in early 1961. But at the end of the first year, pessimism about the program was the rule. One of the principal recommendations for change evoked by the pessimism is that several areas with reasonably good development prospects should be selected as demonstration areas to show the rest of Latin America what can be accomplished. This suggestion is similar to the pattern widely followed in Latin American agriculture of spending large amounts of resources on special demonstration farms or experiment stations of the government to show what can be done. The result is that the projects usually have no impact on training practices in areas immediately joining the experiment stations. The approach doesn't work because the farmer knows that the government is using talent and resources that he cannot duplicate. The test per se is not to produce crops, or build houses, schools, and factories. Everybody knows that this is possible. The test is to show that the institutions and capacity of the underdeveloped countries can become sufficiently effective to do these things on a self-sustaining basis.

The way in which United States foreign aid discovered Northeast Brazil and the traditional political patterns of the region have created unfortunate and unjustified pessimism about the development potential of Northeast Brazil. An objective evaluation of the area, however, supports a position of reasonable optimism. The region will encounter many difficulties, and development efforts will have their ups and downs. But the greatly increased capacity of the Brazilians for developing this area and high quality foreign assistance can produce favorable results for the Northeast and useful experience for the Alliance for Progress in general. The region can be a valuable training ground for foreign aid personnel and an experimental area for improving foreign assistance knowledge and tools, particularly as related to the widespread problem of underdeveloped regions in underdeveloped countries.

Glossary of Abbreviations

ANCAR	Associação Nordestino de Credito e Assistência Rural Supervised Rural Credit Agency for the Northeast
BNB	Banco do Nordeste do Brasil Bank of the Northeast of Brazil
BNDE	Banco Nacional do Desenvolvimento Econômico National Development Bank
CAPES	Campanha Nacional de Aperfeiçoamento de Pessoal de Nível Superior Federal agency concerned with higher education
CBAI	Commissão Brasileira de Aprendizagem Industrial Brazilian-American Commission for Industrial Education
CEMIG	Centrais Elétricas de Minas Gerais, S/A Electric Power Company of Mina Gerais
CHESF	Companhia Hidrelétrica do São Francisco San Francisco Hydroelectric Company
CNAT	Commissão Nacional de Assistência Técnica National Technical Assistance Commission
CODENO	Conselho de Desenvolvimento do Nordeste Economic Development Council for the Northeast
COTEF	Consultoria Técnica de Assuntos Econômicos e Financeiros Technical Office for Economic and Financial Affairs
CVSF	Commissão do Vale do São Francisco San Francisco Valley Commission
DNOCS	Departmento Nacional de Obras Contra as Sêcas National Department of Works Against the Drought
ECLA	Economic Commission for Latin America (UN)
ECOSOC	Economic and Social Council (UN)
ETA	Escritório Técnico de Agricultura Joint Brazil-United States Agricultural Service
ETENE	Escritório Técnico de Estudos Econômicos do Nordeste Office of Technical Studies and Economic Planning of Bank of the Northeast

203

GRUNE	Grupo de Reequipamento Técnico Coordinating Committee for Northeast Universities
GTDN	Grupo de Trabalho Para o Desenvolvimento do Nordeste Working Group for Northeast Development
IADB	Inter-American Development Bank
IBGE	Instituto Brasileiro de Geografia e Estatística Brazilian Institute of Geography and Statistics
ILO	International Labour Organisation (UN)
NEC	Conselho Nacional de Econômica National Economic Council
⌈OEA	Organização Estados Americanos
⌊OAS	Organization of American States
SALTE	Saúde Alimentação, Transporte, Energia Health, food, transportation, energy
SESP	Serviço Especial de Saúde Publica Special Service of Public Health
SPVEA	Superintendência do Plano de Valorização Econômica da Amazônia Superintendency for the Economic Valorization Plan of the Amazon
SUDENE	Superintendência do Desenvolvimento do Nordeste Superintendency for Development of the Northeast

Index

Abbink, John, 90, 123

Accioly Borges, Pompeu, 135

Acre, 37

Act for International Development, 123

Administration: Of development programs, 194; training in, 96, 163

Agency for International Development (AID), 16, 142, 143, 162, 171, 184

Agreements (U.S.-Brazil): *1942*, 122; *1950*, 90; *1962*, 6, 120, 141-43, 193

Agricultural commodities to Brazil, 141

Agricultural credit, 92, 94, 99; ANCAR, 128, 136, 137

Agricultural surpluses (U.S.), 196-97

Agricultural Trade Development and Assistance Act, *1954* (Pub. Law 480), 129n, 130, 141

Agriculture in Brazil, 22, 28-29, 37-43, 124, 172-74

Agriculture in Northeast, 48-51, 73; Furtado report, 109, 111; gains in, 45, 55-56, 180; history, 2; influence of industry on, 158, 174; labor in, 59-60, 63-68; "New Era" approach, 87-88, 136; resettlement projects, 11, 64, 109, 116, 150, 156; role of SUDENE, 115-16, 137, 157, 173; traditional approach, 172-74; U.S. aid, 128, 142, 183-84

Agriculture in U.S., 60, 64, 66, 68, 150, 174, 196-97

Agronomists, training of, 96, 169, 170

AID. See Agency for International Development.

Aid: Foreign (*see* Foreign aid); private sector, 195; public health, 115, 121, 122, 123, 127, 128, 129, 142, 143; technical (*see* Technical assistance)

Airfields, 78, 82

Alagoas, 50, 51, 72

Alliance for Progress, 7, 17, 56, 147, 184, 189, 193; in Northeast, 15, 138-45, 177, 198, 199-201

Almeida, Romulo, 90n, 91, 92, 93, 97, 100, 109, 113

Alto-Piranhas River basin, 173

Aluminum, 85-86, 162

Amapá, 29, 37, 38

Amazon River basin, 20, 21, 30, 122, 149; planning for, 147; rubber production, 37; tax revenues for, 38, 82, 151; U.N. assistance, 133

Amazonas, 37

American International Association, 136

American Technical Mission (*1943*), 81-82, 89, 122-23

ANCAR, 128, 136, 137

Apparel industry, 40, 53

Aranha, Oswaldo, 100

Argentine, 22, 189

Asher, Robert E., 131, 142n

Automobile industry, 25, 27, 40, 147

Babaçu, 41, 49, 50, 53

Bahia: Economic Planning Commission, 161; education, 171; geography, 20, 45; industry, 51, 143; loans to, 130; planning for, 113, 147; products, 7, 30, 49, 53; training in business administration, 163; University of, 170

Bananas, 28, 29, 38, 49, 56, 73

Bank, Inter-American Development, 143, 144, 160, 162, 177, 184

Bank, National Development (BNDE), 93, 102, 116, 130, 135, 160

Bank, World (International Bank for Reconstruction and Development), 24, 85, 124, 138

Bank of Brazil, 94, 99, 136, 152

Bank of the Northeast (BNB), 88, 92-99, 106; and *1958* drought, 73-74; loans to, 143-44; relationship with SUDENE, 113, 116, 145; requests for U.S. aid, 129; role in development assistance, 3-4, 51, 130, 134-37, 156, 160-62, 164; successes and disappointments, 94; tax revenues for, 151; training programs, 172

Barbosa, Raul, 73, 95, 138

Barbosa de Oliveira, Américo L., 91n, 99, 100n, 166n

Bauxite, 29

Beans, 28, 29, 38, 40, 41, 56, 73

Beer, manufacture of, 161

Berenhauser, Carlos, 84, 85n

Berredo, Vinicius, 79

205